Educational Yearning

COUNTERPOINTS

Studies in the Postmodern Theory of Education

Joe L. Kincheloe and Shirley R. Steinberg
General Editors

Vol. 38

PETER LANG
New York • Washington, D.C./Baltimore • Bern
Frankfurt am Main • Berlin • Brussels • Vienna • Oxford

Educational Yearning

The Journey of the Spirit and Democratic Education

EDITED BY
Thomas Oldenski & Dennis Carlson

PETER LANG
New York • Washington, D.C./Baltimore • Bern
Frankfurt am Main • Berlin • Brussels • Vienna • Oxford

Library of Congress Cataloging-in-Publication Data

Oldenski, Thomas.
Educational yearning: the journey of the spirit
and democratic education / Thomas Oldenski and Dennis Carlson.
p. cm. — (Counterpoints; vol. 38)
Includes bibliographical references (p.) and index.
1. Education—Aims and objectives. 2. Education—Philosophy. 3. Spiritual life.
4. Educational sociology. I. Carlson, Dennis. II. Title. III. Counterpoints
(New York, N.Y.); vol. 38.
LB41 .C329   370'.1—dc21   2001038379
ISBN 0-8204-3486-8
ISSN 1058-1634

Die Deutsche Bibliothek-CIP-Einheitsaufnahme

Oldenski, Thomas:
Educational yearning: the journey of the spirit and democratic education /
Thomas Oldenski and Dennis Carlson. –New York; Washington, D.C./Baltimore; Bern;
Frankfurt am Main; Berlin; Brussels; Vienna; Oxford: Lang.
ISBN 0-8204-3486-8
NE: GT

The author would like to thank the following institutions for permission to reprint:

- An earlier version of Chapter 5 "Social Justice, Curriculum and Spirituality" by David Purpel appeared in *Moral Outrage in Education* (1999). New York, Peter Lang. Permission granted by the publisher.
- An earlier version of Chapter 8 "The Critical Discourses of Liberation Theology and Critical Pedagogy" by Thomas Oldenski appear in *Liberation Theology and Critical Pedagogy in Today's Catholic Schools: Social Justice in Action* (1997). Permission granted by Garland Publishing.
- An earlier version of Chapter 9 "Integrating Liberation Theology into Restructuring: Toward a Model for Urban Catholic Schools" by Edward St. John appeared as an article in *Catholic Education: A Journal of Inquiry and Practice*, Volume 2, Number 3, March 1999. Permission to reprint granted by the editors.

Cover design by Joni Holst

The paper in this book meets the guidelines for permanence and durability
of the Committee on Production Guidelines for Book Longevity
of the Council of Library Resources.

© 2002 Peter Lang Publishing, Inc., New York

All rights reserved.
Reprint or reproduction, even partially, in all forms such as microfilm,
xerography, microfiche, microcard, and offset strictly prohibited.

Printed in the United States of America

Acknowledgments

This book began out of an ongoing conversation over the course of several years in the mid-1990s between the two co-editors, Thomas Oldenski and Dennis Carlson. We both had a sense that spirituality or the "spirit" was a central idea, even if typically unnamed and taken for granted, in most progressive, critical, and liberatory forms of educational discourse and practice. We also had a sense that late modern culture is in the midst of a far-reaching transition to the postmodern, and that part of this transition involves a respiritualization of everyday life and education. Finally, we shared a concern that this respiritualization of culture lead in democratic rather than conservative, traditionalist, moralistic, or reactionary political directions. We felt the time was right to bring issues of spirituality back into progressive educational discourse, although we believed—and continue to—that spirituality will need to be talked about carefully and continually questioned. What is the "spiritual"? What is the "spirit"? These are questions that can have no unified or final answer. All we can do, we felt, was try to embed them within particular discursive traditions and political rationalities. That is what we hope this volume begins to do. We recognize at the same time that this is a journey in progress, and that this book—at best—represents a snapshot of what some progressive scholars were thinking about spirituality and democratic education at a particular point in time—which just happened to coincide with the approach of the millennium, a symbolic marker of the transition to the postmodern. Many of the authors in this book participated in one form or another in dialogue among themselves in preparing their chapters, facilitated through symposia on spirituality and democratic education over two consecutive years (1995–1996) at the Bergamo Conference sponsored by the Journal of Curriculum Theorizing. At the University of Dayton, we are grateful to Richard Tankersly for his technical assistance and to Saundra Parker for her editing and word processing skills. We are also grateful to Shirley Steinberg for her encouragement with making this book a reality.

Contents

Introduction
    Yearnings of the Heart:
    Education, Postmodernism, and Spirituality   1
    THOMAS OLDENSKI AND DENNIS CARLSON

Chapter One
    Struggles with Spirituality   10
    WILLIAM DOLL

Chapter Two
    Progressivism, the Millennium, and the New Age:
    Thoughts on Reading James Redfield's Celestine Novels   22
    DENNIS CARLSON

Chapter Three
    Contemplative Spirituality, Currere, and Social Transformation:
    Finding Our "Way"   46
    KATHLEEN KESSON

Chapter Four
    Spiritual Literacy:
    Buddhism, Language, and Health in Academia   71
    GLENN HUDAK

Chapter Five
    Social Justice, Curriculum, and Spirituality   86
    DAVID E. PURPEL

Chapter Six
    Engaging "Mind"fulness: Spirituality and
    Curriculum Connections   103
    ELAINE RILEY

Chapter Seven
Feminist Ethics and Educational Reform
Education for Compassion and Social Justice   120
JEANNE F. BRADY

Chapter Eight
The Critical Discourses of Liberation Theology and Critical Pedagogy   133
THOMAS OLDENSKI

Chapter Nine
Integrating Liberation Theology into Restructuring: Toward a Model for Urban Catholic Schools   163
EDWARD P. ST. JOHN

Chapter Ten
Spirituality of the Crows   179
JANINE PEASE PRETTY ON TOP

Contributors   191
Index   193

INTRODUCTION

Yearnings of the Heart: Education, Postmodernism, and Spirituality

Thomas Oldenski and Dennis Carlson

This book is about the yearnings and desires that lie near the heart of all democratic and progressive forms of education—yearnings towards connectedness with others, the natural world, and the cosmos; yearnings we may refer to as the spiritual: that aspect of human consciousness and will that yearns towards meaning, purpose, and connectedness. For the spiritual is no more than these yearnings, and education proceeds on the basis of yearnings. Ultimately, these yearnings sustain democratic public life and they provide progressivism with its direction—the building of a better world here on planet Earth, a world that is more equitable, just, and caring; a world that is our home and that we must preserve.

    The title of this chapter, *Yearnings of the Heart,* is meant to refer back to a groundbreaking book by Robert Bellah and Associates titled *Habits of the Heart* (1985). It was the central thesis of that book that democracy is not so much a formal system of governance, but rather a way of living together—certain habits and rituals that we participate in and that give meaning to democratic values of equity, social justice, caring, community, and so forth. In the case of democracy, these habits arise not merely out of a rational assessment of how to organize our everyday lives together, but more importantly, out of what Plato called *thymos*—which he symbolically located in the heart. Thymos is that part of the human spirit that yearns after justice, that longs to connect with others as equals and right social injustices. It is that part of the human spirit that calls us to be more than we are as individuals and as a culture. The yearnings of the heart are also, and in a related way, yearnings after personal meaning and purpose. By ignoring such yearnings after purpose and meaning, educators have been left with a crisis of motivation and meaning in the learning process. To move beyond that crisis, progressives must locate learning within a network of relationships and historical struggles, where the self always "finds" itself in the choices it makes and the values it affirms.

The role of the educator, in this sense, is similar to that of the spiritual guide or shaman—one who poses questions more than provides universal answers or "truths." The educator helps students develop their yearnings and desires for purpose, meaning, and connectedness; she or he helps young people understand themselves as part of an historical becoming, with the responsibility and the capacity to act in the world according to one set of values or another. These are existential and ontological questions. They have to do with our attitude towards the world, the way we dwell upon the earth in relation with others, and the meaning we make out of our everyday lives. They are also questions which people are asking with much greater frequency and much greater concern as we move into a "new age" in which the spiritual, the personal, and the public are no longer separable. This new age has profound implications for public education and what it means to become educated in postmodern America.

The "Enchantment of Everyday Life"

> All in all, postmodernity can be seen as restoring to the world what modernity, presumptuously, had taken away; as a re-enchantment of the world that modernity tried hard to dis-enchant... The war against mystery and magic was for modernity the war of liberation of reason's independence. It was the declaration of hostilities that made the unprocessed, pristine world into the enemy. As is the case with all genocide, the world of nature... had to be de-spiritualized, de-animated: denied the capacity of the subject. (Bauman 1992, x)

We begin with the premise that we are living in a time of transition, one that is often talked about in terms of a shift from "modern" to "postmodern" ways of knowing. One of the most basic shifts associated with postmodernism, as Bauman observes, is a rejection of the modernist disenchantment and despiritualization of the world. Modernism objectified the world as "out there," as detached from the knowing subject. In doing so, it also reduced the world to an "object" that was viewed in terms of an instrumental logic of exploitation and domination. "Nature" was no longer seen as anything but a "natural resource" waiting to be developed and exploited. This disenchanted view of the world leads people to look at a river as Heidegger (1977) suggests and to think that it is "wasted" until it is dammed up and made to generate power, until it is "tamed" and made to irrigate crops. The reenchantment of the world is thus consistent with the return of ecological ways of knowing. Ecological ways of knowing the world place people back into the world as a spiritual, inhabited space—a space that is understood in terms of wonder and awe, joy and care, and always in terms of connectedness to everything. Once contemporary culture is reenchanted, it becomes possible once more to look at the river and see something else entirely, to view it aesthetically, poetically, spiritually, and as part of a living creation. This does not mean returning to an idealized aboriginal past of spiritual connectedness. Indeed, dams across rivers may still be needed and serve an important role in a reenchanted world. But an enchanted way of knowing would respect and care for the river, dwell upon its banks poetically, and no longer erect rigid boundaries between the river "out there" and an inner world of experience.

As a despiritualized form of modernism continues to dominate the cultural landscape in the late twentieth century, we are experiencing what David Purpel has called a "spiritual and moral crisis." This crisis is part of a broader crisis of purpose and motivation in advanced capitalist culture. One of the consequences is a decline in democratic public life and community and a retreat into crime and drugs, "yuppie" consumerism, and political apathy. The disenchantment of the natural world has also produced an ecological crisis that may only be effectively overcome through new ways of knowing and inhabiting the earth. This means that educators have an important role in helping people begin to think outside of the box of a technical rational mindset, to bring enchantment back into the learning process. We take postmodernism to be a descriptor of the cultural terrain of this new historical era we are entering, one full of dangers but also hope. One of the hopeful signs is the growing sense that things are "out of kilter," along with a search for something beyond instrumentalism to reconnect us to each other and to a world we have become so distant from.

That "something else" that so many people are searching for today is often named the "spiritual." To bring talk of the spiritual into progressivism is to some almost sacrilegious. But what is often forgotten is that progressives have always—or at least until recent times—talked of the "human spirit," the "democratic spirit," the "spirit of justice," and so on. So part of what we want to do is demystify this word "spiritual" and ground it in progressive traditions and values. We want to view spirituality as a way of giving meaning to our "being here" in ways that move us beyond the idea of the autonomous self (an idea that has been pervasive in the modernist era) and allow us to see ourselves as inseparable from everyone and everything else. Spirituality, then, may be defined as the self's authentic sense of connectedness and purpose. As Karl Marx would say, we are animals whose "species being" is one of experiencing an uninterrupted connectedness to the natural world and each other. But, even talk of an "authentic" spirituality may be misleading and overly idealistic. Our perspective is generally consistent with postmodern theories of culture that view the self as a product of culture and history. Spirituality, as the self's authentic sense of connectedness and purpose, likewise, is always expressed in ways that are particular to cultures and to historical eras. That is, there is no essential or natural form that spirituality takes. Rather, its expression is regulated and limited by discourse and, thus, culture. We are always talking about some culture's expression of spirituality within a given historical period, and even more particularly, somebody, or some group's expression—that is, masculinist or feminist, working class or middle class, democratic or authoritarian and dominating, and so on.

Spirituality, in democratic and empowering forms, also involves being aware of one's own "throwness," to use Heidegger's (1977) term, and the necessity of making one future rather than another. It confronts us with the necessity of acting in the world to advance one project rather than another, to advance one set of truths and values over another. Spirituality is the name we give to the visioning or visionary aspect of the self, which guides the projection of the self in history towards a "good society." Spirituality has an ethical dimension. That is, once we realize that we are here in the world, we are confronted with questions of how to act and for what purposes. Democratic forms of spirituality may be associated with ecological, caring ways of being in the world, along with commitments to social justice and equity. When we use the language of spirituality, consequently, it is with an awareness of just how slippery this term is, and that some notions of spirituality are quite conservative and even reactionary. Furthermore, spirituality implies a way of being in the world that is beyond explanation in mere words. It is an aspect of one's existential experience of the world and thus, indescribable. We are reminded of this by two eastern tales as recorded by Anthony deMello in *The Song of the Bird* (1982):

> A disciple once complained, "You tell us stories, but you never reveal their meaning to us." Said the master, "How would you like it if someone offered you fruit and masticated it before giving it to you?" No one can find your meaning for you. Not even the master.
>
> And, the second tale states that . . . The master was asked, "What is spirituality?" He said, "Spirituality is that which succeeds in bringing one to inner transformation." "But, if I apply the methods handed down by the masters, is that not spirituality?" asked the disciple."It is not spirituality if it does not perform its function for you. A

blanket is no longer a blanket if it does not keep you warm." "So what was spirituality once, is spirituality no more. What generally goes under the name of spirituality, is merely the record of past events."

If it is impossible to define the spiritual experience, we can and must distinguish between different conceptions of spirituality. What meaning, then, might progressives give to the notion of spirituality? One answer, although one that immediately begs clarification, is that progressive conceptions of spirituality are about the *transcendence* of human consciousness and culture. In one usage, the word "transcendence" carries with it certain orthodox religious connotations that progressives often find unsettling. It suggests a transcendence of this life and the struggles to build a better world here and now and a yearning, or longing, to return to a supposed realm of pure spirit—symbolized in orthodox Christianity as heaven. We find this same basic understanding of transcendence behind the recent Heaven's Gate cult suicide in which cult members sought to leave their earthly "vehicles" behind and leap into a higher spiritual realm of existence. In the eastern traditions, transcendence tends to imply a journey "within" through meditation, which is aimed at a radical reconnection to the cosmos—a sense of oneness with the universe and all life. This, in our view, can be progressive if the journey inward leads outward again, with a renewed sense of engagement in life and a sense of being reconnected to others. The trouble is that the journey "inward" may lead us to get "lost in ourselves."

In its most progressive forms, the idea of transcendence has been linked to the Hegelian and Marxist traditions. Within these traditions, history is understood to advance through the transformation of human consciousness, so that each historical era transcends the limitations of the past one. Of course, this is a bit overly idealistic and naïve, and it oversimplifies complex historical developments. But, it contains a kernel of important truth as well. In much of the new age, or millennium mythology, the notion that we are about to transcend the modern era and enter a new era—what Brianne Swimme and Thomas Berry (1992) call the Ecozoic era—is quite progressive. The transformation of human consciousness may even be necessary to the maintenance of the democratic vision. So the question is not so much whether or not progressivism in education should include a language of transcendence, but what we mean by this term, what traditions we ground its usage within. We want to view spirituality in ways that do not separate the spiritual from the material, the "soul" from the body, subjectivity from spirituality, in ways that are consistent with the notions of the democratic spirit and the human spirit, a spirit in the process of historical transformation.

As we noted earlier, spirituality has not been a subject about which progressive educators and scholars have had much to say—at least until recently. Partially, this is because spirituality has, in the past, been commonly associated with organized religion—and the political right has been the strongest supporter of returning religion to the classroom. In recent years, fundamentalist spirituality has become a powerful new force in this country. In local school boards around the United States, fundamentalists are having a very significant impact on curriculum decision making. They envision either pushing public schools to recognize and teach fundamentalist religiosity, or doing away with public schools and replacing them with church-affiliated religious schools supported by public vouchers. As the spiritual crisis of contemporary western culture deepens, the new right's call for a return to fundamentalist, authoritarian form of spirituality may be expected to have an even stronger appeal. All the more imperative, then, that a democratic progressive alternative to this articulation of spirituality with rightist politics be formulated. This book is dedicated to furthering such a project.

One way to articulate spirituality with progressivism is through the idea of a "good society." In the end, there is nothing that different between democratic and progressive visions of a good society and the visions of a good society that undergirds "liberation theology" and some emerging forms of religiosity. Both affirm what Cornell West calls a "prophetic vision." When Martin Luther King, Jr. told those assembled at the March on Washington, the crowning moment of the Civil Rights Movement, that he had a dream, he was engaging in prophetic visioning, linking up the words of Moses, leading his people out of a long bondage, with a democratic vision of an American future. It was a vision of a multicultural American future, of an America that cares enough not to let people live in poverty, an America where people actively stand up against the ugly spectre of bigotry, scapegoating, and exploitation of one individual or group by another. It is a vision of an America of equal opportunity, and of a community in which diversity is not only tolerated, but also actively cultivated. This vision is still a compelling one.

A democratic and progressive form of spirituality thus assumes both a prophetic stance that affirms a vision of a better world, and a stance of outrage that is directed at injustices in contemporary society. However, a democratic and progressive spirituality must go beyond critiquing society to engage people in the active reconstruction of culture and in their own relationships to the world. As Purpel observes, "It is important to remember that the prophetic voice is one that speaks not only to criticism; it is also a voice of transformation" (1989, 81). And as Peter McLaren reminds us, "We need to teach dangerously, but to live with optimism. We need to be outrageous, but to temper our outrage with love and compassion. We need to be warriors for social justice" (1994, 299).

We find many of these themes in diverse religious traditions, such as the ancient Hebraic prophetic tradition. Heschel (1962) describes the prophets of the Hebrew scriptures as advocates "speaking for those who are too weak to plead their own cause" and calling upon others to be also "champions of the poor" (205). The prophets were concerned for justice with "an urgency of aiding and saving the victims of oppression" (204). The words of the prophets may often have begun with a message of doom, but they concluded with a message of hope. "The prophets do not stand aloof of the people, but identify with the people"—the prophet's theme is, first of all, "the very life of a whole people" (6).

The theme of solidarity with others, particularly those who are represented as the "Other" within modern culture—people of color, women, the poor, gays and lesbians, and others—may also be located in Martin Buber's (1958) notions of "I-It" and "I-Thou" relationships. The former is a relationship in which the other becomes an "Other," which is to say, a thing, an object, something to be exploited, something completely detached from the self and distanced "over there." An I-Thou relationship, by contrast, is one marked by a rupturing of the boundaries that separate self and other. This involves recognition of the uniqueness of the other, respect for the other as an equal, and a communion with the other. For it is only, Buber suggests, through the other that we find ourselves.

Struggling with the issue of "how are we to do theology in a meaningful—that is, life changing—way," Soelle (1993) proposes that theology must be considered in terms of four steps: praxis, analysis, meditation, and renewed praxis. It appears that these four steps are also the dynamic of the biblical prophetic tradition, as lived and voiced in the lives of the Hebrew prophets. However, these four steps are not only limited to the prophetic tradition. They are related as well to liberation theology, which "starts with the context of our experiences, our hopes and fears, our 'praxis'" (x).

Liberation theology is rooted in the biblical prophetic tradition of the Hebrew and Christian scriptures, but understands these words in relation to the current and recent historical settings of oppressed peoples and our own lives. There is no doubt that liberation theology includes a movement from being critical to a position of possibility and hope as this becomes a theology in practice—a theology whose goal is to ameliorate the lives of the oppressed. Liberation theologians claim that liberation must first take place before theology can actually happen. It is a critical theology and a critical process of what is and what can be. In these characteristics, liberation theology echoes the themes of the biblical prophetic tradition. Casaldaliga and Vigil (1994) claim that it was "from the spirituality of liberation, lived out day by day, in poverty, in service, in struggle, and in martyrdom, that the theology of liberation arose, which has systematically reflected on this life and its motivations in faith" (xix).

These developments have a direct bearing on democratic curriculum development in these unsettling times, and this book is dedicated to engaging progressive educators in dialoguing about these struggles and their implications for curriculum. It brings together educational scholars working in a variety of disciplines and fields, each of whom explore the connections between spirituality and democratic conceptions of education grounded in notions of caring and connectedness and commitments to struggles for social and economic justice. The coeditors, along with the authors contributing chapters to this book, share a general poststructural, or postmodern, interpretive frame, although we mean to use these terms as signifiers that are porous and flexible enough to include many diverse discourses and perspectives.

The essays collected here explore recent trends in some of the most important of these traditions, including the Judeo-Christian traditions of prophetic visioning and liberation theology, the eastern traditions of Buddhism and Hinduism, American Indian traditions of nature and cycle-based spirituality, Platonic and Hegelian traditions in western philosophy, feminist and critical theory traditions in the social sciences, the "new science" of chaos theory and fractal physics, and various "human potential" movements. The common conviction that runs throughout these essays is that progressivism, as an educational and cultural movement based on a yearning for a better, more just world, cannot afford to ignore the respiritualization of culture and cannot afford to let the fundamentalist right define spirituality.

In Chapter 1, William Doll struggles with spirituality as the sense of mystery and wonder. Dennis Carlson expresses his reactions to popular cultural representations of spirituality, the millennium, and the new age (chapter 2). The focus of chapter 3 is Kathleen Kesson's search for integrating contemplative spirituality with the curriculum, and social transformation. In the next chapter, Glenn Hudak dialogues with notions of spirituality, Buddhism, and the health of academia. David Purpel focuses upon the integration of social justice, curriculum, and spirituality in chapter 5. Elaine Riley proposes a sense of interconnectedness of spirituality and curriculum through a process of engaging mindfulness (chapter 6).

In chapter 7, Jeanne Brady turns our attention to feminist ethics and education for compassion and social justice. Thomas Oldenski examines in chapter 8 the critical discourses of liberation theology and critical pedagogy as a framework for including the spiritual within the educational process. Edward St. John explores the relevance of liberation theology to the discourse on restructuring schools, and more particularly to the Accelerated School Project (APS) (chapter 9). In the last chapter, Janine Peaslee Pretty on Top shares the spiritual experiences of her Native American people, the Crow. It is our hope that these chapters can begin the dialogue among teachers and other educators along with their students as they struggle to articulate the yearnings of the heart with the realities of the present times.

References

Bauman, Z. (1992). *Intimations of Postmodernity.* London: New York: Routledge.
Bellah, R.N., R. Madsen, W.M. Sullivan, A. Swidler, and S.Tipton. (1985). *Habits of the Heart: Individualism and Commitment in American Life.* Berkeley: University of California Press.
Buber, M. (1958). *I and Thou.* New York: Scribner.
Casaldaliga, P., and J. M. Vigil. (1994). *The Spirituality of Liberation.* Kent, UK: Burns & Oates.
deMello, A. (1982). *The Song of the Bird.* Garden City, NY: Image Books.
Heidegger, M. (1977). *The Question Concerning Technology and Other Essays.* New York: Harper & Row.
Heschel, A. (1962). *The Prophets.* New York: Harper & Row.
McLaren, P. (1994). *Life in Schools: An Introduction to Critical Pedagogy in the Foundations of Education.* New York: Longman.
Purpel, D. (1989). *The Moral and Spiritual Crisis in Education: A Curriculum for Justice and Compassion in Education.* Granby, MA: Bergin & Garvey.
Soelle, D. (1993). *On Earth as in Heaven: A Liberation Spirituality of Sharing.* Louisville, KY: Westminister/John Knox Press.
Swimme, B., and T. Berry. (1992). *The Universe Story.* San Francisco: Harper Collins.

CHAPTER ONE

Struggles with Spirituality

William Doll

> As the archeology of our thought easily shows,
> man is an invention of recent date.
> And one perhaps nearing its end.
> —Michel Foucault, *The Order of Things*, 1973

We humans have always known our personal and physical existence to be temporal—we are born, live, and die. This is what it means to be an individual human being. But we have not thought of our species—*Homo Sapiens*—in the same temporal terms. Even with our acceptance of Charles Darwin's thesis that humanity is an evolving form—"descent with modification" is his way of phrasing (1859/1964)—we have not seriously considered that our species evolution might be into extinction. We have, of course, worried about the nuclear destruction of life, but even in this catastrophe, we have assumed some life forms would live—eventually to transform themselves into the human. Again, the species, as species, has not been considered as evolving *toward* extinction—yet this is a natural consequence of the life process.

Entropy, the other dominant Evolution of the nineteenth century—in its popular form, the cooling of the sun and hence the dying of our solar system—is quite universally accepted.[1] Yet we have almost never put these two E's—evolution and entropy—together to recognize that it is not unnatural to consider not only ourselves, but also our species as temporal, maybe even

---

1. While entropy is almost universally accepted—Arthur Eddington (1928) says it occupies "The supreme position among the Laws of Nature" (74)—it does have a history of originating in the nineteenth century mechanical, closed systems. Thus, some scientists have, at the very least, raised fundamental questions about it. See, for example, Ilya Prigogine and Isabel Stengers (1984); Doll (1993); Paul Davies (1995); and George Johnson (1996).

"nearing its end." If our solar system is temporal, why should life on one of its planets not also be temporal?

In fact, how could life on a planet in the solar system exist, if the system itself dies? For centuries, we have operated (theologically, at least) on the assumption that God is securely fixed in "His" firmament with the Devil located in "His" hell. Both figures have been portrayed as male and very, very permanent. Our cosmology, if not our science, has been based on this idea of permanence. Nature is—by its very nature—permanent, simple, and, as Isaac Newton said, consonant and "comfortable to Herself" (1730/1952, 397). In fact, Newton's "law of gravity," that mathematical formula ($F=GMm/r^2$) which describes both falling terrestrial apples and revolving planetary spheres, shows just this conformity. *One* law uniting the whole universe, as Pierre Simon de la Place said, with Newton being "the most fortunate of all men," for he had discovered this law (quoted in Burtt 1932/1955, 31). Before Albert Einstein, gravity was the organizing law of the universe—entropy being dissipative not organizing law.

Einstein (most unwittingly) destroyed this concept of a universe consonant, comfortable, simple. While he was indeed "the last great Newtonian," it is his theories which have helped others (us) see a subatomic world filled with millions of weird "objects(?)," some of them "living" for only a billionth of a second; and his theories have also helped us "see" a celestial world filled with black holes, exploding stars, bursting galaxies, and tumultuous new creations. In fact, we now see ourselves not as "Lords of the Universe," but as accidental inhabitants of a rather tiny planet, located "on the edge of a humdrum galaxy among billions like it scattered across vast megaspaces (Kauffman 1995, 4).

How does all this scientific thinking, based as it is on a fundamental acceptance of change, influence our thinking about God, religion, spirituality, based as it is on a fundamental acceptance of permanence? We have here, Jacques Derrida would say, an *aporia*—a basic contradiction, an essential opposition. Already we have lost Hell—few find it a reality—and with the loss of Hell has come the lessening of the persona of the Devil and of his evil power. What for the Puritans was reality is for us, three centuries later, mythic. The representation of Hell which Dante (1915/early fourteenth century) gives us in his Divine Comedy—nine levels or circles of damnation lying in the bowels of the earth's fiery, volcanic core—is now seen only as mythic, and not a very appealing myth at that. Scientifically we now realize that Hell will ultimately "freeze over." Hell freezing over! It will happen, and in less geological time than we might realize. Our sun is likely beyond the half-way point in its own temporal existence—metaphorically it is into middle-age, maybe even advanced middle-age (Davies 1995, 63). As it continues to age, the earth's crust will harden, ice, and its volcanic core (hell) will, indeed, freeze over.

Theologically we may be ready to accept the nonexistence of Hell and the Devil. Both appear far less in our contemporary church sermons than they did in the sermons or jeremiads of the Puritans. The Devil is now seen to reside more within us than as an active deity in his own right. If God is not dead, I think it fair to say the Devil is.

God may well be dead in the sense in which Frederick Nietzsche pronounced him dead,[2] but He is certainly not dead in people's minds. Religion in its traditional sense is much alive, albeit maybe not well. Our theological thinking here is not ready, I believe, to accept a nonexistent (really nonanthropomorphic) God. We still accept theology, which sees God rooted permanently in His Heaven, itself located in celestial space. If Hell has gone, Heaven remains. But where is Heaven? The celestial and magnetic blue we take to be Heaven with its puffy, white clouds is, we now know, a thin layer of atmosphere surrounding our planet. A unique surrounding? Our planet is, of course, but one of (supposedly) nine in our solar system, while the solar system is itself located in a thin galactic band we call the "milky way." How many galaxies are there—is billions too large or maybe too small a number? How about billions of billions? As for our uniqueness (an arrogant thought) in this vast vastness, what will speculations about past life on Mars do to it? Are we alone in the universe (Davies 1995)? Did life exist at one time on Jupiter's moon, Europa?

What do such musings, speculations, theories, and facts do to our concepts of God, salvation, and permanence in Heaven? Is the God who inhabited Mars—a warlike God, I assume—still alive? As the solar system darkens and deadens, will God still be "there"? Where? What is it like to conceive of a God ruling over a "dead" universe? Does God like the dark? Let There Be Light! Where? Or will God leave this solar system, maybe this galaxy and move to others? Was the creation of this system and us mere whim, our species no more than "randomness caught on the wing?"—to use Jacques Monod's colorful phrase (1971, 98). Finally, what does it mean to our contemporary concept of Christianity to realize that the permanence we had assumed to underlie our religion and spirituality does not exist?

The argument I am making here is that our accepted concepts of God, religion, and spirituality assume a type of permanence—a cosmology of per-

---

2. For a good analysis of what Nietzsche meant by his famous remark, and ways to interpret it, see Mary Elizabeth Quinn 1997, chapter. 2. See also Martin Heidegger, on whom Quinn draws, 1954/1977, Part II.

manence as it were—we no longer find valid. Our scientific theories have changed to accept change as a fundamental feature,[3] but our theological theories have not so changed. Our science is postmodern; our theology is modern. What will postmodern theology/spirituality look like?

If we consider that our theology, religion, and spirituality are rooted strongly in modernism, we might legitimately consider that our theology, and religion. Spirituality has been and is anthropocentric and anthropomorphic—we have created and centered "God" around "Man"[4]—in "our image and likeness." The God of our Judeo-Christian representation is humanly male—as a loving Father, as Moses, as Christ.

Can we accept a nonanthropocentric view of God, religion, spirituality, and theology? What will happen to these words and the values they represent if we do not? Here lie my struggles with spirituality. These struggles, of course, carry over to my concepts of teaching and curriculum design, areas I have devoted my professional life to exploring and areas I believe will be strongly affected by our general (albeit slow) move from anthropocentric sense of spirituality to one more cosmologically and ecologically oriented. I firmly believe a new sense of value must be found, but that this new sense cannot be rooted in an individualistic or humanly skewed frame. We are part of a larger ecological and cosmological frame—a frame Gregory Bateson (1979) calls "mind," with our minds and us as subminds. As do Bateson and Thomas Berry (1988, 1992), I believe our theoretical, theological, and operational frames need to focus on the universe itself and its ways of operating. The universe has its own patterns, and as Bateson says, they "connect." The patterns do connect into a unified whole. Further, Bateson argues, "If you fight the ecological system you lose—especially when you win" (in Berman 1981, 257). Too much of our fight this century has been a fight of us against nature, and the more we have won, the more we have lost.

To move from the personal and social to the ecological and cosmological

3. I realize this statement can be taken (1) as a deification of science and (2) as part of that broad historical tradition—one C.A. Bowers (1993, 1995) rightly rails against—which has equated science with change and both with progress. While I approve of science, change, and progress, I do not wish to imply a simple relationship here, nor an automatic one. Science is but one and only one of the three Ss—Science, Story, and Spirituality—framing my pedagogy. Obviously, change can be for the poorer as well as for the better, and "progress" has brought with it much that is destructive, as well as much that is constructive. The relationship among science, change, and progress is complex and fragile.

4. Margaret Wertheim notes that Laplace, following Newton, believed an "Intelligence" could predict all future events if it had the exact state of the universe now. Wertheim wryly notes that this "intelligence" seemed much like a "supervision of himself" (1995, 145).

means, in an epistemological sense, is to move toward thinking in a relational way. It is the relations between and among objects that becomes the focus (G. Bateson 1979; G. and M. C. Bateson 1987; Berry 1988, 1992; Bowers 1993, 1995; Whitehead 1925/1967, 1929/1978). The patterns exist not in the objects, but in the relations among the objects. It is through the relations among the objects, particularly their differences, that we begin to understand the objects themselves—those temporary permanencies we call facts. A sense of the sacred arises—a *mysterium tremendum* (to borrow from Mary Elizabeth Quinn 1997)—when we look at the complex of relations we find in nature and at the power and generativity of the process of creation. When we shift our gaze from the particular to the interconnected and to the generativity of all life and creation, a sense of awe arises. It is this focus, rather than our own personal salvation, I am advocating we adopt—a focus on the "pattern which connects," rather than on the individual objects connected.

Such a shift in focus lets us see the order in nature (complex), the symmetry (recursive), and the balance (dynamic). In a sense, Newton was right, nature is conformable to herself, but it is neither a simple conformity nor a stable one. It is the conformity of a system continually transforming itself, regenerating itself, and creating itself. "The process [of creation] is the reality" to quote Whitehead, and we are, as says Bateson, the active Creatura within the process. There is no outside/inside; all is one—a dynamic, turbulent, ordered/chaotic process of connecting patterns. In such a process, stochastic Bateson (1979) calls it, change is fundamental, even foundational; but it is change, which operates through the dynamic interaction of stability and flexibility intertwined (Kauffman 1995; Doll 1997). God is now no longer a person, but a word we apply to the *mysterium tremendum* of this creative process. "His," "her," or "its" reality lies within the pattern of patterns or the creativity of creating patterns. Indeed, "God" may even be the pattern of patterns or the creativity of creating patterns.

Traditional theology has not seen God within this patterned fabric, but rather outside the fabric, the creator of the fabric. Being outside, "He" has been permanence in opposition to change; neither permanence through change nor permanence entwined with change. The either/or morality of a system where the permanence (God) lies outside the system is a morality based on power. He (recently also she) who has the most power becomes the determiner of rules. While we have clothed this determiner of rules in religious and/or traditional garments, the validity, or sacredness, of the rules has really been determined by the power the determiner has held. "Power is power only when, and only so long as, it remains power-enhancement and commands for itself more power" (Heidegger 1954/1977, 78). The history of the Christian/Catholic church is a living example of this fact (Wertheim 1995). "Christianity," says Derrida, "has not yet come to Christianity" (in Quinn 1997)—the spirit of Christianity has not yet infused Christian organizations.[5]

The question of values (morality) is, I believe, the most important question we as a society (or collection of societies) face today. Certainly it is an issue receiving a lot of attention in educational, social, and religious circles. Many want or believe we can (re)institute the "values" we had or did not have in the past. This, though, can not be done. As Douglas McKnight (1997) has clearly shown, our country's social values and educational institutions (especially its public schools) were organized around Puritan-Protestant concepts.[6] America grew and as these concepts attained fulfillment they also became dissipated. Their very success led to their being assumed and hence, a loss of their driving forces. As Bateson says: Any attempt to maximize a single variable within a system (including purposive rationality) will force the system into a "runaway" state, capable of destroying itself and its environment (in Berman 1981, 256). The Puritans did try to maximize their single view of life and its way. In fact, as McKnight (1997) says: The Puritans believed that via "correct moral thoughts [they] could arrive at right moral action and [hence] change the terrain of the world" (47).

In the middle of this century, Martin Heidegger saw that we in the West had lost our souls and human values,[7] not so much to technology (the subject of his essay, 1954/1977, Part I) as to our hopes and aspirations for technology. Technology lies, of course, at the heart of the Industrial Revolution—it and its new breed of man—the engineer—forming the social hope

5. This statement by Derrida is appropriated from the (martyred) Czech philosopher, Jan Patocka, and appears in Derrida's *The Gift of Death* (1995, 28). For myself, the comment, while accurate institutionally, should not be considered to denigrate the millions of wonderful persons—female and male—who have and are working within the Spirit of their religion and religious feelings. The compassion humanity does currently display owes much to these people.

6. This comment is not meant to overlook the contributions to our American culture and community made by Native Americans, African Americans, Spanish Americans, Huguenots, Chinese Americans, and Cajuns (to name but a few ethnic groups). However, the dominant power within the American culture was formed in the northeastern part of the United States, where Puritan-Protestant values reigned supreme and where the American public school movement received its origins and from which it still acquires much of its driving force.

7. An ironic comment considering Heidegger's own loss of soul, both to the Nazis and to an ethereal idealization of the ancient Greek concept of *poiesis*. See Richard Bernstein's analysis of this development in chapter 4 of his *The New Constellation* (1991).

for the Enlightenment. Heidegger points out, in "The Question Concerning Technology" (1954/1977), that in this too exalted hope, we have separated means from ends, envisioning technology merely as a device separated from its underlying essence. We have believed we can control technology—a "neutral" tool—for our own (good) ends. This was our justification for the atomic bombs dropped on Japan. The result of this "mentality" has been our becoming subservient to (or "enframed" by) the essence of controlling. Our being is now wrapped up in control—to be we need to be controlling. We accept the controlling mode, an offshoot of praxis, as the way to be. As we control, we accept the idea of control and become, ourselves, controlled.

This is the same argument I am making regarding technology. As we have separated ourselves from God, placing "Him" outside and us inside, we have become susceptible to an inferior-superior, competitive enframing. Our values are, and have been for centuries, ones of "winning" our salvation. This has made us competitive with the very "others" we so desperately need for our understandings of self. In this power game, we, as a species, are bound to lose. Our evolution to extinction may happen naturally or slowly; our movement to extinction may happen sooner because we misunderstand what it means to be a human species.

Our past, competitive, individualist values we cannot recover, nor should we wish to do so. We need another enframing, a brand new paradigm, or as Thomas Berry says, "a new story" (1988, 123). For Berry, the new story is the old, old one of the universe. It is also a radical story, for as Berry says, "We must go far beyond any transformation of contemporary culture. We must go back to the genetic imperative from which human cultures emerge" (207). We need to go back to the "primordial experience" of creation to focus on an "all-pervading mysterious energy" and awaken ourselves to "an awesome universe filled with mysterious power" (24)—the *mysterium tremendum* Quinn

---

8. The Oxford English Dictionary attributes the English use of this phrase to Harvey (1923) in his translation (Ch. 4) of Otto's *The Idea of Holy* (1917). The Oxford English Dictionary definition *(tremendous mystery)* expresses the "overwhelming awe and sense of unknowable mystery felt by those to whom this aspect of God or being is revealed" (Oxford English Dictionary 1989, vol. 10, 173). Derrida in his *The Gift of Death* (1992/1995, ch. 3) calls it a "frightful mystery, a secret to make you tremble," and, playing off the idea of tremble not tremendous, takes the origins back to Soren Kierkegaard (1843/1983) and his *Fear and Trembling*, itself coming from St. Paul (Philippians 2:12) and his exhortation for Christians to "work out your own salvation with fear and trembling."

  I prefer the O.E.D. thrust which I find akin to William James's sense of "an unseen spiritual order" (1897/1956, 52), and to Paul Tillich's reference to the *mysterium tremendum* as a "presence which remains mysterious in spite of its appearance, and exercises both an attractive and repulsive function on those who encounter it" (1957, 53).

develops so well.[8] This shift is away from the "anthropocentric life attitude which has been our story for so long" (67) in favor of an even older (but not developed in Western thought) life attitude present in cosmological creation. We are part of that creation and have our role in it.

This creative process, Berry believes, is neither determined nor random. Its essence lies in the act of creation itself (1988, 199). Bateson, a scientist not a theologian, sees the creative process as the actual integration of determinism with randomism, randomism with determinism. This integration he calls "the Great Stochastic process," (in Berman 1981, ch. 7). Whitehead says simply, "It lies in the nature of things that the many enter into complex unity" (1929/1978, 21). All three agree the process to be one where creation is emergent—the universe coming out of itself—in a mysterious but natural way.

Stuart Kauffman (1993, 1995) also sees the process as emergent and natural—one that can be seen in DNA replicating itself and studied through the use of computers and the patterns developed over time as randomness is iterated upon itself over and over. Whether the computer situations Kauffman develops of order emerging from randomness is a valid example of DNA replicating itself is an open—maybe even personal—question. Using this as a model (or a metaphor) for all creation is even more speculative. But, in this analogic process, Kauffman is moving from the known and manipulable (computer programs) to the *mysterium tremendum* of all creation. I do not believe Kauffman is trying to find the essence, origin, or source of the tremendum. I do not see him trying to see into "the mind of God," but rather to show analogically that a connection might be made between the order which arises spontaneously (under certain constraint conditions) in computer programs and the creative order we find in our universe. Will other universes have different orders?

For me, as I interpret Kauffman, the mystery of how order arises (spontaneously, not by imposition) remains a mystery. It is not defined, merely shown—along with its constraint conditions.[9] In Whitehead's terms "it lies in the nature of things that the many enter into complex unity." Or as Paul Davies (1995) has suggested, there may well be an innate tendency in nature to evolve more complex structures—what he calls the "law of increasing organized complexity" (103). Again, this may well be the *mysterium tremendum*—the natural and innate tendency of nature to create in ever increasing complexity.

What is our responsibility, our morality in the tremendousness of creation? As educators, do we bear any special responsibility?

9. The use of computers for the study of natural development is maybe the mother of all *aporias*.

A God Disappears, Divinity Remains (Paul Tillich 1957, 18)

Responsibility—the state of being responsible (Latin, *respondére*), answering to, being according for, usually to another, according to the Oxford English Dictionary. Even a cursory look at contemporary society shows that traditional sense of responsibility, authority, and morality no longer hold. "Kids just don't respect anymore," they do not "respond" as we (in power) believe they should. The prevalence of such comments shows that many, too many I fear, wish us to return to the past (real or imagined) where the Puritan-Protestant ethic dominated. Not only can this not be done, the very concept of responsibility inherent in this ethic may well be "not thought right through."[10]

Responsibility as we have envisioned this concept has essentially been responsibility *to*—an Other, a God, an Ideology, a Tradition. It has been responsibility to that which lies above or beyond us in our mundane being. This sense of responsibility, which Derrida (1995) calls "sacrificial responsibility" (76), is "the most common and everyday experience of responsibility" (67). It is, in many ways, a "monstrous" responsibility, for its relationship—of us to other—is a power relationship, one of us subjugating ourselves to the Other and hence, willing to sacrifice ourselves and our loved ones to the demands of the Other—just as Abraham "sacrificed" Isaac, or as God sacrificed His Only Begotten Son. It is this sense of responsibility, "our most common and everyday experience of responsibility," Derrida feels we have "not thought right through."[11]

The responsibility of sacrifice, of subjugation is monstrous not only in the act it honors—everywhere, everyday—but also in the moral justification it gives to those acts. We not only kill, we explain (justify) such killing with a term like "cleansing"—in our Puritan-Protestant heritage, a term of purity and morality. Remember that the Puritan trial for witches was "dunking," reminiscent of baptizing, of washing, and of cleansing. Cleansing and words like it are not mere language plays; they represent a morality that hides immorality, a responsibility that justifies irresponsibility. We firmly believe our cleansing to be justified and moral.

Can we begin to develop a "new responsibility"—one announced by the *mysterium tremendum* (28)? The *mysterium tremendum* is, of course, undefined and indefinable. But, associated historically as it has been with a fear-

---

10. I borrow this phrase from Derrida (1995, 32) who borrows it from Patocka. I approach my own attempts at "thinking right through" my next comments with trepidation. Still, I feel an obligation (responsibility?) to begin such a venture. I ask the reader's indulgence and welcome comments. The issues I'm about to raise are important ones, I believe.
11. Idem.

inspiring (fear-demanding, fear-requiring?) Christian God, it has overtones of dread in it. However, I am using the phrase in a different manner; not in regard to dreadful but to the awful—to the awesome and mysterious creation present in all life; a mysterious creation we continue to explore. Instead of fear, I place awe.[12] I'm using this phrase to mark the awesomeness, I believe, we feel when we look upon acts of creation—human, ecological, cosmic. These are awe-inspiring, not fear-inspiring, acts, although fear is latently present in observing the intricacy, complexity, and power of creation. But, fear is not the dominant emotion; nor is it intended to be, whereas, many of the acts God commits in the Bible are, I believe, so intended.

In this (new) frame, responsibility takes on a different meaning. It is no longer responsibility *to*—a power relationship, which allows for the legitimacy of irresponsibility under the guise of responsibility—i.e., following other's orders (85)—but, a responsibility *of*. This is not a responsibility to another, as a self, it is a categorical responsibility which comes with the concept of being, with being in life. Derrida talks of "relation without relation" (78). For me, this is, per se, not a relation to (another), but a relation of (being). Relation, per se, is relation (or responsibility) that comes with conscious living; it is the relationship/responsibility we have in being. It is a categorical, not personal, relationship age that is. As categorical, it removes the power-play inherent in traditional relationships—that is, my being "responsible" when I follow the orders of those more powerful than I.

Operationalizing this new responsibility requires me to make a (free) choice; my actions owe allegiance to no other. I am free to be responsible or irresponsible. The choice I make—and it is I who must choose—is dependent only on my sense of being, not on my obligation to an other. Hence, I have a "relation without relation," I am responsible without sacrificing myself or my being to the other. I am freely responsible and within this "free" responsibility there lies the possibility of new possibilities.

The contradiction inherent in this position (the *aporia* Derrida recognizes

12. "Awe" does indeed have a sense of fear associated with it in its dictionary definitions. In fact, in old English awe (aye or aege) is synonymous with fear—"immediate and active fear; terror, dread" is the way the O.E.D. phrases it. However, over the centuries, awe as a word has moved into "reverential or respectful fear" or subduedness in the "presence of supreme authority . . . or mysterious sacredness." Finally, it becomes "solemn and reverential wonder, tinged with latent fear, inspired by what is terribly sublime and majestic in nature" (O.E.D. 1989, vol. 1, page 831). This latest sense is the one Harvey (note 8) uses, referring to the "overwhelming sense of unknowable mystery." The tremendousness of this mystery appears both revealed and yet hidden the more we understand the universe's "design." A final understanding (a T.O.E.) is, of course, quite contrary to what I'm both describing and arguing for in the *mysterium tremendum*.

so well) is that this ideal can never be. On the one hand, an ethics which has no relations is (or easily can be) an "ethics" of selfishness. Again, hardly an ethics. Yet, the possibility inherent in this intriguing impossibility is inspiring.

My position in being in-the-world then, as I see it, is that of being free to be irresponsible and yet freely choose "the other" course, that of responsibility. I make this choice not out of personal concern for the other—hence, obligating myself to the other and the other to myself—but because I am. Because I am of being.

With an arrogance known only to fools, I now rush in to the *aporias* of life that Derrida illuminates darkly. I believe our spirituality must be not an infusion of grace or spirit from outside, but a relationship of being we develop, with awe and reverence toward all creation. This relationship is, I further believe, without relations to any particular "other," but is a relationship of being, one we hold as we (freely) choose responsibility. In this "free" choice lies one of life's paradoxes.

Recognition of this paradox is an educational mission. The complexity of this paradox is not easily seen; yet if not seen, our sense of responsibility is no more than a subjugation of weaker to stronger. If we are not to accept this power relationship as responsibility, if we wish a sense of spirituality that enhances rather than subjugates, that opens new possibilities, then we need not only education, but a new vision of education. Education in the sense I am considering is education which focuses on *our being*—on our engagement with life as this manifests itself in humanity, the world, the universe, and the cosmos. Such an education does struggle with the spiritual, and is infused with the spiritual at the same time it infuses the spiritual with us. This is an education which requests the being of all we hold sacred, while at the same time, manifests a faith that questioning will lead us to the sacredness of being.

So begin my struggles with spirituality.

Note

I thank Vikki Hillis, my graduate assistant, for her advice on ways to frame my struggles. The struggles are mine, not hers, but they are more eloquently and accurately stated due to her help.

References

Bateson, G. (1979). *Mind and Nature.* New York: E. P. Dutton.
Bateson, G., and M. C. Bateson (1987). *Angels Fear.* New York: Macmillan.
Berman, M. (1981). *The Re-enchantment of the World.* Ithaca, NY: Cornell University Press.
Bernstein, R. (1991). *The New Constellation.* Cambridge, MA: M.I.T. Press.
Berry, T. (1988). *The Dream of the Earth.* San Francisco: Sierra Club Books.

——— (1992). *The Universe Story*. San Francisco: Harper.
Bowers, C.A. (1993). *Critical Essays*. New York: Teacher College Press.
——— (1995). *Educating for an Ecologically Sustainable Culture*. Albany, NY: SUNY Press.
Burtt, E. A. (1955). *The Metaphysical Foundation of Modern Physical Science*. New York: Doubleday Anchor Books. (Original work published 1932).
Dante Alighieri. (1915). *The Divine Comedy*. H. Johnson, Trans. New Haven: Yale University Press. (Original Latin publication early 14th century).
Darwin, C. (1964). *Origin of the Species*. Cambridge, MA: Harvard University Press. (Original work published 1859).
Davies, P. (1995). *Are We Alone?* New York: Basic Books.
Derrida, J. (1995). *The Gift of Death*. D. Wills, Trans. Chicago: University of Chicago Press. (Original French publication 1992).
Doll, W. (1993). *A Post-modern Perspective on Curriculum*. New York: Teachers College Press.
——— (1997). "Curriculum and the Concept of Control." In W. Pinar (Ed.). *Curriculum: New Ideas in and for the Field*. New York: Garland Press.
Eddington, A. (1928). *The Nature of the Physical World*. New York: Macmillan.
Heidegger, M. (1977). "The Question Concerning Technology." W. Lovitt, Ed. and Trans. in *The Question Concerning Technology and Other Essays*. New York: Harper, Colophon Books. (Original German publication 1954).
James, W. (1956). "Is Life Worth Living?" In *The Will to Live*. New York: Dover Publications. (Original publication 1897).
Johnson, G. (1996). *Fire in the Mind*. New York: Knopf.
Kauffman, S. (1993). *The Origins of Order*. New York: Oxford University Press.
——— (1995). *At Home in the Universe*. New York: Oxford University Press.
Kierkegaard, S. (1983). *Fear and Trembling*, Vol. 6. (H. Hong and E. Hong, Trans. and Eds. Princeton: Princeton University Press. (Original Danish publication 1843).
McKnight, D. (1997). Errand into the Wilderness: Thematic Analysis of the Puritan Influence on American Education. Unpublished doctoral dissertation. Baton Rouge: Louisiana State University.
Monod, J. (1971). *Chance and Necessity*. New York: Alfred A. Knopf. (Original French publication 1970).
Newton, I. (1952). *Opticks,* 4th ed. New York: Dover Publications. (Original work published 1730).
Otto, R. (1923). *The Idea of Holy*. J. Harvey, Trans. Oxford: Oxford University Press. (Original German publication 1917).
Prigogine, I. and I. Stengers (1984). *Order Out of Chaos*. New York: Bantam.
Quinn, M. E. (1997). Faith and Its Crisis. Unpublished doctoral dissertation. Baton Rouge: Louisiana State University.
Tillich, P. (1957). *Dynamics of Faith*. New York: Harper & Brothers.
Wertheim, M. (1995). *Pythagoras' Trousers*. New York: Times Books.
Whitehead, A. N. (1967). *Science and the Modern World*. New York: Free Press. (Original work published 1925).
——— (1978). *Process and Reality,* Corrected Ed. (D. Griffin and D. Sherburne, Eds.) New York: Free Press. (Original work published 1929).

CHAPTER TWO

Progressivism, the Millennium, and the New Age: Thoughts on Reading James Redfield's Celestine Novels

Dennis Carlson

Arthur C. Clarke's epic novel, *2001: A Space Odyssey* (1968), adapted in movie form by Stanley Kubrick as it was being written, ends with the space traveler experiencing his own death and rebirth under the guiding hand of an archetypal cosmic power—represented by a monolith. Reborn as a child of the cosmos with vast new powers, "the baby stared into the depths of the crystal monolith," Clarke writes, "seeing—but not yet understanding—the mysteries that lay ahead." All the child knew was that it could not stay where it was. "The direction, though not the nature, of his destiny was clear before him" (218). With superhuman new powers, and new understandings of the nature of the universe and his own infinite possibilities, the child of the cosmos returns to earth. There, viewing the lush green planet from space, he watches as a "slumbering cargo of death"—an ICBM—is blasted into orbit, about to begin a nuclear war that will no doubt destroy humanity and much of the rest of the earth. Sensing the threat, the child "put forth his will, and the circling megatons flowered in a silent detonation." Clarke leaves the child of the cosmos there, "brooding over his still untested powers," and "not quite sure what to do next."

If there is a defining myth of our time, it is perhaps this myth of the millennium and of cultural transformation. It is a myth in which we cast ourselves as the cosmic child—facing the future expectantly, full of new powers and understandings, yet still uncertain what direction our transformation will take. In saying that the millennium is a myth, I do not mean to discredit or dispel it, or treat it as a falsehood, although some would. For example, the popular science writer Stephen J. Gould argues in *Questioning the Millennium* (1997) that the sense of expectancy that is associated with the millennium has no basis in logic and that the millennium myth needs to be dispelled. All calendars, after all, are based on arbitrary beginning points. Furthermore, the Christian calendar is governed by a purely arbitrary base ten number system, so that decades, centuries, and millennia take on particular importance which they would not have if we used another number base or were Chinese rather than American. Finally, Gould argues that expectations of dramatic events—either for the good or the bad—have their origins in religious traditions—in this case a Christian doctrine, which looks forward to a Second Coming and a final battle between good and evil. As a scientist, Gould suggests we abandon such nonsense and recognize that it is nonsense. We should rise above the myth of the millennium. Unfortunately, while I think Gould and others of a scientific frame of mind who share his perspective raise important concerns, they miss the point about myth. They fall victim to the modernist tendency to understand myth as a falsehood that needs to be revealed as such and then put aside and left behind. The millennium is indeed an arbitrary marker of time, history, and transformation, and it is important that we recognize this. Indeed, as Gould reminds us, for much, if not most, of the world's population, the year 2000 is just another year and, in fact, is not even designated as the year 2000. But because the millennium is a myth, does not mean it is "false," or should be dispelled, or that it is inconsequential. Its "truth" is in its recognition that modern culture is in the midst of transforming itself in ways we are not yet fully capable of comprehending. To this extent, the millennium, like all great myths, needs to be read as a sign of the times, a message we are sending ourselves, a self-fulfilling prophecy.

At the same time, myths—by their very nature—come with no fixed meanings or politics. In the language of cultural studies, myths are "floating signifiers" whose meaning may support divergent and even contradictory claims, projects, and practices. For cultural conservatives, the millennium is a sign of the coming collapse of all moral standards and absolute truths, a collapse that can only be prevented by returning to a Eurocentric cultural heritage and resisting the rhetoric of multiculturalism and diversity. Fundamentalist religious groups look to the millennium as a time of Armageddon, the Apocalypse, the Second Coming, and the Rapture. Their millennial text is the Book of Revelations, in which St. John the Divine reports that he "saw an angel come down from heaven. . . . And he laid hold on . . . Satan, and bound him a thousand years. . . . And when the thousand years expired, Satan shall be loosed out of his prison." Among others, the millennium is a sign that a dramatic new leap in human consciousness is about to occur—as in *2001*. But this is not in itself progressive. The mass suicide of "Heaven's Gate" cultists in 1997 suggests the millennium myth may lead some to disengage from struggles to build a better world here on earth and seek transformation and transcendence by leaving their earthly "vehicles" behind and catching a ride on a passing UFO.

What, then, might the millennium myth mean in a democratic and progressive sense? I begin with the premise that progressives must be about more than criticizing the millennium mythology. They must offer, more proactively, a millennium mythology of their own, including myths of knowing and becoming educated. In this sense, I use the word "myth" in neither a positive nor negative sense, but rather to refer to sets of beliefs, stories, metaphors, and images that govern the way we make meaning out of our experiences and thus, how we organize our everyday lives together. Myths are embedded in the basic structure of our language and everyday rituals. They are thus involved in giving purpose and direction to our lives. They are bearers of cultural memory and meaning. Metaphorically, myths are the cultural lenses through which we view and represent the world. Different lenses reveal the world very differently. At the same time, some represent reality in simplistic, stereotypic, and uncritical ways, or they assume that the world is "naturally" the way it is. Other myths see things more complexly and are serious efforts to grapple with the truth. Some myths represent the perspective of a very limited few, while others are forged out of a democratic dialogue and represent a more comprehensive and inclusive "picture" of the world. Some serve progressive ends, others seek to make us captives of the status quo and inequitable power relations.

If these are fundamentally new times that will call for progressives to re-imagine democratic forms of education and culture in transformative ways, they are also fundamentally unstable times of many competing political and cultural mythologies. To this point, progressives have not been able to articulate a bold new vision of the American dream, and a new vision of what public education—from early childhood to adult learners—could be. It is a time characterized by an exhaustion of the progressive impulse in American education and culture. It is no longer fashionable to speak of transformative change or engage in utopian visioning. Progressives have become more pragmatic and less driven by a purpose and sense of historical mission. But progressivism has not lost its vision entirely. Indeed, I think a new progressive myth of the millennium is emerging in contemporary American culture, one that holds great promise and points us in important new directions as educators and citizens of a democratic culture. It is what I will call, following popular usage, a "New Age" myth of the millennium.

Of course, the notion of a New Age is about as slippery as the notion of the millennium and much gets subsumed under the rubric of the New Age. It has been used to refer to a whole array of diverse ideas and movements in "postmodern" America—some of which are even contradictory—all mixed together in a spiritual pastiche. As a cultural movement, it has been associated with everything from the use of crystals and pyramids to focus and harness energy, to belief in witches and paganism, to a cosmology that is integrating the new physics with spirituality, to belief in UFOs and contact or "communion" with aliens, to self-help forms of therapy based on Eastern forms of mind/body connectedness, to the assertion of an Earth Goddess mythology, and so on. While there is much of value in these movements, they have tended up this point to be "fringe" and "counter-cultural" movements and have become the brunt of jokes from conservatives and progressives alike. Aside from this formidable problem, the New Age movement is, at this point, highly commercialized and commodified. It is a movement grounded in popular culture, which has become increasingly controlled by multinational media conglomerates. The marketing of the New Age moved into high gear by the 1990s, with Hollywood and major trade publishers becoming the major producers of New Age texts. By reducing a cultural movement to "entertainment," by emphasizing stories with happy endings, and by focusing upon personal themes of self-discovery and romance, popular culture has worked to diffuse the progressive political potential of the New Age millennium myth.

Nevertheless, behind the constructed media image of the New Age lie some very basic progressive ideas stated in new and potentially quite radical ways. One of the contradictions of the new multinational capitalism is that it is increasingly dependent on the mass marketing of popular culture, and progressive stories sell—even those that overtly criticize multinational capitalism. If the New Age movement were just a fringe movement of Southern California baby boomers, then New Age novels, self-help books, and films would not be able to construct such a large market. What this audience is buying is a retelling of the progressive story of history, an idealistic story of the reawakening of the democratic spirit to its historic sense of purpose. The reawakening of idealism and a sense of history within the public is, ultimately, what the New Age myth of the millennium is all about. In an age that appeared to have lost its ideals and its sense of history, this must be taken as a hopeful sign.

Because the New Age myth of the millennium has found expression in popular culture, its progressive potentials remain undeveloped and ambiguous. If these potentials are to be developed, young people (and people of all ages for that matter) will need to become more critical readers and consumers of popular culture texts. With regard to New Age texts, we need to ask: In what ways are New Age ideas and mythologies consistent with deeply rooted democratic beliefs and values in our culture? In what ways are they consistent with the advancement of democratic projects at this point in history? And what aspects of the New Age movement currently blunt, or block, its progressive potential to transform culture consistent with the further advancement of the democratic imagination and vision? More particularly, educators need to ask what the implications of New Age ideas are for the way we organize teaching and learning. Progressive educators should not underestimate the magnitude of the change that will be required in public education over the next several decades in order for the idea of public education to survive. Progressive educators will need to think boldly, rather than tinker with the way things are. New Age perspectives on education may help in this regard, for they return us to some very basic and necessary "truths" or insights about democratic forms of knowing and becoming educated that tend to get forgotten in all of the professional concern for how to more effectively deliver a curriculum to students to raise standardized test scores.

The Celestine Insights

To explore these issues, I want to focus my comments upon a New Age bestseller in the 1990s, James Redfield's *Celestine Prophecy* (1993), and its sequel, *The Tenth Insight* (1996). While these are presented as fiction, they are written in the form of a self-education journey, or quest, so they have particular relevance in assessing New Age perspectives on education. Both books were published by Time-Warner, among the largest of the new global media conglomerates, and more sequels and a film have been produced. The first book, in particular, was "packaged" in a way that reflects a concern with the New Age market. For example, it includes a page that informs readers of a Celestine newsletter to which they can subscribe, along with the following: "Also available from James Redfield is an audio tape based on his interpretations of an individual's moon sign and sun sign." The tape supposedly helps people "understand your particular control issues and discover your most inspired, spiritual mission." Perhaps in response to criticism for such an overt marketing approach to the book, no advertisements or other promotional material is included in the sequel. One gets a hint of other criticisms leveled against the first book in an introductory note in the sequel. Redfield writes in the note: "I don't mean to minimize the formidable problems still facing humanity, only to suggest that each of us, in our own way, is involved in the solution." In this simple statement, he points to the central tension that runs throughout the New Age movement—the tension between a naive optimism and a more realistic hope, between believing that the crisis we face in modern culture calls for a collective response and believing change must begin at the individual, or personal, level. If New Age authors such as Redfield tend towards naive hope and individualistic responses to complex global problems, it is perhaps wise to see this as a reaction against the reigning cynicism of the age and the tendency among progressives to emphasize collective state responses—which have their limits as well.

The plot of the two Celestine novels goes something like this. A middle-aged man whose life seems to be moving without clear direction—a purposely nondescript "everyman"—is informed by a friend of an ancient Manuscript that has supposedly shown-up in Peru and that turns out to have been written by Mayans right before their culture rather suddenly disappeared. The Manuscript reportedly speaks of a transformation in human consciousness that is to occur at about this time in history and includes important "Insights" to help the people of the world move into the next phase of their historic evolution. So the central character decides on a whim to go to Peru and see what he can learn. Meanwhile, the Peruvian government, in collaboration with the Catholic Church hierarchy in Peru and presumably other groups, is after the Manuscript. This is really a variation on the myth of the journey of the hero, which is always a journey of self-discovery and self-knowledge. Along the way, our modern-day hero meets others searching for the Manuscript and who know about various parts of it. These fellow travelers reveal, one by one, the ten insights contained in the Manuscript—although the Manuscript itself will remain elusive and some of the insights a bit vague. The first novel ends with the central characters, who have learned nine of the insights, being pursued by the Peruvian police. The protagonists "vibrate" their energy at a higher level (something they learned through one of the insights) and thus are no longer visible to their pursuers. This is something like the idea of being "transported" in the Star Trek series in that it is based very loosely on the new physics, but Redfield also moves into the realm of fantasy and science fiction. Supposedly, the Mayans—the authors of the Manuscript—had achieved this capacity as well and literally vibrated themselves into another dimension. In the sequel, Redfield's protagonist—back in this dimension—continues the journey in search of the Tenth Insight, but this time deep in the Appalachian Mountains. Here, it turns out, sinister forces in the state, in collusion with multinational corporate conglomerates, have begun to harness a new source of power they have discovered in the earth. They are out to have complete control of this new power source. To stop them, the cast of characters has to remember their own previous lives when they had the chance to affect change but for one reason or another were too insecure to act. Working cooperatively, the group is able this time to help save the future—at least temporarily—for the forces of decentralization and democratic, grassroots control of the new power being unleashed.

Around this very sketchy story, Redfield leads the reader through a series of ten "Insights." The Insights get talked about, rather than actually stated, and some are quite ambiguous in their meaning. Nevertheless, taken together, the Insights represent a condensation of some of the major themes woven throughout New Age texts. It is as if Redfield set out to construct the broadest possible audience by taking ideas and themes from diverse sources and presenting them in ways that many people can understand and relate to. Because the characters in the novels are really just convenient foils through which the author is able to expound upon his views, I will not typically identify characters when I quote from the books. Indeed, I do not want to read these books as fiction so much as an introduction to New Age approaches to education and culture.

The First Insight, according to Redfield, "occurs when we become conscious of the *coincidences* in our lives" (1996, 6). In modern usage, coincidences are defined as a sequence of occurrences that appear to have a causal relationship, but, in fact, do not. The sequence of events is presumed to be accidental, or follow the laws of chance. All definitions serve purposes and have effects, and we must, consequently, ask what purpose and effect this modern notion of coincidence serves. One of the effects, if not purposes, of this idea might be to discourage us from looking for meaning in the occurrences of everyday life. By taking coincidences seriously, we are led to reflect critically on the occurrences of our everyday lives and to ask: What is the relationship between the occurrence of these two events? What is the message I am trying to tell myself? As such, seeing and interpreting the coincidences of everyday life is a way of deliberately reflecting upon the world around us and constructing meaning out of events. Redfield asks, how many times have you begun with a "hunch or intuition concerning something" you want to do. Then, "after you had half forgotten about it and focused on other things," you suddenly met someone or read something or went somewhere that led to the very opportunity you envisioned (6). Here, as with other insights, Redfield provides the reader with several possible interpretations. The most literal of these is a metaphysical interpretation. Redfield suggests that there is "some other process operating behind the scenes" (6–7), some spirit world or dimension that is sending us messages or signs in these coincidences. Another interpretation is more consistent with humanistic psychology.

The act of "seeing" connections between apparently unrelated events, of stumbling upon the answer you were looking for, is related to a heightened "wide-awakeness," or engagement, with the world around us—what Heidegger called "attunement." We suddenly "see" new relationships or connections between things, and we simultaneously see how these relationships can help us solve a problem at hand. Professional educators in the twentieth century often talked about the power of intuitive thinking, and some reform movements, such as the "new" math and science of the 1960s, were supposedly designed to foster intuitive thinking. But these efforts have, by and large, been half-hearted and overly preplanned. Real intuitive insights and "discovery learning" only come out of questions and problems we pose or face ourselves, and they require an attunement and focusing of attention that schools often seem to go out of their way to discourage. To promote intuitive insights, education must become about "reading" everyday life and becoming more aware of the world around us. Intuitive thinking is democratic because it focuses our attention on actively making meaning rather than passively receiving meaning or knowledge.

The Second Insight has to do with becoming aware of history as the story of changes in the "World View" of people. It also involves becoming aware that we are historical actors involved in the slow evolution of human consciousness towards greater self-awareness and the achievement of its vision for itself. According to Redfield: "What's really important is the World View of each historical period, what the people were feeling and thinking." Once we understand history in this way, we can see "what our contribution is toward further progress. We can pinpoint where we come in, so to speak. . . . And that gives us a sense of where we are going" (1996, 20). The cultural mythology of the New Age is, in this sense, very Hegelian—very much a mythology of the "spirit of history" moving upward through a series of transformative leaps towards the current age, and leading on from here through new leaps in human consciousness or World View. But largely missing is Hegel's dialectic, the struggle between opposing social forces and ideas. Instead, the spirit of history is represented as advancing primarily through an evolutionary process in which old ways of thinking begin to lead culture towards a crisis, out of which a New World View emerges. This is similar to the process of change that Kuhn talked about in natural science in terms of "paradigm shifts." Redfield's leaps in human consciousness are also represented in a more Platonic sense as leading towards reunification with transcendent truths—and thus, to "pure spirit."

This story of history, as the transformation of human consciousness in a progressive direction, is, ironically, one that many academic progressives have begun to leave behind in the rush to embrace postmodernism and a politics of pragmatism as opposed to idealism. There are, to be sure, good reasons to be suspicious of some tendencies within idealistic accounts of history. They tend to treat consciousness and ideas almost as if they were freefloating without an adequate account of how consciousness is shaped by the material world. This was Marx's major criticism of Hegel's idealism, although Marx remained idealistic in his own way, merely pulling consciousness down into the material world of politics and struggles over power. Both also believed that there was one road of history, and that it was possible to speak of a human consciousness that was evolving and emerging in the world. Postmodernism represents a recognition that there is no unified human consciousness, as such, and that those who have talked of a human consciousness and its historic evolution have generally taken for granted modern Western culture as the highest form of human consciousness. So the New Age cultural mythology tends to construct a unified history of human consciousness that is naturalized to all peoples and eliminates cultural difference. This history simplifies complex and diverse cultural developments and washes away differences by moving the reader along from one great leap in human consciousness to another—from the primal jungle to the early Neolithic and pagan cultures with their female, agricultural gods, to the establishment of authority and authorized truths and patriarchal gods of domination, first by the church and then by science, to the realization that we must reestablish a lost unity, a lost connectedness to the earth and cosmos, that we must deliberately take control of our own evolution as a species.

With all of these problems, it may be that progressivism needs a story of history as the transformation of human consciousness. It just must be one that is less Eurocentric, homogenizing, and naively optimistic. For only by historicizing the present moment is it possible to project ourselves into the future deliberately. It is also important to recognize that there is a global or world culture of sorts emerging, that most humans living around the world went through some pretty dramatic changes in the twentieth century, and that these changes were related to the emergence of new ways of thinking about the world, new world views. Belief in the historical transformation of human consciousness also motivates people to believe that they can play a part in that transformation. The individual feels part of an historical becoming. For those who have become too cynical or "realistic" for such idealism, it is well to remember that those who make history do so because they believe in history.

They also know how to mobilize and use power. Progressivism cannot get by on ideals alone. Idealism must be wedded to a more realistic assessment of what it takes to advance democratic projects. So progressivism speaks in an idealistic language of social justice and human freedom, but also in a more pragmatic language of empowerment and cultural struggle over power. History is not only the story of the transformation of human consciousness, but also the story (simultaneously) of the transformation of power relations in everyday life.

With the Third Insight, Redfield articulates a New Age theory of power or "energy," and many of the remaining insights are concerned with how this energy is to be used in changing human consciousness and culture. According to the manuscript, the millennial transformation in human consciousness and culture will begin to occur when people "learn to perceive what was formerly an invisible type of energy" (1996, 41). The manuscript predicts that people will slowly begin to understand how to tap into and utilize this energy in ways that will revolutionize human relations—although the connection with human relations is not yet made clear. Education, understood as the process of becoming more self-aware, of moving to a higher level of human consciousness, is presented as learning to "see" or be more aware of power in our everyday lives and learning to use power in ways that do not dominate or oppress others.

Redfield grounds his theory of cultural power in a rather free interpretation of the "new" science. We might think of New Age cultural mythology as rupturing the borders that, particularly in the modern era, have separated scientific theory from social theory, and the scientific from the spiritual. From cosmological and quantum physics, Redfield takes the idea that "what we perceive as hard matter is mostly empty space with a pattern of energy running through it." Power, or energy, is thus viewed as the basic stuff of the universe and as the active force in cultural production. This new physics is wedded in New Age cultural mythology with the new ecological sciences. One scientist in *The Celestine Prophecy*, who is studying the effect of directing energy at plants, observes: "We've tried to look at these plants as total energy systems ... What we have found is that the total ecosystem around each plant is really one living system, an organism. And the health of each of the parts impacts on the health of the whole" (1993, 46). This idea is taken from the so-called "Gaia hypothesis," which posits that to understand any part of the earth, or any life on the earth, you have to understand it as part of the whole energy system, which has all the characteristics of a living, sentient being—hence, the name "Gaia," in reference to the early Greek earth goddess (Lovelock 1979).

There are some obvious connections between this New Age theory of energy and a progressive theory of cultural power. And the view that culture may be studied as the distribution and deployment of power is becoming more influential. In the language of the popular social theorist, Michel Foucault (1979), culture—which is to say, knowledge or truth and the ritualization of knowledge or truth—is really the production of power, so that we can speak of culture as characterized by a particular "economy of power"—a distribution and circulation that positions individuals within power relations and attaches itself to their bodies, as well as their minds. This theory of cultural power is very similar to Redfield's theory of energy, it seems to me. When progressives use the language of empowerment or disempowerment, they are, consciously or not, drawing upon the metaphor of an invisible energy field in which power is circulating between and among people. Ecological metaphors of power and energy distribution, so long as they are dynamic rather than static, help us appreciate that we are not autonomous individuals, but part of larger power dynamics which are producing culture.

At the same time, New Age cultural mythology tends to understand ecological principles and the distribution of power as operating primarily at an individual level. Which is to say, it focuses on the circulation and distribution of power among people as individuals rather than as members of class, race, gender, sexual, and other identity groups. So conflicts over power, and power relations of domination and subordination, are viewed as human conflicts.

The Fourth Insight, for example, is an awareness that "we humans have always sought to increase our personal energy in the only manner we have known: by seeking to psychologically steal it from others—an unconscious competition that underlies all human conflict in the world" (Redfield 1996, 66). Redfield argues that when two individuals meet in contemporary culture, two things typically happen simultaneously. One person receives power from the other and comes away from the encounter feeling stronger and empowered. Simultaneously, the other party is drained of power or energy and comes away feeling weak and disempowered. "Dominating another makes the dominator feel powerful and knowledgeable, but it sucks the vital energy out of those who are being dominated" (1996, 88). The key to the Fourth Insight is thus, to become aware of contemporary culture as a "vast competition for energy and thus, for power" (89). Unfortunately, Redfield relates none of this to historic struggles, so its politics of everyday life is an individualized politics. To its credit, though, it does shift our attention to everyday life as the real "scene of the battle" in culture. One of the dilemmas of progressivism in the modern era, was that it encouraged people to look to a liberal-welfare state to legislate progress. State responses are needed. But it is also becoming increasingly clear to many that legislative progress may not translate into "real" progress unless we redirect more of our focus on everyday life. This suggests, among other things, an increased emphasis on the study of interpersonal relations in educational institutions.

In order to develop these thoughts on interpersonal relations further, Redfield takes the reader on an excursion into the cosmos and back to the moment of its birth. The Fifth Insight suggests that through such excursions, individuals are slowing learning to "recharge their batteries" without needing to drain power from others. Through a radical reconnectedness to the cosmos involving forms of meditation and re-grounding in the actual experience of "being here," individuals are presumably able to achieve an ecological "balance" in their relations with others. Once more, this is an idea woven together out of various New Age influences. It blends eastern beliefs in the power of meditation with an existential return to experience, and it mixes both of these with the new cosmological science. This cosmological science has given the New Age a myth of origins, a new Genesis story. In Redfield's first novel, the central character has a transcendent experience while sitting on a ridge overlooking a great expanse of the Peruvian forest. The experience consists of reliving the birth of the cosmos from the instant of the "big bang," down through the eons when stars are created and burn out, down through the epochs of geological history and biological evolution on earth, up to the present moment and his present experience of being here. The character experiences reliving this "cosmogenesis" rather than imagining it from an outsider's perspective. He is there at the creation, part of the creative energy that gives birth to the cosmos. According to the Fifth Insight, people will slowly become aware "of what has long been called mystical consciousness. . . . For a growing number of humans, this consciousness would become experientially real—because these individuals would experience flashes or glimpses of this state of mind during the course of their lives." In achieving this state of connectedness to the primordial force or spirit of the cosmos, individuals—according to Redfield—"are receiving energy from another source—a source we will eventually learn to tap at will" (1996, 106).

This is all very similar to ideas popularized in the human potential movement within psychology, which is perhaps most associated with the influential work of Abraham Maslow (1962) regarding a "hierarchy of needs." At the top of this hierarchy, which corresponds to stages in the evolution of human consciousness, Maslow places the state of "self-actualization." According to Maslow, "self-actualizing people, those who have come to a high level of maturation, health, and self-fulfillment, have so much to teach us that sometimes they seem almost like a different breed" (67). He associates self-actualization with "peak experiences." During such experiences, everything is seen as a whole, and people become nonjudgmental. It is almost as if, Maslow notes, "the universe was conceived to be a unit" (70). Everything is also bathed in a "richness of detail," a detail that is only possible with this kind of "absorbed, fascinated, fully attending cognition" (71). This is also similar to what William James called the "varieties of religious experience," and what Freud called the "oceanic experience"—the experience of being part of a cosmic ocean in which the ego is dissolved. In Maslow's words, through peak experiences, individuals may become "ego-transcending, self-forgetful, egoless." They can be "desireless, unselfish, non-needing" (74). In the mythology of self-actualization, we may also see the influence of what, in philosophy, is called Platonic idealism. At the top of Plato's (1955) "ladder" of ways of knowing the world, the ego dissolves through transcendence of the ego and reconnection with the unity of all truth and knowledge—something philosophy set as its aim. But, whereas Plato tied this transcendent experience, this egoless state, to the attitude of highly educated philosophers and mathematicians, Maslow and the New Age movement tie peak experiences to a recuperation of an expressive and connected self that modern forms of education may actively stifle.

Peak experiences also, and in a seemingly contradictory manner, are associated with acceptance of the world as it is with all of its shortcomings and injustices. Acceptance of the world, and with it a "letting go" of the ego, is one of the features of eastern spirituality that has always separated it from progressivism in the West. How, after all, can we work to build the "good society" and fight injustices if we learn to accept the world as it is? Furthermore, everyone has interests, and those interests are what lead people to change the world. Those who claim to rise above their egos are not necessarily to be trusted. These are significant issues for progressives to address. But, it may well be the case that those who have fought hardest against injustices are those who have also learned to accept the world as okay, with all of its problems, and see beyond the current battle to a broader unity of all people. Redfield writes: "The West is correct in maintaining that life is about progress, about evolving towards something higher. Yet, the East is also correct in emphasizing that we must let go of control with the ego. We can't progress by using logic alone. We have to attain a fuller consciousness . . . because only then can our evolution towards something better be guided by a higher part of ourselves" (1996, 142). This suggests a contradictory, but potentially powerful, form of Zen progressivism—based on finding the energy to change the world by accepting it as it is, in all its wonder.

It is impossible to schedule peak experiences in the school day or the course syllabus. The only way for education to promote peak experiences is to provide the context in which individuals might be led to experience reconnectedness to the cosmos. Native American peoples traditionally went on "vision quests" to have peak experiences, to meditate, fast, and commune with nature. In the second Celestine novel, a Native American serves as a guide as the central character prepares to undertake a vision quest into the Appalachian Mountains. In contemporary culture, we provide the young (or the old for that matter) with few such opportunities. To promote peak experiences, education would need to move (at least occasionally) outside the confines of the classroom and campus, back into the natural environment. More time would be needed for meditation and self-reflection, and then for periods of reengagement in the world with a renewed sense of purpose and direction.

In the Sixth Insight, Redfield links peak experiences with changes in interpersonal relations. According to the manuscript, as people become more connected to the cosmos, they will begin to understand their own particular way of controlling others. "This style is something we repeat over and over again. I call it our unconscious *control drama*" (1996, 121). Human service professionals will recognize this insight as a variation on themes popularized in "Transactional Analysis" (TA) and other client-center counseling and conflict-resolution approaches. These approaches are based on interpreting human relations in terms of their "game" structure and in terms of "scripts" individuals repeat over and over in the games that structure their relations with others (Berne 1996; Steiner 1990). A prominent control script in TA is that of the intimidator or persecutor. Its opposite is often called the "poor me" script. A game begins when an intimidator meets a person living the "poor me" script. Redfield writes: "Each drama needs a matching drama to be fully played out. What the intimidator needs in order to get energy is either a poor me, or another intimidator" (1996, 204). So in a sense, both parties are attempting to control the other to validate their scripts. The ideal interpersonal relationship, from this perspective, is one in which the cycle of codependency is broken and both parties recognize each other as equal, autonomous adults. Although these ideas have been applied to many types of interpersonal relations, including teacher-student relations, they have been most associated with couple counseling. According to the theory of codependency, we expect the other person in the relationship to make us whole and complete, to make us happy, to give our life meaning and purpose, and so forth. According to Redfield, "the problem with this completed person, this O, that both people think they have reached, is that it has taken two people to make this one whole person . . ."

In the end, "both people want to run this whole person they have created," which means that this type of relationship always breaks down into a power struggle. "But we are waking up now. No one wants to be subservient to anyone else any longer" (1996, 194).

This emphasis upon a transactional analysis of interpersonal relations is very consistent with what one sees in much of the self-help literature available in popular culture today, and the New Age movement has been closely linked to various approaches to self-help counseling. All of these various traditions offer individuals ways to analyze their everyday relations with significant others. All are optimistic in the sense that they believe people can change once they become aware of the scripts or roles they are playing, all affirm relationships between equals, and all believe people should become less dependent upon other people for their happiness and learn to take back control of their lives. Since the 1970s, community counseling agencies throughout the country have begun to rely more and more upon these approaches to counseling clients, at least partially because the basic principles of such approaches, such as TA, are very easy to teach prospective counselors. Schools and colleges have also begun to teach these skills to students in peer counseling and mediation programs so that they can resolve their own conflicts.

This concern in the New Age movement for change at the level of interpersonal relations says something important about the cultural politics of the movement. Historically, progressivism has been associated with a cultural politics that places the emphasis upon group relations. The concern has been with challenging power relations of domination and subordination between groups of social actors defined by their gender, class, race, and sexual identities. This has led to a politics of political mobilization and lobbying for legislation to lessen, or overcome, historic inequalities between groups. I do not want to discount, in any way, the importance of this concern for relations between groups of social actors. It has, and must continue, to be an essential part of the progressive agenda. But, we must also, I think, face up to its limitations. A century of progressive legislation has brought about some important changes. But, it has also proven how difficult it is to legislate how people relate to one another in their everyday lives. The reaction against affirmative action provides a good example of this.

At the same time, the almost exclusive focus in New Age literature on the politics of everyday life is limited as well. Not only does it fail to recognize the importance of mobilizing and exerting power within the state to affect change in everyday life—the civil rights laws of the 1960s are a good case in point—it tends to discourage us from seeing group inequalities. Relations tend to get reduced to situational relations between individuals, so we fail to see the broader context of their relations. Those who are victims are presumed to actively "seek out" persecutors to fulfill their "poor me" scripts. Now it certainly is true that some battered women, for example, consistently seek out relationships with abusive men because they lack a positive sense of self-worth and feel they deserve nothing better. But it is not very useful to understand abuse as merely the result of two people seeking each other—a persecutor and a victim—and seeing both as equally at fault. Historically, women have been cast in the role of victim. It is also the case that they have resisted and struggled against abuse more than they have sought it out. But, properly linked to a politics and a history beyond the merely personal and situational, an analysis of the "games people play" can, I think, provide an important and heretofore missing component of a progressive cultural politics. It implies a much more active role on the part of individuals, outside the framework of a welfare state, in sustaining the conditions for freedom and democracy through their interpersonal relations with others. This, in turn, suggests a much more important role for education in teaching people what Foucault called the "ethics and practices of freedom"—ways of relating to one another that allow the other as much freedom as possible and that replace domination with negotiation and a sharing of power.

The Seventh and Eighth Insights relate to educational concerns perhaps most directly, for they point to the importance of learning how to deliberately reflect on our experiences, our beliefs, and the culture we inhabit. One might say this strikes to the very core of progressive educational concerns with helping individuals learn to direct their own education, to no longer be captive to beliefs and rituals or to take them for granted, to develop the capacity for *reflexivity*.

The Seventh Insight says, among other things, that in order to understand, or interpret, our various thoughts "we must take an observer position. When a thought comes, we must ask why? Why did this particular thought come now? How does it relate to my life questions?" (Redfield 1996, 169). From such a position, we examine events in terms of their significance, in terms of "a message that somehow pertains to our questions" (178). This relates closely to the First Insight, regarding coincidences and using intuitive thinking to make connections between seemingly unrelated events. This time, however, the emphasis is on a more deliberately reflective process involving a capacity to assume the role of the outside observer. This is the stance of the phenomenologist, the anthropologist, and the social scientist—"bracketing" or stepping outside of the everyday life world and looking back on it analytically. This is also a stance that has come under a good deal of criticism by postmodernists, and I think rightly so. We cannot step out of our lives so easily, and there is no neutral place "outside" of our lives from which we can observe what is going on. On the other hand, it is still useful to learn how to "step back" a bit from the everydayness of our lives so that we can reflect upon events from a bit less immediate and involved perspective. Once more, this deliberate reflection can lead in one of two directions. It can lead almost exclusively into a dwelling on one's own experience, an almost obsessive narcissism that is to be found in some New Age literature, which takes the form of journeys of self discovery. In this form, self-reflection leads to a more "positive" outlook on life. Thus, Redfield observes that through self-reflection, "soon, negative images will almost never happen" (169). A more progressive form of self-reflection must link personal meaning-making with the making and remaking of culture so that it is placed within a broader context, and it must be critical as much as "positive." Redfield certainly seems to understand self-reflection in this sense, for the novels are primarily about connecting one's personal life to a larger history of struggle to advance certain beliefs about how we might live more equitably together, in an ecological and caring culture. This is another of the central tensions or dilemmas that run throughout the novels—the tension between a cultural politics that is reduced to the power of positive thinking and a cultural politics that calls for critique of current beliefs and practices and is involved in struggle over power.

The Eighth Insight counters Redfield's emphasis upon self-reflection as an individual process by locating reflexivity within dialogue as well. According to the Manuscript: "As the members of a group talk, only one will have the most powerful idea at any given point in time" Others in the group, if alert and focused, "can feel who is about to speak, and then they can consciously focus their energy on this person, helping to bring out his [sic] idea with the greatest clarity." As the conversation progresses, according to Redfield, "someone else will have the most powerful idea, then someone else and so forth." The trick is to "concentrate on what is being said" and intuitively "feel when it is your turn" (1996, 214). Albeit in very simple language, this is a fairly good description of a progressive theory of dialogue. Everyone is attuned to what is being said, all voices are heard, and no one dominates the conversation. Dialogue allows individuals to express their own beliefs and interests at the same time that it encourages individuals to question their own beliefs and interests as others react to them. It reveals that there are multiple truths, multiple ways of making sense out of events and experiences, at the same time that it encourages the construction of a collective truth or meaning—even if that truth or meaning must also be open to change and revision as the dialogue continues. Dialogue is likely to become a more important feature of progressive forms of education in the twenty-first century as people increasingly recognize the importance of multiple truths or perspectives on issues. Unfortunately, what is missing from Redfield's New Age theory of dialogue is recognition of the need to include diverse voices within the dialogue. Aside from a Native American, all the central characters in the books are European American. This tendency towards Eurocentrism, including a romanticization of the "Noble Savage" and appropriation of Indian cultural mythology, is a deep current in the New Age movement, and one that needs to be seriously addressed—for it significantly limits the progressive potential of many New Age ideas.

From the concreteness of dialogue and reflection on the events of everyday life, Redfield, once more, pulls the reader back to a bigger picture, which has to do with advancing a "vision" for the world. The Ninth Insight predicts that around the time of the millennium, people around the world will begin to grasp "how human culture will change in the next millennium as a result of conscious evolution" (1996, 222). There are really two parts to this insight—that humans are about to achieve "conscious evolution," and that because of this, human culture will change in some fundamental ways. The idea of "conscious evolution," is, once more, very Hegelian. For Hegel (1910), the end of history finds the Self finally reaching full self-consciousness, recognizing that nothing fundamentally holds it back, that it is the maker of its own destiny. No longer captive of illusions, no longer insecure and beaten down, humanity would finally realize its full human potential. From his vantage point in the early nineteenth century, Hegel believed humanity finally was approaching such self-consciousness. The New Age cultural mythology merely extends Hegel's time frame. The Celestine novels talk vaguely about humans becoming capable of "conscious evolution" sometime in the next millennium.

The utopian vision of a postmillennium world that Redfield describes is based on a pastiche of cultural influences. There is Hegel's vision of a future that is more spiritual and humane. There is also Marx's vision of a future beyond capitalism where people share equally in the fruits of their labor and machines have freed individuals of the need to devote most of their lives to routine, menial, degrading forms of work. Finally, there is an ecological vision of once more living in harmony with the natural world and caring for Gaia. "By the middle of the next millennium," Redfield writes, "the means of survival— foodstuffs and clothing and transportation—will be totally automated and at everyone's disposal." People will live together in harmony, and "no one will consume excessively because we will have let go of the need to possess and to control for security." Instead of the constant pursuit of materialism, "our sense of purpose will be satisfied by the thrill of our own evolution" (1996, 223).

A "spiritual economy" will prevail in which people give money to those who give them spiritual truths and help them evolve. All of this future will be possible because the scarcity of resources of energy will be overcome, and because automation will free us of work. Which brings us to the Tenth Insight. This Insight has to do with "maintaining our optimism and staying awake" to the possibilities of the moment, realizing that our lives are part of a "long history of human awakening" (Redfield 1996, 234–235). The plea here, simply, is for individuals to keep the vision alive in their everyday lives, which means to advance a dream. One lives attuned to the present moment, but the present moment is also viewed as part of an historical process of becoming, so that one sees possibilities in everyday life to advance a vision of what the future could be.

Progressive Mythologies of the Spirit

Ultimately, the New Age movement and mythology speaks of a respiritualization of the progressive project. But respiritualization is neither "good" nor "bad" as such. It all depends upon what form respiritualization takes, and how we understand spirituality. So I want to conclude with a few thoughts on democratic and progressive forms of spirituality. I want to proceed by presenting a typology of cultural mythologies of the spirit, all of which are to be found in one form or another in the Celestine novels, and briefly discussing the cultural politics of each. The first cultural mythology of the spirit, and one most people think of when they hear the word "spirituality," is what I will call a *metaphysical spirituality*. Metaphysical discourses of the spirit speak of God and Satan, heaven and hell, of angels, astral zones, the afterlife, and a God who intervenes in history—sometimes to destroy (as in the "great flood" myth of Genesis) and sometimes to save (as in the myth of "Jonah in the whale"). Metaphysical discourses are governed by an interrelated set of binary oppositions or dichotomies—oppositions that separate the spirit world from the material world, the spirit from the body, this world and the afterlife. Often God, or various spirits, are presumed to have "plans" for people's lives—which, in its negative form, is associated with fatalism and the belief in predestination. So when we "open the door" by entertaining the idea that there is a spirit world parallel to the material world, we have to be aware of what we may be letting in the door along with this idea. It can very quickly lead to a new fatalism—a belief that the gods or spirits are pulling the strings. In Redfield's novels, there clearly is a spiritual world apart from the material, and coincidences are represented as messages or signs from this other dimension. At the same time, the spirit world for Redfield and many other New Age writers is no more than the afterlife of the self, so that if we receive messages from an afterlife, it is messages we are sending ourselves. Still, I think the New Age respiritualization of culture is not primarily the recuperation of metaphysical spirituality.

A second cultural mythology of the spirit is what is most often called Platonic idealism and which I will call the mythology of *idealistic spirituality*. While Plato is often associated with the rise of modern scientific and mathematical ways of knowing, he is also associated with a form of idealism that comes very close to being metaphysical. Plato accepted the notion that there is a spirit world—a world of pure truth, pure ideas, pure reason, pure knowing, pure unity of mind—which one returned to briefly after death, before being born again. Education, from such a viewpoint, is mythologized as a process of remembering—in this case, remembering the truth we knew when we were in the spirit world and which we forget when we were born back into the world. Now, this is very close to what Redfield suggests is going on in the Celestine novels. The task of each person is to remember the vision for his or her life and for the planet that they knew when they were in the afterlife, before they were reborn. One of the problems with such idealistic spirituality is that it tends to treat life as a poor substitute for the world of pure spirit or ideas we will return to upon death. So it is that Socrates, on his deathbed, presented the world he was about to return to as more real and substantial than the world and the friends he was saying good-bye to. Rather than fear death, Socrates almost seemed to embrace it, to seek it out—although he also felt unfairly condemned to die. We find a similar form of ascetic Platonism in some elements of the New Age movements. It took an extreme form in the "Heaven's Gate" cult mass suicide, for example. While Redfield has been influenced by Platonic idealism, he also backs away from it a bit, and in a progressive direction, I think. He does not, for example, represent the afterlife as a place of unified, all-knowing spirituality. Rather, he presents the reader with an afterlife that is peopled with spirits in various stages of working through their problems by reflecting on their previous lives and planning out the next. This focuses attention on bringing spirituality into this world and on the reconstruction of this world to make it more consistent with our visions and ideals.

Yet a third cultural mythology of the spirit is what might be called *subjective spirituality*. The subjectivist tradition in the Modern Age has been associated with an existential return to experience, and with this, a return to feeling, intuition, mysticism, and the ontological question of how we experience our "being in the world." Particularly in American culture, subjectivism has appealed to an individualistic ethic which places the self at the heart of the meaning-making process. Education is about self-knowledge, to "know thyself." The tendency in subjective spirituality, and in many New Age narratives of the "journey of the spirit," is that the self gets lost in its own narcissistic pleasures—telling its heroic story. The self gets lost in self-exploration and self-management; it comes to believe that it is a "free spirit" and that knowledge is found by turning inward to listen to the "real me" within. But the self is never a free spirit, and the inward journey ultimately must involve finding ourselves within culture, as both produced by and producers of meaning. This implies finding oneself within cultural struggles along a number of axes. Often, subjectivism is motivated by a desire to remove oneself from these struggles, to find meaning in a self-exploration alone. In education, we are witnessing a growing shift towards a subjectivist curriculum; and, in contrast to the objectivist curriculum that is the norm still in public education, the return to narrativity, story-telling, autobiography, and aesthetic and spiritual experiences must be considered progressive. But narratives of self discovery are not sufficient unto themselves. Subjectivism, to the extent that it represents the flight of the self into itself, might even be antiprogressive, for in such forms, it blunts efforts to develop a public consciousness or empathize with the struggles of others.

This suggests the influence of another cultural mythology of the spirit—one I will refer to as a mythology of the *spirit of history*. This too is an idealistic tradition, but not in the sense of positing an afterlife of pure ideas and transcendent truths. Within philosophy, this is a form of spirituality most associated with Hegel, and in somewhat less idealistic, but more politically radical, form with Marx. Hegelian idealism, more than Marxism, has had the strongest influence on the New Age movement. To some extent, this is reflective of the tendency in the New Age movement to see ideas as the dominant force shaping history, a notion most associated with Hegel, whereas Marx emphasized the primacy of material culture in shaping ideas. With the demise or near demise of Marxism by the late twentieth century, there has been a corresponding rise in influence of Hegelian idealism. Once more, ideas and visions are shaping history. But in Hegelian idealism, the influence of the material culture and world does not disappear, it is just not viewed as determinant. In both Marx and Hegel, there is a sense of dialectic, of the interplay between consciousness and material culture, and of the self as simultaneously produced by culture and the producer of culture. Hegel's spirit of history is an embodied spirit, living in a particular culture at a particular point in its history and seeing things from a particular perspective in that culture rather than a unified perspective. The spirit is simultaneously the language that frames our thinking and embeds our knowing in a cultural context along with the agency or will that is using language, and using language in new ways to express new meanings.

At base, notions of a "spirit of history" or a "democratic spirit" give rise to and are a reflection of the historic struggles of peoples to control their own destinies. We find such a construction of spirituality already developing in Western culture in the Greek myth of Prometheus, the rebel who brings the powers of the gods to humans. In Greek mythology, Prometheus is bound to a rocky crag where carrion birds pick at his flesh as punishment for attempting to steal some of powers of the gods (symbolized by fire) and bringing this power down to people to use. Interestingly, in some of Maslow's late writings that have been recently published, he identifies self-actualized individuals as Promethean. "In these people," he wrote, "there is a greater optimism about human nature and the human condition." They do not assume that destiny will win out. This is a stance "only for those who have no gods to be impotent before. These are the individuals who must look for the godlike in humanity itself" (1996, 58). Albert Camus saw in Prometheus the archetype of the rebel in Western culture, one who asserts that there is some spirit within him which is "worthwhile and must be taken into consideration," that is godlike and "confronts an order of things which oppresses him with the insistence of a kind of right not to be oppressed" (1956, 14).

This is a cultural mythology of the spirit that we find in much great democratic literature of the past and present. We find it, for example, in Dostoyevski's "The Grand Inquisitor"—a story embedded within *The Brothers Karamazov*. In this short story, Christ suddenly reappears in sixteenth-century Spain, during the height of the Inquisition against heretics. At this particular time, in this particular town, a hundred heretics have just been burned at the stake *en masse,* in front of the townsfolk. When Christ appears in the crowd, everyone immediately recognizes him. Symbolically, or metaphorically, Christ is a symbol of every man and every woman who sees that God is within, and that they have the power to heal themselves without the authority of the Grand Inquisitor or the Church. When the Grand Inquisitor appears upon the scene, he immediately orders that Christ be detained, and much of the rest of the story involves the rather one-sided conversation between the Grand Inquisitor and a silent Christ. The Grand Inquisitor, the symbol of all authoritarian and oppressive regimes and institutions, knows that Christ has come back to free people to make their own choices rather than look to the authority of Church dogma and leaders. This is the freedom to define ethics not in terms of abstractions and absolutes, but in terms of making complex choices in concrete situations. Democratic culture in general has always been grounded in a belief that people wanted and would thrive with such freedom. The Grand Inquisitor argues, in contrast, that people really want to be told what to do and how to live their lives, and that they will gladly give up their freedom to anyone who can offer them *miracle, mystery, and authority*. At the end of the story, the Inquisitor looks hopefully to Christ for some sign; but Christ merely bends over and kisses him. The Inquisitor tells Christ, "Go, and come no more.... Come not at all, never, never" (1956, 199). Christ is banished once more and humanity is turned over to the Grand Inquisitors. Redfield suggests that he is not unfamiliar with this classic text of the democratic spirit of history. One of his characters in the first novel is a cardinal in Peru who is leading the effort to retrieve the Manuscript before its Insights become widely distributed. The cardinal, in a final, confrontational dialogue with the leading character, remarks that the Manuscript would "undermine our basic structure of spiritual authority. It would entice people to believe that they are in control of their spiritual destiny" (Redfield 1996, 237). People he asserts do not really want such freedom.

Which returns us to the New Age myth of the millennium. In its most progressive usage, the millennium myth is an enticement for people to believe they can control their destiny, that they can make and remake themselves and culture rather than be passive victims of fate. It is also about keeping the democratic and progressive vision alive through our own agency, and through the recognition that we are part of a larger agency in the process of becoming. Andre Malraux's epic novel of the Spanish Civil War of the 1930s, *Man's Hope* (1938), ends with the antifascist army marching down a long road, along with the prisoners it had captured in a battle. As part of this moving force, the central character Manuel "felt the seething life around him charged with portents, as though some blind destiny lay in wait for him." He heard, as if for the first time, "the voice of that which is more awe-inspiring even than the blood of men, more enigmatic even that their presence on the earth—the infinite possibilities of their destiny" (422–423). This belief in the infinite possibilities of the human destiny is the essence of democratic spirituality.

Now we are beginning to realize that the road of history is much longer than we had ever imagined it could be and that we are not exactly center stage in the cosmos. We cling to a small planet in a relatively uninhabited, backwoods section of a medium-sized galaxy at a particular moment in the 15 billion-year (give or take a few billion years) history of the universe (Reuther 1992; Swimme and Berry 1992). This may lead us to believe that our struggles and lives are insignificant in the great scheme of things. But it need not. Indeed, quite the opposite seems to be happening. We are becoming more aware of our own radical freedom out here, "lost in space," to make our own histories and define ourselves. And we are also beginning to grasp the idea that somehow what is going on here, at this moment, at this place on planet Earth, is part of a larger becoming and is connected to everything in the universe. This is surely the message we are sending ourselves with the millennium myth. It is about the reawakening of the democratic spirit to its historic project, and about the reawakening of each of us to ours. At the same time, the cosmos makes us aware that we cannot wait for the end of history for some utopian vision of the good society, in order to enjoy life. So the millennium myth is about a heightened awareness to the world, awe in the face of its wonder, and the return to experience. Manuel, in Malraux's novel, contemplates the infinite possibilities of human destiny even as he becomes more aware of "the sounds of running water in the street and the footfalls of the prisoners, profound and permanent as the beating of his heart" (1938, 423).

References

Berne, E. (1996). *Games People Play: The Psychology of Human Relationships*. New York: Ballantine Books.
Camus, A. (1956). *The Rebel*. New York: Alfred A. Knopf.
Clarke, A. C. (1968). *2001: A Space Odyssey*. New York: New American Library.
Dostoyevsky, F. (1956). *The Brothers Karamazov*. New York: Dell Publications.
Foucault, M. (1979). *Discipline and Punish: The Birth of the Prison*. A. Sheridan, Trans. New York: Vintage.
Gould, S. J. (1997). *Questioning the Millennium: A Rationalist's Guide to a Precisely Arbitrary Countdown*. New York: Random House.
Hegel, G.W. F. (1910). *The Phenomenology of Mind*. J. B. Baillie, Trans. London: George Allen & Unwin Ltd.
Lovelock, J. E. (1979). *Gaia: A New Look at Life on Earth*. Oxford, UK: Oxford University Press.
Malraux, A. (1938). *Man's Hope*. New York: Random House.
Maslow, A. (1962). *Toward a Psychology of Being*. New York: D. Van Nostrand.
——— (1996). *Future Visions: The Unpublished Papers of Abraham Maslow*. Edward Hoffman (Ed.). London: SAGE Publications.
Plato (1955). *The Republic*. H. Lee Harmondsworth, Trans. London: Penguin Books.
Redfield, J. (1993). *The Celestine Prophecy*. New York: Warner Books.
——— (1996). *The Tenth Insight*. New York: Warner Books.
Reuther, R. (1992). *Gaia and God: An Ecofeminist Theology of Earth Healing*. San Francisco: Harper Collins.
Steiner, C. (1990). *Scripts People Live: Transactional Analysis of Life Scripts*. New York: Grove Press.
Swimme, B., and T. Berry. (1992). *The Universe Story*. San Francisco: Harper Collins.

CHAPTER THREE

Contemplative Spirituality, Currere, and Social Transformation: Finding Our "Way"

Kathleen Kesson

The Postmodern Spiritual Landscape: March 30, 1997

As I write these words, the newspapers and television screens are filled with purple shrouded images of thirty-nine human beings who ended their lives in a collective quest for spiritual advancement to a "level above human." Heaven's Gate, a media described "millenniallist cult," maintained that humanity is doomed and that flying saucers await a fortunate few. According to the testimony they left in the wake of their deaths, they counted on a spaceship trailing in the wake of the Hale-Bopp comet to transport them to a new dimension of experience. This tragic occurrence reminds us yet again of the fragility of reason in the face of passionately held belief, and it brings into high relief our fears of charismatic spiritual leaders, of the surrender of rationality, and of heretical and idiosyncratic spiritual ideas. In spite of these fears, however, the postmodern spiritual landscape teems with novel religious ideas, and continues a trend towards differentiation and pluralism.

Today's edition of the *New York Times* notes that there are at least 2,000 distinct religious groups in America, according to J. Gordon Melton of the Institute for the Study of American Religion. The proliferation of *esoteric* religions, or religions concerned with *hidden truths* (the "occult"), accounts for a significant portion of recent growth. In addition to these "new religions," there are estimated to be thousands of small cults throughout North America. In terms of UFOs, the *Times* cites Professor Lucas, editor of a forthcoming scholarly journal of alternative and emergent religions, as saying that there are at least 100 groups whose spiritual interest focuses on flying saucers (Niebuhr 1997). Most of these groups see the world as hopelessly corrupt, even doomed. The tragic events in Rancho Santa Fe, California, rather than being seen as merely an aberration, must be understood in this context of a somewhat desperate collective quest for meaning, intimacy, transcendence, and spiritual purpose.

Mainstream religions occupy a largely secular center of the postmodern spiritual landscape. But these face a widespread decline in authority, sacred and secular, notes the *Times,* as well as a rise in the number of people looking for something new. In response to the secularization, the "despiritualization," if you will, of mainstream religions, highly charged developments on both the conservative and the radical ends of the spiritual spectrum enliven the landscape with an eclectic array of premodern, modern, and postmodern spiritualities, many of them characterized by a kind of millennial fervor.

On the right of the spectrum, globally, there is a rise in fundamentalism of all stripes and a "recycling of medieval ontologies" (Horkheimer's phrase), with an increasingly politicized and often militant focus to these movements. These fundamentalisms usually rely on literal interpretations of authoritative texts, and they are imbued with critiques of modernity, including criticism of state intrusion into private life, unbounded capitalism, secular education, and the proliferation of a "promiscuous" media. They react to the complexities of the present and the uncertainties of the future with reversions to past value structures, dogmas, and forms of social relationships, and they represent perhaps the most insistent calls for a return to the dominion of patriarchy, whether the voices be those of the Christian or the Islamic patriarchs.

On the counter-cultural left, a more experimental impulse dominates: cultural cross-fertilization has created a smorgasbord of opportunities for contemporary spiritual aspirants: spiritual seekers can attend workshops on animal totems, urban shamanism, nature worship, aligning the cakras, creating their own reality, and balancing their inner (or outer) female (or male). Spirituality is largely psychologized, and dominated by what Paul Heelas (1993) calls "self-religiosity," a kind of historic foundationalism which places the New Age firmly within the modernist trajectory of romanticism:

> The self—individuated or cosmic—provides a powerful meta-narrative, of a kind which stands in sharp contrast to the 'de-centered' self theorized by advocates of the postmodern condition. (110)

In this chapter, I examine the problem of the *centered/de-centered* self in some depth.

Despite Heelas's modernist characterization of the New Age spiritual landscape, it paradoxically exhibits many of the characteristics of the *postmodern* consumer culture: a somewhat disorienting collage of signs and images; the mixing and matching of codes; depthlessness; intense affect-charged experiences; the playful immersion in unconscious processes; participation in virtual realities; the compression of time (many workshops promise absurd psychological and metaphysical results in a few hours of seminar work); the loss of a sense of reality and history; and the de-centering of the subject. The New Age seems particularly susceptible to the seductions of capitalism: advertisements in New Age magazines offer workshops on such things as "The Art of Enlightened Shopping" and "Channeling Your Way to Prosperity." Elsewhere, I have warned of the difficulties of orienting ourselves spiritually in a fragmented, capitalist culture (1996), and it is vulgar excesses such as these that provide fodder for the political left's critique of spirituality and mysticism.

Less susceptible to criticism from the left, various forms of liberation theology provide a theological home for liberatory social movements. Although this movement is considered radical within the framework of traditional Christianity because of its Marxist sympathies, it is spiritually conservative, rather than experimental, in its preservation of Western, modernist ideas such as the autonomy and freedom of the individual, progress, and salvation.

The postmodern spiritual landscape, then, encompasses a crazy quilt of beliefs: the traditional and the novel, the fundamental and the experimental, the radical and the conservative. It is a mix of organized religion and its offshoots, cults, and individualized spiritual practices. Despite the intentions of Christian fundamentalists to return our society to earlier norms and practices, I suspect that our spiritual landscape is altered beyond return. Though some people might liken this state of affairs to the Tower of Babylon, I would suggest that the chaos of competing beliefs and practices may be a fruitful one, with opportunities opening up to embrace new ideas and freedoms.

Over the last few years, I have participated in a number of seminars and symposia devoted to the issue of spirituality and education, or spirituality and curriculum, at the annual meetings of the American Educational Research Association, the American Educational Studies Association, and the Journal of Curriculum Theory Conference. I am quite astounded at the level of interest in the topic, which, until recently, was more or less taboo in the academy. The emphasis on empirical and quantitative data in the social sciences, coupled with the rejection of speculative metaphysics in the modem academy, makes it difficult, in these forums, to speak about the qualitative, often ephemeral, intuitions that constitute spiritual experience. Subtle and personally meaningful insights can wither under the onslaught of language, especially the technical and instrumental language of the social sciences. Inevitably, the conversations condense into a desire for definition: What is spirituality? Is it different from religion? Does spirituality require belief in a Creator? Once the difficulties of discourse are acknowledged, the conversations usually branch from these unresolved questions of definition into discussions about the difficulty of finding common ground from which to teach ethics and morality, the importance of teaching about religions in a way which fosters tolerance and respect, or the necessity of creating caring communities in schools. The dominant concern of liberal educators is the preservation of the boundaries between church and state, an important and interesting postmodern dilemma, which, however, abdicates responsibility for a serious rethinking of educational ideas in terms of what we are coming to understand about spiritual development, and in terms of the veritable explosion of spirituality in the culture outside of academia.

As educators, we will have to come to terms with a radical pluralism of belief, and clearly, one of our foremost tasks will be to assist in the cultivation of tolerance and respect for difference, crucial assets for living with religious and spiritual diversity. I want to suggest in this chapter, however, that educators must become more spiritually sophisticated, more attuned to the philosophical assumptions of the emergent beliefs that characterize postmodern culture if we are to become effective at helping our students cope with the chaos of conflicting ideologies. While it is most certainly not the role of public educators to teach specific beliefs or practices, it is in their domain to cultivate in our students the capacities for discrimination and discernment that will help them evaluate the spiritual options that they are faced with, both now and in the future. In this paper, I want to explore a range of theoretical issues that might contribute to the project of educating educators about spirituality. I will examine the place of "ontology" (the study of "being") in curriculum theory; differing conceptions of the self in Eastern and Western traditions; some differences between religion and "process," or contemplative spirituality; some connections between postmodern ideas about the self and contemplative spirituality; the possibilities of social action within contemplative traditions; and last, some implications of this spiritual perspective for educators. It is my hope that the amplification of understanding about the "spiritual impulse" will help educators both nourish their students' search for meaning, intimacy, transcendence, and spiritual purpose, and foster the kind of critical awareness and discrimination that will protect them from the spells of spiritual charlatans and hucksters.

Curriculum Theory and Spirituality

Ontology—the philosophical study of the nature of *being*—is one of the primary categories underpinning the study of education, along with *epistemology* (the study of the nature of knowledge) and *axiology* (the study of the nature of value, and value judgments). Ontological investigations have remained largely in the realm of theologians, however, and while educators all operate out of a set of assumptions about human nature, these assumptions are often tacit, rather than theorized. What we believe about the nature of human *being*, whether these beliefs are consciously or unconsciously held, affect many of the curriculum decisions we make. We may believe that a child is a "blank slate," waiting to have the knowledge of the culture inscribed upon it, or we may believe that a child embodies a "divine spark," waiting to be lit. These fundamentally different assumptions suggest radically different pedagogies.

The relationship of theological understandings to education is explored in the genre of "curriculum theory as theological text" (Pinar et al. 1995). The focus of much of the writing in this genre seeks to reclaim the moral, ethical, and prophetic voices usually associated with religious scholarship in order to amplify the understanding of curriculum as a profoundly moral and spiritual endeavor. The term "theological" here implies a particular framework for approaching questions of spirituality. According to *Webster's II,* theology is 1) the study of the nature of God and religious truth, especially by an organized religious community; 2) an organized, often formalized body of opinions concerning God and man's [*sic*] relationship to God; or 3) a course of specialized study, usually at a college or seminary. Much of the writing that has been done in this genre of curriculum theory is understandably influenced, if not dominated, by the milieux of Western Judaeo-Christian religious forms with which the writers are most familiar. One main theme of this genre is the development of "historically grounded self-consciousness," a theme grounded in Hegelian/Marxist notions of dialectical self-development. The emphasis here is on the construction of identity, the development of will and purpose, and the assertion of increasing individual rights and freedoms.

This idea of the "self" and "self-consciousness" is a foundational, if controversial, concept in curriculum theory. Curriculum theorist James Macdonald once said (1995a) that "the self as a concept has suffered at the hands of everyone from behaviorists to analytic philosophers . . . neither comes to grips with what allows them to perform at all" (80). Macdonald was concerned with the inability of the major curriculum perspectives, or as he called them, "ideologies" (traditional, romantic, progressive, and Marxist), to identify a source of value other than rational, explicit knowledge. Drawing upon the ideas of William James and Carl Jung, he proposed a new ideology of education which he termed the "transcendental developmental," moving the field of curriculum theory into territory formerly claimed by theologians. Macdonald called for an "inner dialectic of the self" (80), in which the ego-bound personality might engage in an exploration of the unconscious mind to uncover a spiritual, or transcendent, source of value. He called this ontological process "centering," providing us with a concept of the self that opened up pathways for the disciplined exploration of human *being* in the field of curriculum.

The disciplined study of the self has been carried out most deliberately within the autobiographical genre of curriculum theorizing popularized in the 1970s by William Pinar and Madeline Grumet (1976). This mode of inquiry is denoted by the Latin infinitive of the word curriculum—"currere," *to run the course*. Pinar and Grumet describe currere as the existential experience of schooling, a method by which experience is disclosed "so that we may see more of it and see more clearly. With such seeing can come deepened understanding of the running, and with this can come deepened agency" (Pinar et al. 1995, 518). Following the pathways laid out by Macdonald, Pinar, and Grumet in their studies of the human subject, I want to problematize the notion of self and self-consciousness, and suggest that the Western theological understandings of the self most familiar to curriculum theorists are vulnerable not only from the perspective of a postmodern philosophical critique, but from the perspective of some Eastern spiritual philosophies. At the same time, I want to keep in mind the potential excesses of self-negation in what I am alternatively calling process spirituality and contemplative deconstruction. My double-edged critique thus runs the risk of leaving me standing nowhere on the issue of the self. However, I hope that my argument circles us back to a more theorized, complexified understanding of what Macdonald called the process of "centering."

Eastern Understandings of the "Self"

In this chapter, I rely on an understanding of the self first proposed by post-Shaevic Tantric teachings, which originated around 5000 B.C. and were then systematized into Astaunga Yoga by Patanjali about 100 B.C., and out of which developed various schools of Buddhism, Zen, Tantra, and Taoism. My understanding of this perspective grows out of my own studies in Asian philosophy, mostly Tantric, Buddhist, and Taoist thought. My explorations have been both academic and experiential—I have practiced sitting meditation in the Tantric tradition for the past 30 years. These archetypal spiritual practices provide a distinct contrast to Western theological understandings of the self and the nature of being.

Despite important differences between them, these contemplative paths share an understanding of the self as a nondualistic continuum of fluid experience, ranging from the dense expression of the body to the more subtle and ephemeral expressions of mind and spirit. At the level of the body and the individual ego, there is a sense of separation, isolation, and a false sense of permanence, which is termed "maya" or illusion. The entire constellation of personal memories, experiences, reactions, mental habits, and desires constitute this enclosed aspect of the self. By utilizing specific practices and disciplines (meditation, concentration, mindful attentiveness, mantra, chanting, etc.), one comes to understand the illusion of this isolate self and begins to move beyond such limitation into a genuinely somatic awareness of the interconnectedness and the dynamism of all creation. This exquisitely subtle form of understanding, the elimination of the subject/object dichotomy, is "the diamond that cuts through illusion" (Nhat Hanh 1992). The various traditions have names for the state of mind which is achieved when one gets beyond the consciousness of the limited self: *nirvana, nirvikalpa samadhi, savilkalpa samadhi, moks'a, enlightenment.* What is paradoxically evident and what cannot be understood without being experienced, is that as the tentacles of the ego-bound self are loosened, there is a gradual awakening to the subtleties and unimagined depths of experience—we literally come to "see the world through childlike eyes" with a sense of newness and appreciation and a profound aesthetics. Freed from the bondage of surface desires, and socially constructed identities, fears, and strivings, the aspirant discovers a kind of fluidity of perception that enables a radical decentering of the self.

This notion of "fluid boundaries of the self," in addition to the deliberately nonrational aspect of contemplative traditions, is seen as problematic by many Western people. Thus, the efforts to bring this perspective on spirituality into social, political, and educational discourse meets with stiff resistance for a variety of compelling reasons. Murray Bookchin (1995), one of the most vociferous leftist critics of the "ever-widening landscape of spiritualism and mysticism" (110), worries about the submersion of individual identity and rational thought into a mushy identification with "Cosmic Oneness," a totality which he feels could lead to an ever stronger centralized state. He decries the demise of the New Left political counter-culture of the 1960s, which left a vacuum quickly filled by "intuitive and mystical notions" (92):

Vaporous 'feelings' displaced the 'mindbending' challenges of rationality, while the delights of mythopoesis and mystery displaced the cold demands of secularity and intellectual clarity. (93)

Bookchin appears to think that one cannot be engaged in introspective practice and maintain the ability to reason thoughtfully. This sort of exclusionary thinking has no counterpoint in Tantric philosophy, however. Noted British scholar of Sanskrit and Tantric history, Sir John Woodroffe, notes the impossibility, within this tradition, of separating rational and spiritual truth: "Truth is one and what is unreasonable must be rejected, whoever says it, 'even if he be the Lotus-born'" (1969, 325). Mystics in this tradition have, for many thousands of years, gathered empirical data from introspection, applied techniques of analysis and discrimination to the data, balanced experiential and revelatory knowledge, and engaged in the collective pursuit of meaning from these experiences. In this chapter, I want to challenge the idea that a contemplative spirituality necessarily leads to the loss of rationality or political regression. With the explication of some political dimensions of contemporary Tantra and the Taoism of the Tao-te-Ching, I hope to persuade the reader of the consistency of these practices with important elements of a postmodern, radical democratic project. Why is this particular inquiry important in a book about curriculum?

The discourses of the self, of spirituality, and of emancipatory politics all have a home in the reconceptualized field of curriculum (Pinar et al. 1995). These particular discourses are, for good historical reasons, uneasy housemates. I believe it is safe to say that the field, taken as a whole, advocates for increasing freedom, justice, equality, and respect for diversity in our society and in our classrooms, values clearly aligned with the project of radical democracy. Given this commitment, any discussion of spirituality and curriculum must necessarily take into consideration the political dimensions of the ideas generated. It is an extremely complicated topic. Let me begin this consideration by foregrounding an issue which inevitably comes up in discussions of spirituality and education—the difference between religion and spirituality.

Disentangling Religion and Spirituality

One of the fundamental concepts in this emergent discourse on spirituality and education is the distinction between spirituality and religion. While I would maintain that religion is certainly a principle manifestation of spirituality, and vice versa, I want to cautiously uncouple the two domains for analytical.

purposes. Many people who disdain adherence to an organized religion engage in one or another forms of spiritual growth. There are many explanations for this. In the *New York Times* article cited in the beginning of this paper, Robert Bellah is quoted as saying that people who prefer noninstitutional forms of belief do so because it is "'formless' and guided by whim, unregulated by clergy members or bounded by time-honored liturgies" (Niebuhr 1997). The tone of Bellah's remarks suggests his opposition to individualistic spiritualities, understandable in light of his ongoing interest in the development of community. I am somewhat more sympathetic to the rejection of institutionalized religions, however, for a variety of reasons.

First, although religions and religious rituals are largely constructed around *someone's* primary mystical experiences (or the eruption of material from their unconscious), later participants in the rituals do not necessarily participate in the energy of the original experience. Meaningful rituals often become, over time, dry and lifeless forms. Psychologist Carl Jung, who studied the religious impulse in humans for much of his professional career, noted that the repetition of rituals that represent original mystical experiences need "not necessarily mean lifeless petrifaction" (1958, 9), but may continue to provide a vital context for genuine spiritual experience for centuries. However, most religious traditions "resist further creative alterations by the unconscious" (Jung 1964, 253) and remain reproductions of one person's mystical experience. I would suggest that it is this incapacity to sustain a dynamic link between their mythic/symbolic constructions and the contemporary psychological processes of their adherents that account, at least in part, for the diminishing relevance of formal religion in many peoples' lives. The important distinction here is between spirituality as a dynamic, exploratory process and religion as the structured form that emerges to contain, and to some extent, control the process.

Thus, religion serves to codify and *sanctify* particular spiritual experiences, especially those that serve social needs for order, continuity, and stability. This conservative function highlights another important reason that people have rejected institutionalized religion. Historically, religious leaders and institutions have colluded with other vested interests in society to resist change and to oppress various groups and individuals, and people are now justly suspicious of clerical authority. The Church, for example, has played a major role in sustaining patriarchy, a fact which has been illuminated by feminist theologians and other critics. Many people view churches as upholders of the status quo, and are deeply committed to a worldview and belief system that has brought our culture to the brink of disaster. The Christian church, for example, is perceived as deeply implicated in the environmental crisis with its assertion of human dominion over the Earth. So, while some people may be acting on "whims," I would argue that for many of us, the choice to pursue noninstitutional spirituality is carefully considered, and undertaken in response to both reasoned critique and deeply felt intuitions.

Many religions are responding to the various critiques of their institutions and changing both their belief structures and their practices in significant ways in an effort to enhance their contemporary appeal. I suspect, however, that a large portion of the population will continue their exploration of novel spiritual pathways. Both libertarianism and experimentalism are deeply embedded in the Western psyche, and these impulses characterize many traditional and contemporary "process spiritualities."

The framework I have developed for this discussion relies on some fundamental analytic differences between religion and spiritual process, summarized in the table below.

While these categories may appear to be diametrically opposed, they should not be thought of as mutually impenetrable. Their relationship is rather more like the Chinese symbol of Yin and Yang, in which apparent opposites

Religion	*Process Spiritualities*
God as separate Being	Spirit immanent in creation
Explanatory—revealed knowledge	Exploratory—experiential knowledge
Institutionally embodied beliefs	Personal beliefs and practices mediate collective beliefs and practices[a]
Conformist	Self-Creative
	Personal
Adaptive—religions have to live in the world in order to have an impact on it	Transformative—Spirit breaks loose from the world (Kovel 1994)
Exoteric	Esoteric
Social	
Emphasis on discrete categories (matter, spirit)	Emphasis on interpenetrating processes[b]
Continuity, stability	Novelty, disruption, disequilibrium
Seeks absolute truth	Truth is contingent, partial

a. Process spiritualities are certainly not always individualistic; rather, they are often steeped in traditional practices and rituals. The differentiation that I am noting here is the emphasis on experience and process over belief.
b. Many spiritual process philosophies do indeed contain categories. The carefully delineated "kosas" or layers of mind of Tantra are examples of such categories. The emphasis, however, is on a *continuum* rather on discrete elements. Examples of interpenetrating processes can be found in the new work in holistic health on the mind-body continuum.

flow into each other. Profound mystical experiences of the Divine often occur in the context of a specific religious commitment (Underhill 1990, 95). As well, the history of religion is full of instances in which the radical, destabilizing insights or revelations of mystics engaged in spiritual processes (who are often scorned, expurgated, tortured, or executed) come to play a major role in the stable dogmas of a faith system (Jesus of Nazareth is only the most obvious example). Joel Kovel (1991) speaks of the transformation of Christianity from a

> religion radically open to spirit-being to one of logos and modernity . . . the original religion of Jesus was, if not erotic, certainly ecstatic, which is continuous with the erotic, and therefore partially subversive to the rationalized building of religious institutions. (120)

Tantra, a traditional process spirituality, includes a description of characteristics which differentiate religion (which Tantrics associate with *philosophical idealism*) from spirituality, which these scholars understand as an *introspective science*. Contemporary Tantric philosopher P. R. Sarkar is critical of religions to the extent that they command followers to abide by their tenets rather than supporting logic or clear thinking. Religion's basic defect, he states unambiguously, is that proponents inspire fear and subjugation in people with their self-interested interpretations of scripture. He decries the damage to humanity that has been done as a result of the innumerable conflicts generated over religious differences (1987, 20–21).

Other Tantric scholars (Tadbhavananda and Kumar 1985) suggest a number of characteristics that distinguish spirituality from religion: "[S]piritual science is comprehensive and consistent, resolving the contradictions that exist in Idealism between the physical, mental, and spiritual spheres of life . . . it involves practices which transform the human personality, developing the faculty of intuition and creating the scope for direct experience of Supreme consciousness. Spirituality has always had social application, though in the past it lacked a detailed social philosophy" (33).[1] Process spiritualities tend towards the personal while religion tends towards the social and the institutional. Process spirituality, with its emphasis on exploration, maintains the capacity to undermine dogma and rigid faith systems. Historically, mystics pursuing esoteric spiritual pathways have been positioned on the margins of our collective experience. Perhaps this accounts for the assumption that spirituality and a committed politics are incompatible. I would suggest just the

---

1. This lack of a detailed social philosophy has been mitigated in contemporary Tantra, which has a comprehensive social, political, and economic philosophy. See for example, *PROUT: Neo-humanistic Economics* (1989), by Dr. Shambbushivananda.

Contemplative Spirituality, Currere, and Social Transformation 57

opposite—that the margins are useful places from which to critique the dominant social institutions and from which to conceptualize a radical, spiritual politics. The radical potential of process spirituality may explain why educational discourse has focused on theological and religious ideas, rather than on a mystical spirituality. Religion is, if controversial, at least socially acceptable, and generally supportive of the status quo.

Process Spiritualities and the De-centered Self

For some time, I've been interested in questions concerning the compatibility of process spirituality and the postmodern philosophical project. I want to confess up front some genuine theoretical difficulties in thinking this through. The very content, the substance of this thinking is akin to an infinite hall of mirrors, in which reflections reflect upon reflections, which, in turn, reflect back reflections. This occurs, I believe, because the project, at least in terms of the spiritual process, is to get beyond thinking into a state of unconditioned awareness—so to even talk about the topic merely reinforces the thinking patterns one is attempting to transcend. You see the dilemma?

I have come to agree with Linda Woodhead (1993) that most of the emergent ("new age") forms of process spirituality owe more to modern thought than to postmodern. Many of the narratives invoked have essentialist underpinnings (such as the stable, eternal self) and experience-based epistemologies, which assume nonlinguistic and ideologically untainted experiences. David Griffin (1988) and his colleagues at the Center for a Postmodern World, for example, are working to synthesize ecology, feminism, and "new science" into a "postmodern spiritual paradigm." Their "reconstructive postmodernism" is posited in opposition to a deconstructive postmodernism, which has been associated with literary criticism. While I find much of value in this work, I detect in it elements of modernity such as those noted above, and thus I want to grapple with the notion of a deconstructive spirituality for the purposes of this chapter. The late James Moffett, in his groundbreaking book, *The Universal Schoolhouse: Spiritual Awakening through Education,* talks about some compatibilities between destruction and contemplative spirituality.

> Today's concept of "deconstructing" culture catches, rather well, the efforts of spiritual disciplines to find the hidden "subtexts" of the manifest world and to recognize how it seems real or true because we constructed it in the first place. The Hindu notion of the manifest world as *maya,* or illusion, has always assumed the *constructionist*

view of knowledge that reigns today in cognitive psychology circles, that is, that humans *make* knowledge or meaning, collectively and individually, by putting together their perceptions of the world according to their needs, bents, lights, fears, desires, and circumstances of time and place. Any human version of reality is thus always situational and relative. The antidote is to undo, or deconstruct, one's personal and cultural conditioning. This awakening of mind and liberating of behavior would be an education indeed. (1994, 28).

I'm intrigued with this similarity between the process of deconstruction, which uses language itself to reveal the multilayeredness of texts, and the process of contemplative spiritual process, in which the self uses the self as its own instrument of deconstruction. It is precisely this effort "to undo or deconstruct one's personal and cultural conditioning" which is at the heart of most contemplative spiritualities.

The issue of language and nonlinguistic perception is a complicated topic in terms of process spiritualities. An important postmodern idea, as I understand it, is that all "consciousness" is constituted by language. We literally can not think something unless we have *named* it. Tantric philosophy includes a sophisticated analysis of acoustic roots, the vibrational frequency of sounds, and the relationship of sound perception to consciousness. While this philosophy sees a necessary connection between language and cognition at many levels of mental activity, it does not agree on the unidirectionality of this activity—there is no law that words or names must come first and then thoughts. It acknowledges the necessity of language for such mental activities as description, comparison, analysis, inference, classification, induction, and deduction. The absence of language is noted, however, in intuitive perception (we do not have to name something in order to perceive it) or intuitional ideation (the formation of a mental image in the mind). Of course, the moment one decides to describe or analyze such experiences, language is necessary.

One of the intentions of spiritual practice, or *sadhana,* is to elevate the mind above the constant stream of mental chatter—to bring the mind to a point of stillness. Often, when people reach a point of stillness and silence, they have subtle mental experiences, which they have difficulty talking about—the experiences seem to be beyond language. This difficulty, however, may be due more to the paucity of the English language when it comes to describing states of consciousness than to any inherent linguistic problem. The Sanskrit language, evolved over thousands of years as the language of introspection, has a rich vocabulary for describing exquisitely subtle mental and spiritual experiences. In the lexicon of postmodernism, these introspective practitioners have developed a "discourse community" that enables the naming of supramental experiences. Having words for experiences undoubtedly facilitates the process of having these experiences—but it is also true that people have such experiences without having words for them.

In another postmodern vein, I want to briefly explore Deleuze and Guattari's (1983) notion of a "nomadic subject" for its metaphoric utility in thinking about the differences between the "theological, or religious, project" and the "spiritual project." In regards to the former, one important purpose of religion has been to channel the unconscious—that prepsychological, presocial, and preontological milieu that psychologist C. G. Jung suggests is the source of the religious impulse, and that Joel Kovel suggests is the source of the "wish to be free" (1958, 167) into socially acceptable streams. From paternalistic religious points of view, the unconscious is seen as dangerous, uncharted territory, and adherents of the faith are warned against the tasting of forbidden knowledge. I believe this repression is what Deleuze and Guattari refer to as "territorialization." On the other hand, most process spiritualities engage in the deliberative process of revealing and coming to terms with the material in the unconscious, which is one way that I understand their term "deterritorialization." In *Anti-Oedipus,* Deleuze and Guattari make the case for unleashing the unconscious, and they elucidate a theory of desire that is linked not just to persons or isolated objects, but to the "entire surroundings that it traverses, the vibrations and flows of every sort to which it is joined, introducing therein breaks and captures—an always nomadic and migrant desire, characterized first of all by its 'gigantism' (292). . . we always make love with worlds" (294). I relish this phrase of theirs—'we always make love with worlds'—because it begins to capture the quality of a continuum of mystical experience that traverses and embraces the territory between the erotic and the ecstatic. The body of the Tantric *literally* is the cosmos, the libido and the kula-kundalini,[2] but different aspects of a vibrational frequency, but the awakening of the multiple and interpenetrating layers of what Merleau-Ponty called "Flesh"—that juncture where *matter* opens into *being.* "Making love with worlds" suggests a profound sort of *connectedness* with all of creation, a connectedness that is an important aspiration of contemplative spirituality.

Spiritual process, as anyone who has spent much time engaged in it will attest, is fraught with difficulties and entrapments. Krishnamurti, the eminent Indian philosopher, has pointed out how all experience, even experience

2. Kula-kundalini is the latent spiritual energy in the human body (residing at the base of the spinal column) which, when aroused, accounts for mystical experiences as it rises through the subtle psychic centers (cakras and nadis), which correspond to the nervous ganglia along the spine. This experience, encompassing as it does the physical, psychological, mental, and spiritual dimensions, accounts for the nondualistic nature of Tantra.

directed towards self-annihilation, actually serves to strengthen the self. As long as there is an "I" who seeks to get beyond the self, there is a self. It is all a process of continuous isolation. Like Feuerbach in Western philosophy, Krishnamurti asserts that all of our beliefs about God, the timeless state of immortality, are merely projections by the self of something that, it is hoped, will destroy the self:

> You have not really destroyed the self, but only given it a different name, a different quality; the self is still there, because you have experienced it. Thus, our action from the beginning to the end is the same action, only we think it is evolving, growing, becoming more and more beautiful; but, if you observe inwardly, it is the same action going on, the same 'me' functioning at different levels with different labels, different names. (1954, 81)

The idea of freedom, then, in this mode of experience, is qualitatively different from the Western ideal of the development of the autonomous self as an agent of intention and fulfilled desire. Freedom, in this Eastern sense, implies freedom *from* the chains of desire (which can only be attained by mindful attention *to* the sources of desire), and from the very notion of a self (attained through a process of introspective deconstruction). Don Cupitt, a radical English theologian, sees Madhyarnika Buddhism as one of the few important spiritual expressions of the postmodern philosophical sensibility:

> For this is a spirituality which realizes the ultimate unreality and transitoriness of all which common sense regards as real and solid. There is no self, no experience, no objects "out there," no God, no "presence" there is only an ever-shifting and changing flow of signs. Spirituality consists in being able to let go of our lives, to stop looking for depth and meaning and permanence. To accept "Isunyata," emptiness, the void. (quoted in Woodhead 1993, 176)

In the Prajnaparamita Diamond Sutra (Nhat Hanh 1992), the Buddha says to his disciple "If . . . a Bodhisattva holds on to the idea that a self, a person, a living being, or a life span exists, that person is not an authentic Bodhisattva" (38). These four perceptions, which are at the core of Western ideological commitments, are, from the Buddhist perspective, the erroneous perceptions that are at the root of all our suffering!

This fallacy of the objective world, which Cupitt refers to in the above quote, is an idea which has gained currency in postmodern thinking. This epistemological problem is addressed in Tantra, although its understanding of the "void" doesn't have the nihilistic overtones of Madhyarnika Buddhism.

The Gayatri-Mantra, one of the holy scriptures in this tradition, discusses the stages of mental experience aspirants go through as they come to understand this fallacy. At the most elementary level is the ordinary condition of consciousness, in which the outer world appears to be stable, objective, and independent of consciousness. With some reflection, one understands that these seemingly independent objects, are, in fact, utterly dependent upon our senses, which are constituted in particular ways. The notion of objective stability wears off. Subjectivity begins to assert itself, and the "seer," seeing, and the seen are internalized, subjectified, and unified. We come to realize that though the objective world is largely dependent on the *relationship* between our sensory apparatus and the "things out there," and there is some organizing factor which directs the senses to perceive one thing rather than another out of the myriad of phenomena presented to us from moment to moment. This organizing factor is the self, the nature of which we then begin to ponder. This self is the only factor in the triad (world, senses, and attentive self) which can operate independently of the other two. The nature of perceived objects is dependent upon our sensory apparatus, and the direction of the senses is dependent upon the attentive mind with its preconceived ideas. The self, however, has the capacity to evolve both objects and senses, for example, in the dream state, and these objects seem quite real as long as the dream lasts. It is not so great an epistemological step to begin to see the objective world in somewhat the same way as we perceive the dream world—as relative, contingent, and causally related to the contents of our consciousness. This concept, as I have stated it here, is vastly oversimplified, and I refer the reader to the Tantric texts (Anandamurti 1993; Pandit 1968; Sarkar 1987; Woodroffe 1969) listed in my bibliography for a more comprehensive treatment of the subject.

Tantrics suggest that the human mind has a natural tendency towards objective thought, but the goal of Tantra is the redirecting of thought, away from the objective world towards infinite, *unqualified consciousness,* which resides (though dormant) in every human being. The meaning of evolution, in this context, is "the liberation of the spirit, or inner self, from all which obscures its essential freedom" (Woodroffe 1969, 342). This liberation of the spirit, which derives from the progressive *deconditioning* of the mind, is the essence of the practice of all of the Eastern contemplative traditions. While human freedom thus appears to be an objective shared by contemplative spirituality and an emancipatory politics, it is this withdrawal of attention from the material world that gives rise to the critique that introspective, or contemplative, spirituality is incompatible with the emancipatory political project. It is to this dilemma that I turn next.

Spirituality and the Emancipatory Political Project

> A fundamental change in society can happen only if that society begins to be based on total freedom from partiality and exclusivity, that freedom which comes from recognizing the unconditional goodness of human nature . . . the acknowledgment of the unconditioned aspect of human nature, which translates experientially as the freedom from the conjecture of a "self," the discovery of this freedom, at first in occasional glimpses, and the aspiration to fully realize it, are the foundation of genuine change in society. (Hayward 1984, 275)

This idea, that freedom from *the conjecture of a self* might serve as the ground for genuine social change, is a radical one indeed to Western ears. Our notions of freedom and democracy are so intimately interwoven with notions of the individual that it is difficult indeed to conceive of a politics less dependent on modern Western notions of the self.

As I have suggested above, spiritual processes are primarily concerned with revealing the relationship between being and nonbeing, or qualified and unqualified consciousness. In this same sense, the emancipatory political project, unable or unwilling to shake its Hegelian roots, has concerned itself with unrealized possibilities, or that which has not yet come into being. Hegel, of course, posited the existence of an Absolute Other, with which the finite self was engaged in a dialectic of realization towards its own divinity. While Marcuse derived his concept of negativity from Hegel, following the Feuerbach/Marxist inversion he "concentrated on the realization of potentiality within the historical realm of existence rather than some ultimate ontological sphere at the end of history" (Hewitt 1995, 115). However, the historical materialist orientation of critical theory has continued to rely on a metaphysic of unrealized human capacities for its dialectic between the existent and the possible.

Joel Kovel, in *History and Spirit* (1991), elaborates a critical theory of spirituality and refines the understanding of the dialectic with a slight movement away from its structuralist roots:

> . . . the notion that truth and being alike emerge from the conflict, that non-being gives birth to being, that the negative determines the positive and co-exists, with it). . .[the dialectic is] not a master plan [but rather] an opening of being, and a clearing of false, encrusted Egoic being. (109)

This idea of a "clearing of false, encrusted Egoic being" contrasted with an "opening of being" is certainly compatible with the Eastern perspectives discussed in this paper. Kovel views history as an unending dialectic of splitting and the overcoming of splitting, the splits being created by domination within categories such as race, class, and ethnicity; and gender "Spirit," he presumes, occurs in the motion of the dialectic as splitting is overcome:

> Spirit is not opposed to matter, or the flesh; rather it is revealed, indeed created, in the freeing of matter and flesh; that is, in the overcoming of splitting. And Spirit is not a by-product, or an indicator of this overcoming; it is the lived process itself. Thus, liberation is a spiritual project, and spirituality is emancipatory. (1991, 3)

The quest for freedom, says Tantric philosopher P. R. Sarkar, is the motive force behind social evolution. Freedom is the "progressive elimination of all elements—physical, psychic, or social—which obstruct the unfoldment of the mind towards real knowledge, free from all bondages and limitations" (in Kritashivananda, undated). Tantric social theory, thus, differentiates between mere *change* and genuine *progress,* which is a meaningful concept only insofar as the movement is associated with the evolution of the mind towards the spiritual goal: new technologies and products may be sophisticated, but distract the mind away from spirituality; new products may be useful, but destroy the environment upon which life depends; new ideas in the intellectual sphere may be intricate, but they may not expand the mind; new social or institutional structures may only serve to consolidate the power of a few at the expense of the many. The criterion for real progress is "whether or not each member of the society is helped in the march towards real freedom—beyond all limitations" (Kritashivananda). Freedom, in this tradition at least, encompasses all spheres: material, social, mental, and spiritual. Tantra, thus, embodies a radically egalitarian philosophy, thus represents a spiritual philosophy that delineates a value base for a spiritual politics.

I would suggest that the discussion of freedom has been limited by the focus of the West, including the critical project, on the "being," or material, side of the equation. It could reasonably be argued that Eastern understandings have suffered to the same degree from their emphasis on nonbeing, which can lead to passivity and the acceptance of the status quo. It is a misconception, however, to assume that all contemplative forms of spirituality are necessarily passive in terms of the emancipatory political project. The socioeconomic theory of contemporary Tantra, far from passive acceptance of the status quo, asserts that economic freedom is part of the natural right of every human being. It is passionately antiexploitative, and intent on the removal of disparities in all spheres, especially in social, economic, and political life. In this last section, I want to highlight some ideas which argue for the compatibility of the foci (on being and nonbeing)—indeed, for the notion that they might serve as "correctives" for each other's excesses—as we think about the development of a spiritual politics.

Contemplative Spirituality and Social Transformation

I want to state a bias here, in terms of an emancipatory political project: I share with many other scholars and activists a commitment to the increase of radical democracy in our social world (Trend 1996), a viewpoint which (among other things) calls for the redistribution of power away from bureaucracies, the state, and large corporations into the hands of citizens and decentralized citizen groups. I view contemporary anarchist thought, having incorporated discourses such as radical ecology, feminist theory, spirituality, and postcolonial theories into its infrastructure, as possibly the most compatible basis for social organization within a postmodern philosophical framework. I am inclined toward an organicist, ecological anarchism, a contemporary form of anarchism characterized by voluntarism, communitarianism, and antiauthoritarianism (Clark 1984). This said, I want to attempt to draw some theoretical links between postmodernism, spirituality, and the anarchist project.

Moving the critical Marxist/psychoanalytic project away from its structuralist tendencies, Deleuze and Guattari, in *Anti-Oedipus,* elaborate upon the revolutionary nature of desire:

> And, if we put forward desire as a revolutionary agency, it is because we believe that capitalist society can endure many manifestations of interest, but not one manifestation of desire, which would be enough to make its fundamental structures explode . . . we believe in desire as in the irrational of every form of rationality, and not because it is a lack, a thirst, or an aspiration, but because it is the production of desire: desire that produces—real desire, or the real in itself. (1983, 379)

While Deleuze and Guattari have provided a brilliant political analysis of the psychological subject and of the revolutionary potential of the release of "desiring-production" upon the world, their work does not provide an accessible, practical method for revealing the nature of desire or assessing appropriate action which might arise from such an awareness. Indeed, their writing is deliberately obscure and confusing because of our limited understanding of the concept of "desire." Perhaps an examination of this notion of desire from the perspective of contemplative spiritual practice will shed some light on their proposal.

Contemplative spirituality is, in one sense, a method of self-exploration that involves careful attention to small psycho/physiological events—*points at which desire emerges from the unconscious into awareness.* In Vipassanya Buddhism, for example, the meditation practice involves simply paying attention to the sensations of the body while regulating the breathing. Corresponding with this attention to the emergence of desire, the act of "witnessing" separates one from the force of desire, loosening the bonds of the ego upon consciousness. One becomes aware of the source of desire, while at the same time becoming progressively freer of its hold. This subtle discrimination acts to sort out what is real, or genuine, from what is merely socially constructed, and enables the spiritual practitioner to act from a state of compassionate, expanded awareness.[3] This foundation of compassionate awareness is a more inclusive position from which to determine political action than the usual narrow, ego-bound sentiments based on vested class or economic interests, geography, social group, or dogma.

For an intriguing analysis of the interrelationship between desire, purpose, action-in-the-world, and social transformation, I turn to John Clark's commentaries on the Tao te Ching in his book *The Anarchist Moment* (1984). He notes the growing number of anarchists who have adopted an organicist, ecological anarchism which "coherently synthesizes theory and practice, metaphysics and critique" (166). Unlike other organicist philosophies which posit the existence of an eternal timeless "One," the Tao suggests a dynamic "process of becoming in which both being and non-being are enduring presences" (170):

> 'Non-being' names this beginning of Heaven and earth; 'Being' names the mother of the myriad things. Therefore, some people constantly dwell in "non-Being' because they seek to perceive its mysteries, while some constantly dwell in 'Being' because they seek to preserve its boundaries. These two ['Non-Being' and 'Being'] are of the same origin, but have different names. . . . (Young and Ames, quoted in Clark 1984, 169)

According to most commentators on the Tao te Ching, each individual being has its own Tao, and its own internal sense of unfolding, a kind of immanent "telos" (not to be confused with the various authoritarian teleological philosophies from Plato to Hegel to Marx). The Sanskrit word "dharma" has a similar meaning in Tantric philosophy—signifying the organic evolution of an individual being or a social entity in accordance with a dynamic cosmic principle. I want to tentatively suggest an affinity between the notion of such an immanent telos and the process of desiring-production set forth by Deleuze and Guattari, and further suggest that the utopian organic anarchist community, which fully embraces humanity and nature, might signify the realization of their revolutionary project.

John Clark (1984) provides the definition of an anarchist political theory with which I am most in accord. He states that the essential elements of such

---

3. The notion that there is a level of experience below the social construction of reality runs counter to postmodern suppositions. It is perhaps the notion of the existence of an "indwelling spirit," then, that lies at the bifurcation point of postmodernism and spirituality.

a theory are: (1) a view of an ideal, noncoercive, nonauthoritarian society; (2) a criticism of existing society and its institutions, based on this anti-authoritarian ideal; (3) a view of human nature that justifies the hope for significant progress toward the ideal; and (4) a strategy for change, involving immediate institution of noncoercive, nonauthoritarian, and decentralist alternatives (126–127). Certainly, theoretical and practical anarchism has no possibility of realization in a society dominated by the notion of individual self-interest. Overcoming individual self-interest requires an extraordinary conceptual shift, one for which process spirituality is uniquely designed. I view the deconstructive spiritual process, with its dedicated effort to reveal the very microparticles of desire as they "come-into-being," and its movement towards "freedom from conjecture of a self" as an integral component of the "bringing-into-being" of the radically democratic, ecological anarchist community. My guiding assumptions here are that (1) the individual good is inextricably bound up with the social good—that is, there is a relationship between individual and social *dharma;* and (2) when we realize our interconnectedness through contemplative spirituality, these categories (individual and social) no longer seem dichotomous. If these assumptions seem overly optimistic, I refer the reader to a closer examination of the values and commitments that have grown out of these contemplative traditions. While it is beyond the scope of this chapter to lay these out in detail, they hold in common a reverence and respect for all life forms, and the cultivation of altruism, humility, compassion, and social responsibility.

I have suggested that contemplative spirituality is more individualized than institutionalized. Any spiritual politics, however, is necessarily a social activity. Learning to "dialogue across the differences" of our spiritualities is a crucial component of a spiritual politics. Clearly, a "hermeneutic of introspection" is essential—akin to the ancient communities of Tantrics, Jnana Yogis, and Taoists, who engaged in such collective discussions for literally thousands of years of introspective experiments. The insights gained from their collective analyses form the bases of the spiritual process technologies that have evolved over the centuries into more or less systematized spiritual practices and social commitments. The integration of individual spiritual practice with a hermeneutic analysis could, in the same way, provide the grounding for the emergence of a radically democratic, anti-authoritarian form of social organization. I think such a dialectic is what the writer of this passage from the Tao te Ching had in mind:

> Heaven and earth unite to suffuse sweet dew. Without commanding the people, equality will naturally ensue. (Mair 1990, p. 99)

This notion of an "immanent telos" which might guide collective decision making, seems surely counterintuitive, if not downright dangerous, to Western thinkers grounded in notions of the autonomous individual, rational decision making, and the need for external authority and control. I put it forth for consideration as an alternative ontological paradigm, one that offers opportunities to connect below the surface of our differences in a "common ground" of being.

Currere Revisited

Interestingly, curriculum theorist James Macdonald argued for a *bounded anarchy* as the only viable approach to political circumstances in schooling (1995, 151). He suggested that while maximizing freedom is a noble educational goal, the process needs to occur within a structure conceived to foster self-discipline and meaningful choice. While I do not know whether or not Macdonald ever drew the connection between the notion of bounded anarchy and the process of centering, I believe there is a compelling link. James Moffett (1994) has outlined a radical plan for providing an education that is consistent, in principle, with theories of spiritual development and with the notion of bounded anarchy. His plan calls for maximizing student choice over learning options, full access to decentralized educational and artistic resources, the full integration of social services into education, the development of community-wide learning networks, and new counseling and facilitative roles for teachers. His proposals support the highly individualized, yet socially responsive approach to curriculum inherent in the notion of "currere." While he doesn't pretend to have all of the answers to questions that will inevitably come up in response to such a radical rethinking of schools, his book is valuable because of his courageous efforts to bring spirituality (not religion) fully into educational discourse. It is an excellent starting point for the conversation. All educational ideas have, at their heart, an idea of the good life and a social vision. I believe that the notion of bounded educational anarchy is consistent with a social vision of a spiritually focused, nonexploitative, radical democratic community. Theoretical and practical anarchism, after all, are primarily concerned with maximizing freedom, but the ideal is tempered by any number of social, practical, and ecological limits. If we can agree on the general parameters of such a radical social vision, then we can begin to think about what *bounded anarchy* might mean in the context of learning environments, and what habits of mind we need to foster in order to realize its social promise.

In closing, I want to linger for just a moment on some intriguing linguistic connections. Victor Mair, in his translation of the Tao te Ching based on the recently discovered Ma-Wang-Tui manuscripts, explores the archaic roots of the word Tao, while arguing for its early connection with Indian spiritual concepts. The archaic pronunciation of Tao, he states, sounded like *drog* or *dorg,* which links it to the Proto-Indo-European root *drogh* (to run along) and the Indo-European *dhorg* (way, movement). The nearest Sanskrit cognate is *dhrajas* (course, motion) and *dhraj* (course) (Mair 1990, 132). I am struck by the similarity of these linguistic roots to the meaning of the Latin infinitive of the word curriculum—"*Currere*" *to run the course.* All signify movement along a pathway.

As a philosophical concept, the Tao is the "all-pervading, self-existent, eternal cosmic unity, the source from which all things emanate and to which they return" (Mair 1990, 132–133). Similarly, in Tantra, Brahma is the all-pervading entity, and the process of emanation and return is called *saincara* and *pratisaincara*. Just as the Tao is immanent in all living creatures, so is Brahma, and the process of *sadhana,* or contemplative spiritual practice, serves to connect the individual divinity *(Atman)* with the cosmic principle. This process of union is "*Dharma.*" Carefully considered, these concepts might greatly amplify our understanding of human development across the life span. They suggest, as well, a spiritual dimension to the notion of currere. Macdonald reminded us that "if we accept Dewey's concept of providing experiences that both interest people and contribute to their long-range development, it is clearly essential that the kind of long-range development be identifiable" (89). The notions of the Tao and of Dharma express subtle understandings of how the "Way" or "Course" or "Path" unfolds for each of us. Process spirituality is an important method of attuning ourselves to and deepening our understanding of our unique pathway in life. It suggests both centering and de-centering of the self, and implies an understanding of freedom quite beyond our usual understandings. A German proverb, quoted by Mair, asks:

Was hilft laufen, wenn man nicht auf den rechten Weg ist?
What is the use of running when we are not on the right way?

Indeed, how might we find our "Way" into and through the complex discourse of spirituality and the postmodern curriculum? The proverb for me suggests the importance of a deep personal and collective examination of the values, purposes, and direction of the education we provide for children. We need to develop our understanding about the complex nature of spiritual development so that we can better assist our students in their search for meaning, intimacy, transcendence, and spiritual purpose—that is, in finding their "Way."

References

Bookchin, Murray (1995). *Re-enchanting Humanity*. London: Cassell.
Clark, John (1984). *The Anarchist Moment: Reflections on Culture, Nature, and Power*. Montreal: Black Rose Books.
Deleuze, Gilles, and Felix Guattari (1983). *Anti-Oedipus: Capitalism and Schizophrenia:* Minneapolis: University of Minnesota Press.
Griffin, David Ray (1988). *Spirituality and Society*. New York: SUNY Press.
Hayward, Jeremy W. (1984). *Perceiving Ordinary Magic: Science and Intuitive Wisdom*. Boston: Shambala Publications.
Heelas, Paul (1993). "The New Age in Cultural Context: The Pre-modern, the Modern and the Postmodern." *Religion*. (23). 103–116.
Hewitt, Marsha Aileen (1995). *Critical Theory of Religion: A Feminist Analysis*. Minneapolis: Fortress Press.
Jung, C. G. (1958). *Psychology and Religion: East and West*. London: Routledge and Kegan Paul.
——— (Ed.) (1964). *Man and His Symbols*. New York: Dell Publishing.
Kesson, Kathleen (Summer 1996). "The Foundations of Holism: Some Philosophical and Political Dilemmas." *Holistic Education Review, 9.* (2) 14—24.
——— (Autumn 1994). "An Introduction to the Spiritual Dimensions of Curriculum." *Holistic Education Review. 7.* (3) 2 – 6.
Kovel, Joel (1991). *History and Spirit: An Inquiry into the Philosophy of Liberation*. Boston: Beacon Press.
Krishnamurti, J. (1954). *The First and Last Freedom*. Wheaton, IL: Theosophical Publishing House.
Kritashivananda, Ac. (undated text). *Elements of Progress*. Denmark: Proutist Universal.
Macdonald, James (1995a). "A Transcendental Developmental Ideology of Education." In Bradley J. Macdonald. (Ed.). *Theory as a Prayerful Act: The Collected Essays of James B. Macdonald*. New York: Peter Lang.
——— (1995b). "Curriculum as a Political Process." In Bradley J. Macdonald (Ed.). *Theory as a Prayerful Act: The Collected Essays of James B. Macdonald*. New York: Peter Lang.
Mair, Victor H. (Trans.) (1990). *Tao te Ching*. New York: Bantam Books.
Moffett, James (1994). *The Universal Schoolhouse: Spiritual Awakening through Education*. San Francisco: Jossey-Bass.
Nhat Hanh, Thich (1992). *The Diamond That Cuts through Illusion: Commentaries on the Prajnaparamita Diamond Dutra*. Berkeley: Parallax Press.
Niebuhr, Gustav (March 30, 1997). "Land of Religious Freedom Has Universe of Spirituality." *New York Times*.
Pandit, M. P. (1968). *Kundalini Yoga*. Madras: Ganesh & Co.
Pinar, W., W. Reynolds, P. Slattery, and P. Taubman (1995). *Understanding Curriculum*. New York: Peter Lang.
Pinar, W., and M. Grumet (1976). *Toward a Poor Curriculum*. Dubuque, IA: Kendall-Hunt.
Sarkar, P. R. (1987). *Neo-humanism in a Nutshell*. (Translated from the original Bengali by Aca'rya Vijaya'nanda Avadhu'ta and A'carya Mantreshwarananda Avadhuta). Calcutta: Manasi Press.
Shambbushivananda (1989). *PROUT: Neo-humanistic Economics*. West Germany: Dharma Verlag.
Tadbhavananda, Ac. and Jayanta Kumar (1985). *The New Wave*. Calcutta: Orient Press.

Trend, D. (1996). *Radical Democracy: Identity, Citizenship, and the State*. New York: Routledge.
Underhill, Evelyn (1990). *Mysticism: The Preeminent Study in the Nature and Development of Spiritual Consciousness*. New York: Doubleday.
Woodhead, Linda (1993). "Post-Christian Spiritualities." *Religion*. 23 (2), 167–181.
Woodroffe, Sir John (1969). *The Garland of Letters: Studies in the Mantra-Sastra*. Madras, India: Ganesh.

CHAPTER FOUR

Spiritual Literacy: Buddhism, Language, and Health in Academia

Glenn Hudak

Do not force others, including children, by any means whatsoever,
to adopt your views, whether by authority, threat, money,
propaganda, or even education.
—Thich Nhat Hanh (1993), *Outer Being*

And if you are sure that you are a guide to the blind,
a corrector of the foolish, a teacher of children,
having in the law the embodiment of knowledge and truth,
you, then, that teach others, will you not teach yourself?
—Romans 2:19–21 (New Standard Revised Version of the Bible)

And how do we, professional educators—academics, teach ourselves? In her recent book, *Other People's Children* (1995), African American educator Lisa Delpit discusses her journeys "into understanding other worlds, journeys that involved learning to see, albeit dimly, through the haze of my own cultural lenses" (9). Here she discusses insights gained as she explored other cultures, particularly the lives of native Alaskans. Her goal is an attempt to gain understanding of what it means to be "multicultural"—to be different and yet connected—to bridge the gap with another culture. What is most astonishing about Delpit's journeys are her struggles with research epistemologies such as "the narrow and essentially Eurocentric curriculum" (181) found in many teacher education programs, which tend to objectify and assume an air of superiority when encountering non-Western cultures. Indeed, she writes that one lesson she received during her stay with Native Alaskans was

> learning to be part of the world rather than trying to dominate it—on learning to see rather than merely look, to feel rather than touch, to hear rather than listen: to learn, in short, about the world by being still and opening myself to experiencing it. If I realize that I am an organic part of all that is, and learn to adopt a receptive, connected stance, then I need not take an active, dominant role to understand; the universe will, in essence, include me in understanding. (92)

Notice Delpit's emphasis on "stillness," on being "receptive," on being "connected," on being "part of all that is" as a way of knowing and understanding, a way that does not intend to control, or to cling to, or to dominate others. It is an epistemology that amplifies freedom, respect, and love; it is also an epistemological stance that amplifies a non-Western perspective on learning.

Upon reading Lisa Delpit, however, various "loose ends" in my thinking began to tie together: Like Delpit, I am concerned with the ways in which we train future teachers to teach other people's children. Like Delpit, I too have found that the ways in which we academics go about teaching teachers with our rational, dualistic, Cartesian epistemology serves most often to create disconnection between people rather than connection, disequilibrium rather than balance, fragmentation rather than wholeness, pathology rather than health between ourselves as faculty as well as with the students we teach. And finally, like Delpit, I have found much inspiration, insight, and understanding from non-Western epistemologies. For me, Buddhism has been particularly helpful, especially Tibetan and Zen Buddhist thought.

I begin with these insights from Lisa Delpit as a way to situate my essay on Buddhism, language, and health in academia, because her observations evoked in me various insights gleamed from Buddhist thought. While I have been a student of Buddhist thought for over two and a half decades, it has always remained something of a puzzle for me to work out how to integrate Buddhist epistemology into my workplace—academia. My aim in this essay has been to cast a wide net, so to speak, in hope of getting a good catch. My logic is intentionally circular, rather than linear. I begin by circling around something very basic to all academic research—our relationship with words and concepts.

Admittedly, without "words and concepts" it would be extremely difficult for us academics to do our jobs. But further, as I hope will unfold, our relationship with words and concepts reflects practices and attitudes that can obscure rather than reveal healthy relationships. For my observation has been that we tend to become possessive of our ideas—words and concepts—and that this sense of ownership of our ideas serves most often to reinforce what we, progressive educators, claim we are ideologically committed to eradicate. That is, a good deal of the "turf" issues and power struggles among faculty are related to an obsessive clinging to ideas as if they were the final truth. In contradistinction, this essay represents less of a formal research paper and more of a rumination—something read with morning coffee—on academia and Buddhism inspired by Thich Nhat Hanh and Chogyam Trungpa, among others.

As such, I have divided this essay into two sections. The first section attempts to provide "context," to situate the discussion on Buddhism, health, and academia. In the first part I do not discuss health issues directly; rather drawing upon Nhat Hanh, Delpit, and others I "playfully" explore words and concepts in academia. I have written and published some of these ideas earlier (Hudak 1998); however, my thinking about this topic continues to develop as part of my journey in academia.

In the second part, I begin to circle around the notion of "linguistic" health in academia as a sort of "spiritual literacy." Here it must be made clear from the start that the terms "spiritual," "literacy," and "health" are loaded with ideological assumptions which often mask very contested political terrains. However, this essay is not the place for me to discuss current trends and debates regarding these terms. Instead, I want to simply state operating definitions used. First, drawing from the work of educator and theologian Dwayne Huebner, "spirituality" is conceived as a sense of "moreness" found in everyday life. That is, there is "more" to our lives than what we conceive through and by the ego, "I"; what transcends (as well as includes) the ego, and all constructs (including concepts and words), is spirit. Next, I'm defining literacy as a social practice, which constitutes more than simple reading and writing. Here, I view literacy as embracing two interrelated modalities. One modality sees literacy as dialogical and draws from the tradition of critical consciousness, Marxist praxis, and liberation theology—that is, from the works of Paulo Freire. The other modality of literacy is practices that involve the reading and writing of Silence, of Listening, of Un-saying. This tradition is referred to in mystical traditions (both Christian and Buddhist) as "apophatic." For this essay I draw from this second tradition of literacy, for I want to suggest that when we become nonattached to words and concepts, is it possible to (re)connect with ourselves, with others, with the world, and this "lived-experience" of literacy is health. Finally, then, I am thinking of "health" in terms similar to Buddhist scholar Chogyam Trungpa, who writes of achieving and realizing the "basic goodness" of our lives. Here basic goodness is close to the experiencing of the Buddhist notion of *shunyata,* emptiness, and where one directly experiences the nondual, interrelatedness beyond the fabric of language. Finally, I want to draw to the reader's attention the fact that arguments are presented in "broad" strokes, suggesting contours and avenues for further, more precise analysis at a later date.

Words, Concepts and Buddhism: Liberation, Cure, or Addiction?

Thich Nhat Hanh is a Vietnamese Zen Buddhist master who currently lives in France. He has served as chair of the Buddhist peace delegation to the Paris Peace Talks during the Vietnam War and was nominated for the Nobel Peace Prize by Dr. Martin Luther King, Jr. He is the author of over 70 books. In *Cultivating the Mind of Love* (1996), Nhat Hanh writes in alternating chapters of love and of Buddhist epistemology. The chapters on love present vignettes of Nhat Hanh's falling in love with a Buddhist nun many years ago in his youth. He writes:

> Monks do not usually share stories like this, but I think it is important to do so. Otherwise, how will the younger generation know what to do when they are stuck? As a monk, you are not supposed to fall in love, but sometimes love is stronger than your determination. (21)

The chapters on love do not attempt to explain what love is in an analytical way. Rather, as a Dharma Talk (Buddhist Teachings), they are intended to be heard, listened to, with our whole being. This mode of listening is very similar to Delpit's sense of "being still and opening myself," being completely receptive to the experience of those around us. For, as Nhat Hanh writes, we must learn to listen with the whole of our being, not just with our intellects:

> Seeds of love and understanding buried deep within [our] consciousness [are] touched, and I could see that [you are] listening not just to my talk, but [yours] as well.... When you listen to a Dharma Talk, just allow the rain of the Dharma to penetrate the soil of your consciousness. Don't think too much; don't argue or compare. (3)

"Don't think too much." This sounds strange for us in academia to hear, yet Nhat Hanh's intent is that thinking, the intellect itself, can get in the way of our experiencing reality directly. For Nhat Hanh there is a difference between mediated and unmediated realities. As such, the Dharma Talk is like the Zen saying, "the finger that points to the moon is not the moon." The finger, words, and concepts point beyond themselves to what lies beyond the horizon of language, of words, concepts, and notions. Likewise, the interconnectedness between us and the world—love—lies beyond the concept, the word "love." Love is not simply a state of *understanding*, but rather the direct *realization* of our being connected with the universe.

Love and liberation from suffering lie in a realm beyond language; they are directly experienced, immediate, not concepts. As such, Nhat Hanh's concern is not to gain an intellectual understanding of love, but rather to evoke the poetic experience of it through his writing. To this end the chapters on love include love poetry, and other heartfelt moments in his struggle with being in love. However, Nhat Hanh's intent is not discursive; it is not simply to discuss the issue of falling in love, nor is it simply to instruct us on Zen Buddhist epistemology. Instead, he suggests through the form of the text (i.e., the alternating of chapters, first on his experience of love and then a chapter on Buddhist epistemology) that the ways in which we cling to another person when we claim to have fallen in love, are similar to the ways in which we cling to words and concepts. In either case, we are unable to directly experience the world around us, to be connected to it. Instead, our grasping of concepts, such as "love," mitigates, again, our actually realizing the very love, the very connectedness with the universe we desire in our lives.

There is a strong pedagogical undercurrent within the text, instructing, pointing to human liberation—living in love and freedom. For Thich Nhat Hanh, learning is not the accumulation of knowledge; instead, it is the letting-go of concepts and ideas that stand in the way, mediate our encounters with the world. In *Cultivating the Mind of Love* (1996) he writes:

> Notions and concepts can be useful if we learn how to use them. Zen master Un Chi said, "If you see the Buddha on your way, kill him." He means, if you have an idea of the Buddha that prevents you from having a direct experience of the Buddha, that object of your perception catches you, and the only way to free yourself and experience the Buddha is to kill your notion of the Buddha. This is the secret of the practice. If you hold onto an idea or a notion, you lose the chance. Learning to transcend your mental constructs of reality is an art. *Teachers have to help their students learn how not to accumulate notions* (my emphasis). If you are laden with notions, you will never be emancipated. Learning to look deeply to see into the true nature of things, having direct contact with reality and not just describing reality in terms of notions and concepts, is the practice. (53–54)

This pericope tells us first that Zen Buddhist epistemology is not antilanguage, antiword. Rather, concepts and notions can be helpful if used skillfully, if they aid in our initial understanding of reality. The cautionary note, is that our concepts can prevent us from direct perception of Buddha himself. This is an interesting note in that, for Buddhists, killing is prohibited. One wonders here if "metaphorical killing" is the exception to the rule. Or is there another intent here. Namely, even the probation "no killing" is itself a notion, and, as such, if we become infatuated, fixated with these precepts then, once again, we become disconnected with our environment. Here we perceive the reality of no killing through words, not through the direct experience of being connected with the universe. Hence, the only way to free oneself and experience reality is to kill all notions, including the notion to kill all notions. This task can become painfully regressive, as we willfully attempt to extinguish the metadialogues in our heads, telling us to be silent.

While concepts and notions serve a pedagogical function to teach and instruct, it is wrong to view reality as equivalent to signs—notions and concepts. In an earlier work, Nhat Hanh (1995) writes:

> The ultimate dimension of reality has nothing to do with concepts. It is not just absolute reality that cannot be talked about. Nothing can be conceived or talked about. Take, for instance, a glass of apple juice. You cannot talk about apple juice to someone who has never tasted it. No matter what you say, the other person will not have the true experience of apple juice. Concepts and words cannot describe things. They can only be encountered by direct experience. (140)

For Nhat Hanh, the idea is for us to use concepts and notions skillfully, without getting caught by them. Here Nhat Hanh refers to Wittgenstein's famous analogy of language as a "ladder" to explain his point (139). That is, we can use words to climb to a certain point, and when we arrive, we no longer need the ladder. Thich Nhat Hanh refers to Buddha's teachings as a "raft" to remind us that all teachings are constructs that aid us "crossing" various rivers of life, and that after the crossing, we must learn to "let go" of all true teachings of the Buddha and, not to mention, all teachings that are not true. There is more to the universe than can be captured in conceptual, intellectual understanding.

Indeed, educational theorist Dwayne Huebner (1996) writes of the "spirit" as that sense of "moreness" found in everyday life. It is argued that language paradoxically communicates "more" than it is able to express. Huebner elaborates this point, in his article, "Education and Spirituality":

> There is more than we know, can know, ever will know. It is this "moreness" that takes us by surprise when we are at the edge and the end of our knowing. Call it what you will. . . . One knows of that presence, that "moreness," when known resources fail and somehow we go beyond what we were and are and become something different, something new. . . . It is this very "moreness" that can be identified with the "spirit" and the "spiritual." Spirit is that which transcends the known, the expected, even the ego and the self. It is the source of hope. It is manifested through love and the waiting expectation that accompanies love. (15–16)

Huebner's sense of the spiritual-as-moreness suggests the possibility of there being more to heaven and earth, so to speak, than language. And that the

Spirit exists as a moment of waiting, patiently, possibly in silence. Indeed, Huebner suggests that the Spirit transcends knowledge, in that we begin to live by love and faith. Living by love and faith does not negate knowledge or communication; rather, this is a moment of transcendent living: living beyond the expectations of "even the ego and the self," as Huebner puts it. Indeed, as soon as we claim to know something, there is something more and unexpected that can occur, something that lies beyond our horizon of awareness—beyond language.

From Huebner and Nhat Hanh we see that living fully as human beings entails a letting-go of conceptual frameworks such that we can experience that sense of "moreness" in everyday life. While the "spiritual" discussions reflected in Huebner's and Nhat Hanh's work move towards a letting-go of conceptual frameworks, trends within the educational research community reflect a move towards greater accumulation of ideas as something to be possessed, as cultural capital to be exchanged within the marketplace of the university. A simple observation here: While nothing is monolithic, I can bear witness that, at times, life in the academy is far from peaceful, particularly with regard to the politics connected with "turf issues." Challenge someone's epistemology, ideology, or words and there is likely to be sparks flying, even if the challenges are initially intended to be helpful!

Now, my point is not to belabor conflicts in the academy; rather to make the observation that as academics, we spend a good deal of time writing and speaking. Words and ideas are the basic tools of the trade, so to speak. Our words perform many functions. Among them, words are a form of capital which we use as a means to establish our place in the academic hierarchy: publish or perish, merit pay increases, and so on. Thus we invest much time, effort, and personal sacrifice in our writing and our thinking, not only to connect with others, but also to satisfy the conditions of our job. It is no great mystery that we can become protective of what we write or say.

But it is one thing to become protective, to guard against unfair attacks, and yet another thing to become infatuated with our words. To become infatuated with our words means, to a certain degree, we have fallen in love with them. Here, our words and ideas take on the role of a loved one; they are our lovers. We love our words, which is fine; they are our creations. However, the pathology occurs when we cling to them like a jealous lover, reifying our words to such an extent that it becomes virtually impossible for us to see, hear, or touch others or ourselves. Nhat Hanh (1996) writes:

> Because of our tendency to use notions and concepts to grasp reality, we cannot touch reality as it is. We construct an image of reality that does not coincide with reality itself. . . . In Western philosophy the term "being-in-itself" is very close to the

> Buddhist term "suchness," reality as it is, free from conceptions or grasping. You cannot grasp it, because grasping reality with concepts and notions is like catching space with a net. (41–42)

Likewise, as Delpit observed:

> We educators set out to teach, but how can we reach the worlds of others, when we don't even know they exist? Indeed, many of us don't even realize that our own worlds exist only in our heads and in the cultural institutions we have built to support them. (xiv)

When we are seduced by our own words, we hear what we want to hear and see what we want to see; reality is in our heads.

This sense of how epistemologies, ways of knowing, can disconnect us from each other within the academic context of teacher education is further illustrated by some of the arguments presented in the book *The Struggle for Pedagogies* (1993). In this text, Jennifer Gore uses Foucault's analysis to try to come to terms with the ways in which so-called progressive pedagogies, specifically derived from Marxist and feminist thought, have generated their own hierarchies within the academy. That is, here we have progressive thought used against itself to create yet another repressive structure within schooling. Here Gore underscores Foucault's claim that all knowledge can become dangerous—that is, knowledge can be used, transformed, transmuted, for strategic purposes within a field of power. Simply to evoke Marx or feminist (or Buddhist) thought provides no immunity from one using these notions or concepts for larger political purposes or advantages. For Gore (and Foucault), there is no inherently liberating pedagogical thought; knowledge comes without fixed guarantees. As such, questions of liberation have to be addressed by looking at the larger political picture, and how a specific knowledge form is circulated, say, within the school. Here, Gore comes very close to Nhat Hanh's concern of being attached to concepts, or notions, as a fixed sort of truth—the Law—when she writes:

> My concern is that when discourses of critical or feminist pedagogy present themselves as fixed, or final, or "founded" form, that form soon protects them from rethinking and change. It turns what was once "critical" in their work into a kind of norm or law—a final truth, a final emancipation. As a teacher educator practicing critical and feminist pedagogy, I wanted to believe that what I am doing is right—it is certainly more difficult to live with uncertainty. (11)

It is worth noting how Gore's desire to do right, to have certainty in one's actions, especially when teaching future teachers about other people's children, can lead to the constitution of laws, norms, final truths that, again, act as laws controlling what we see, hear, and understand.

Indeed, Delpit, Nhat Hanh, and Gore all suggest that embedded in our notions of "liberating" epistemologies, there is, simultaneously, a double play at work in our thinking. Namely, liberation, from a common sense perspective, implies a freedom from suffering from oppression. And, at the same time, this movement away from suffering implies a sort of certainty—that is, liberation will cure suffering. More specifically, if, for example, we employ a Marxist or feminist epistemology, the intention is that we will be working towards alleviating social and economic injustices; these epistemologies promise to "cure" injustice. Along similar lines of thinking, we can say that Zen Buddhism promises to "cure" suffering, by transcending the cycle of birth and death.

Notice how "uncertainty" itself can become normalized, static, once we begin to tack onto liberation epistemologies a telos—a specific grand purpose to cure. And notice further, once a liberation epistemology becomes a cure, then, like some precious "drug," it is possible to barter this drug as a possession within current relations of power. That is, for example, we, the teachers of teachers, may become "experts" on liberation, on how to cure suffering; as such, we may gain prominence in society, earn a healthy salary, gain respect from our peers, and, in short, live a comfortable, secure (certain!) lifestyle. What began for us as a "raft" to cross the river of suffering becomes a comfortable upper-middle-class lifestyle. To this point, Krishnamurti (1953) writes:

> If we are being educated only to be scientists, to be scholars wedded to books, or specialists *addicted* to knowledge, then we shall be contributing to the destruction and misery of the world. (11, emphasis added)

That is, the point of education is to humanize the world, not simply study it. When liberating epistemologies become cures, it is possible, within the current play of capitalist power relations, to become addicted to that knowledge—*to become dependent not only on the content of knowledge, but more, the contextual lifestyle that can be construed around the "expert" who possesses that cure.* Here, liberation becomes its own enemy. If you meet "liberation" on the street, kill it! "Liberation" can be an addicting epistemology. However, Eve Sedgwick (1994) notes that within the contemporary play of signifiers, any activity can be labeled as addicting. "What is startling," Sedgwick writes, " is the rapidity with which it has now become commonplace that, precisely, any substance, any behavior, even any affect may be pathologized as addictive" (132). We may have come to the point in American culture where liberation epistemologies and theologies in postmodern societies embrace Jacques Derrida's (1995) notion of the *pharmakon*. That is, within the context of a consumer-oriented society, it becomes difficult to distinguish liberation, the "cure," from the "poison."

Consider the way in which "media Buddhism" appears to consume the older, more "authentic" notions of Buddhism. For the line between remedy and poison is thinly drawn in the postmodern culture of Media America, even for Buddhism. Consider the current media rage over Buddhism in America. In an issue of *Time* magazine (October 13, 1997), Buddhism made the cover page. The article tells of two movies—*Seven Years in Tibet,* and *Kundun.* Throughout the article, we are told of the plight of Tibetans in China. Of how celebrities are using money and influence to push for Tibetan independence. Of how Zen Buddhists in San Francisco run two well-respected AIDS hospices. Of how Thich Nhat Hanh's book, *Living Buddha, Living Christ,* has sold over 100,000 hard-cover copies. Of how large numbers of middle Americans meditate, chant, and observe Buddhist teachings. In short, the article tells of how Buddhism is, once again, fashionable. (Buddhism was fashionable both at the turn of the century and in the 1950s with the Beat movement). These efforts to help others are, of course, commendable; however, the postmodern moment lies in the way in which the media, within a capitalist discourse, are now framing the "phenomenon" of Buddhism.

Indeed, it is becoming increasingly difficult to distinguish Thich Nhat Hanh, the engaged Buddhist monk who struggled to bring peace to Vietnam, from Thich Nhat Hanh, the media image in *Time* magazine. As boundaries blur, the multiplex of possibilities makes one dizzy, for everything can become potentially something infused with meaning—even in locations once thought of as devoid of spirit—for example, suburban shopping malls.

Towards a Spiritual Literacy

As Thich Nhat Hanh suggests, words and concepts need to be used skillfully and without attachment. For the point that must be stressed is that all concepts can aid, as well as obscure, in our journeys to connect with others. Indeed, as Eve Sedgwick points out, even the term "addiction" can become its own poison, a mode of hegemonic thinking, a label used to contain, control the behaviors of others. Here Sedgwick and Nhat Hanh come very close to contemporary postmodern thought on language and literacy. Knoblauch and Brannon (1993) write of language as an endless play of signifiers, "proliferating meanings without ever delivering on the promise that they point to something beyond the tangles of language" (167). Language is conceived as a sort of "leaky" system, forever composing and subverting the world; a sort of "joker" who seems, at first glance, to be stable, have a presence—however, under scrutiny to be tricky, mysterious, slippery stuff. If, for instance, we attempt to pin down the meaning of a term, instead of coming up with a single definition, we instead are referred to yet more terms. The point being, language is utterly interdependent where each word is related to another to such a degree that it is virtually impossible to understand one word without knowing the larger sociolinguistic universe within which it is a part. As an interdependent system, it is difficult to experience the moreness that lies beyond the linguistic universe.

Now, while it is possible to discuss other dimensions of language (e.g., language and ideology, subjectivity, social reality), I want to continue along the path of language as referring to, as Huebner and Nhat Hanh suggest, a reality that is beyond language. That is, if we accept for the sake of argument Huebner's definition of spiritual as pointing to that "moreness" of living, then it is possible to consider the notion of a "spiritual" literacy. Here, spiritual literacy is, as Huebner and Nhat Hanh suggest, using words skillfully to point to, name that which cannot be named—the transcendent. Admittedly, this is something of a dilemma—naming that which can't be named. This particular form of dilemma is known, within studies of mysticism, as *aporia,* the unresolved dilemma of transcendence. That is:

> The transcendent is beyond names, ineffable. In order to claim that the transcendent is beyond names, however, I must give it a name, 'the transcendent.' Any statement of ineffability, 'X is beyond all names,' generates the *aporia* that the subject of the statement must be named (as X) in order for us to affirm that it is beyond names. (Sells 1994, 2)

The designation of this language of "unsaying" is known as apophatic. Notice the similarity in this quote between the apophatic tradition and Nhat Hanh. Namely, Nhat Hanh refers to using concepts skillfully to point to something beyond, something transcendent. The transcendent, in turn, once named, is no longer the transcendent, but rather runs the risk of being reified, fixed within boundaries. Hence, apophatic language attempts to "say" what cannot be said, by "un-saying."

We can proceed further in our investigating of unsaying, for one of the paradoxes of unsaying is that the transcendent is realized within the immanent. Within, so to speak, a grain of sand lies the whole universe. That is:

> [A]t the heart of that unsaying is a radical dialectic of transcendence and immanence. That which is utterly "beyond" is revealed or reveals itself as most intimately "within" . . . When the transcendent realizes itself as the immanent, the subject of the act is neither divine nor human, neither self nor other. . . . This moment in which the boundaries between divine and human, self and others, melt away is

> commonly called mystical union . . . and *[h]owever humble it may appear, is nothing less than the healing of the world, the healing of the relationship between the world and the deity*. . . . (Sells, 7, emphasis added)

Unsaying, then, is part of a larger pedagogical moment, a learning that paradoxically is not found "out there," but rather here in our immediate grasp. In fact, it is so "here" as to go unnoticed; God is everywhere among us. Further, note that the more we attempt to grasp, cling to the transcendent, the less likely we are to apprehend it. This is something of a mystery, where mystery refers to the tension that as soon as one thinks one has "it," one has lost "it." "It is glimpsed only in the interstices of the text, in the tension between the saying and the unsaying" (8). As such, the mystical union is constituted when subject and object form a union. The real trick, the pedagogical moment, is that one cannot will this union, for this would be an act of intention, of ego control and hence, tacitly reaffirming the "objectness" of the other. Nor can one consciously not will this union. On this latter point, we play a sort of sly game with our egos, namely, "I'm really not willing, intending" when we, in fact, are controlling to have no control. It is an endless regressive cycle, unless we learn spiritual literacy. That is, to fully let go and experience the world in a direct way, unmediated by concepts. This level of living is healing, is health.

Indeed, Tibetan Chogyam Trungpa (1986) writes of health as the realization of our "basic goodness":

> It is not just an arbitrary idea that the world is good, but it is good because we experience its goodness. We can experience our world as healthy and straightforward, direct and real, because our basic nature is to go along with the goodness of situations . . . There is a gut-level sense of health and wholesomeness taking place in our lives . . . There is something very real and, at the same time, very rich about our human experience. Out of that feeling, a tremendous sense of health can be propagated to others . . . When we feel healthy and wholesome ourselves, then we cannot help projecting that healthiness to others. (10, 39)

Notice that for Trungpa health and wholesomeness are interrelated to a basic sense of the world as directly experienced as good. Further, when we are healthy, we project health onto others. However, Nhat Hanh (1996) refers to the extreme difficulty of letting go, of experiencing *shunyata*, emptiness. *Shunyata* means direct realization of the interconnectedness of the Universe, and it means all words, concepts, and notions are "empty" of any intrinsic reality. To have our minds cling even to the notion that all is empty is, in Nhat Hanh's observation, to be caught in the poison of *shunyata*. "All other notions can be healed by the notion of emptiness, but when you are caught in the notion of emptiness, the disease is incurable" (43).

If the perspectives of Truhgpa and Nhat Hanh are taken together, we begin to realize this import of proper instruction, of becoming spiritually literate to the path of unsaying. Again, Trungpa (1973) writes that:

> The experience of shunyata cannot be developed without first having worked through the narrow path of discipline and technique. Technique is necessary to start with, but it is also necessary, at some stage, for technique to fall away. From the point of view of the whole process of learning and practice technique is quite unnecessary. We could perceive the absence of the ego at a single glance. But we would not accept such a simple truth. In other words, we have to learn in order to unlearn. The whole process is that of undoing the ego. We start by learning to deal with neurotic thoughts and emotions. Then false concepts are removed through the understanding of emptiness . . . Then surrender and renunciation. Renunciation in this instance is not just throwing away but, having thrown everything away, we begin to feel the living quality of peace. (197–198)

Here Trungpa clearly links a sort of instruction, a literacy with shunyata. And the unfolding of shunyata with a growing sense of health with oneself and with others. Of import is again for us to be aware of the role of letting go of the addicting nature of words and concepts. False concepts are initially removed, then one unlearns to undo the ego! It is a process of beginning with attachments to words and concerns, to detachments, and finally nonattachments to them.

Finally, I want to suggest that spiritual literacy, as health, is also a moment of "grace." The concept of grace is derived from the Greek *charis,* which can be translated as "favor." Indeed, Martin Marty (1992) describes "grace" as a sort of code word for Christian faith and life. Here, the idea is that God was moved out of love to create the universe, to situate humans within it, and to connect with us through his love. Biblical scripture (e.g., Genesis) tells us that as humans we have fallen, that a breach has occurred between God and humans. The overcoming of this breach between God and humans is grace, to the extent that God does us a "favor" by attempting to rectify this rupture, through unconditional love. "This love, unmotivated and spontaneous—which means that it does not need to find redeeming qualities in its object—finds its expression in grace" (210). We can see that grace exemplifies "the revelation of divine character in action and the relation of the divine to human beings" (210). Following this logic, we can say that if spiritual literacy entails learning to experience the world directly, then it follows that the "breach" between subject-object is rectified, unified in that unexpected moment of mystical union. This act of unification, I suggest, is grace, a "favor" that cannot be willed by humans. Further, this act of grace is made manifest because of the mysterious nature of language—namely the moreness of language, of its openness to continual acts of "interpretation." The very fact that language allows for there to be more, more than expected or anticipated, imagined is grace. And so . . .

What does all this mean for us, the teachers of teachers within the context of the academy? It means language, words and concepts, are all tricky. Language can illuminate, as well as conceal. Nothing new here! It also means that we academics tend to place a great deal of import on language, so great as to become addicted to our own words. When we become addicted, we become dependent, fixated by them, and when we become fixated, we no longer experience others, their humanity afresh. Paradoxically, we no longer experience our words, themselves as wondrous—the cure always has the potential to poison; the language this reveals can also blind us to others. Indeed, Delpit writes, "the answers [to problems in education], I believe, lie not in a proliferation of new reform programs, but in some basic understanding of who we are and how we are connected and disconnected from one another" (1995, xv). And who are we? While we, as human, are constituted within language, Nhat Hanh, Huebner, and Delpit remind us that there is always "more" to reality and how we are connected to one another and the world. As such, the answer to many educational problems are not more reforms, if by this we mean more technical solutions, more concepts that obscure reality. Rather, it is about gaining a basic realization of what it means to be human and share the Earth with others in a loving way. This is an act of Love and this is Health.

Further, Thich Nhat Hanh reminds us of the Buddhist notion of Sangha. The Sangha is a Buddhist community, where "the Sangha contains the Buddha and the Dharma. A good teacher is important, but sisters and brothers in practices is the main ingredient for success. You cannot achieve enlightenment by locking yourself in a room" (1995, 71). Sangha is about a community in common pursuit; it is about right relationship with oneself and the world. That we are in a postmodern era, where liberating epistemologies such as Zen can be both cure and food for media consumption, does not alter Nhat Hanh's assertion that we must look beyond the words and concepts, beyond the Law, to our first Love and make eye-to-eye contact with the world around us if there is to be a significant transformation in the quality of teaching, learning, and living.

In the end, spiritual literacy is political. That is, the sense of spirit-as-moreness alerts us to the fact that we are finite, not the whole picture, but rather a part of it. Hence, for Nhat Hanh, Delpit, and Huebner the spiritual transcends the known, the expected, and even the sense of who we think we are. This sense of spiritual-as-moreness is political. For within the current play of power relations within capitalist America—a society that thrives on competition, greed, and self over all others—moreness provides us with a source of hope—that is, there can be more! Moreness provides the foundation for dreams and imagination of a "more" just and humane society. It does this by affirming our presence, while at the same time waking us up to the truly "larger picture," namely that it is a big Universe, and that capitalist America (and the academy) for all its good, for all its bad, and for all its in-betweens, is not the final destination of humanity. There is more to it.

Therefore, this sense of spirit reminds us that we are not the center, but interconnected, related to one another and that no one person has the "whole" story. We all have some partial truths to communicate to each other. Moreness then demands that we dialogue with each other, to collectively construct our worlds and our sense of what it means to be alive. This act is political, especially within the current context, which attempts to divide us, separate us into isolated individuals cut off from ourselves, from each other, and from the Universe.

References

Delpit, Lisa (1995). *Other People's Children*. New York: New Press.
Derrida, J. (1995). *The Rhetoric of Drugs. Points. . . . Interviews 1974–1994*. E. Weber (Ed.). Stanford: Stanford University Press.
Gore, Jennifer (1993). *The Struggle for Pedagogies*. New York: Routledge Press.
Hudak, Glenn (1998). "Addicting Epistemologies? An Essay Review of Thich Nhat Hanh's *Cultivating the Mind of Love*." *Educational Review*, 27 (9), 43–47.
Huebner, Dwayne (1996). "Education and Spirituality." *Journal of Curriculum Theorizing*, 11(2), 13–34.
Knoblauch, C. H., and Lil Brannon (1993). *Critical Teaching and the Idea of Literacy*. Portsmouth, NH: Boynton/Cook Publishers.
Krishnamurti, J. (1953). *Education and the Significance of Life*. New York: Harper.
Marty, Martin. (1992). "Grace." In D. Musser and J. Price (Eds.), pp. 209 – 211, *A New Handbook of Christian Theology*. Nashville: Abingdon Press.
Nhat Hanh, Thich (1995). *Living Buddha, Living Christ*. New York: Riverhead Books.
——— (1996). *Cultivating the Mind of Love*. Berkeley: Parallax Press.
Sedgwick, Eve (1993). *Tendencies*. Durham, NC.: Duke University Press.
Sells, Michael (1994). *Mystical Languages of Un-Saying*. Chicago: University of Chicago Press.
Time (October 13, 1997).
Trungpa, Choygam (1973). *Cutting Through Spiritual Materialism*. Berkeley: Shambala.
——— (1986). *Shambala*. New York: Bantam Books.

CHAPTER FIVE

Social Justice, Curriculum, and Spirituality

David E. Purpel

Preface

There are moments when I find the culture's extraordinary reluctance to respond honestly to the realities of social injustice to be ironic and troubling, but most of the time I am horrified and outraged. This social and cultural amnesia becomes especially vivid during Presidential campaigns, presumably the time for serious public debate on our most basic priorities and commitments. Instead, we get commentaries on the style and persona of the candidates, pious statements of the importance of integrity and firmness, deeply troubled concerns for fiscal responsibility, and fervent devotion to the well being of the global economy. What we don't get is any significant concern for poverty or racism; there is little or no mention of hunger or homelessness; or any sense of outrage at unnecessary human suffering. In a generation we have gone from a war on poverty to a crusade for middle-class tax relief.

Meanwhile, mainstream educators seem to be focused on devising more sophisticated testing and tighter control mechanisms, while many educational critics are engaged in fierce battles over the fate of the universe and the nature of deconstructionism. Some educational visionaries would have us believe that what we really need in education is an end to dualistic thinking and a consciousness of spiritual oneness with nature and the universe. While politicians spin, educators test, critics reflect, and theorists parse, there are people eating dog food, teenagers turning tricks, children dealing in drugs, and families living in boxes. I say all this because I believe that it is intolerable that there be any educational discourse without continuous reference to the presence of the pain and suffering that is rooted in human greed, irresponsibility, and callousness.

The Rise and Fall of Curriculum

Although the field of curriculum theory has been declared moribund, it is perhaps fairer to say that it appears that many theorists have given up on the notion that reforming the formal school curriculum is the key to social, if not educational, reform. In response to this disenchantment with curriculum development, much of what goes on in the name of curriculum discourse today tends to be highly theoretical and ideological in nature. The vacuum of dialogue on what we should teach has been largely filled with discussion of instructional and assessment issues. Indeed, it would appear that even the politicians have discovered the language of the hidden curriculum, as they call for an education that responds to the concerns of competing in the global economy and for "a return to values." The once powerful demands for more demanding science, history, and math courses, as well as for a more academic curriculum, now seem like part of ancient history.

Herbert Kliebard has helped to clarify how the various curriculum controversies have been played out in the schools historically. It is his position that the story of the twentieth-century American school curriculum can be seen as the struggle among four broad competing educational groups: "First, there were the humanists, the guardians of an ancient tradition tied to the powers of reason and the finest elements of Western cultural heritage . . ." [The second group] "led the drive for a curriculum reformed along the lines of a natural order of development of the child" based on scientific data. [Thirdly, there are] "The social efficiency educators . . . also imbued with the power of science, but their priorities lay with creating a coolly efficient, smoothly running society." Finally, there were the social meliorists, who felt that "new social conditions did not demand an obsessional fixation on the child and on child psychology; nor did the solution lie in simply ironing out the inefficiencies in the existing social order. The answer lay in the power of the schools to create a new social order" (Kliebard 1986, 23–25).

Kliebard's conclusion is that none of these orientations ever became dominant as the schools tried to accommodate to pressures from each of these groups: "In the end, what became the American curriculum was not the result of any decisive victory by any of the contending parties, but a loose, largely unarticulated, and not very tidy, compromise" (1986, 25).

This typology helps us to see the continuity of our educational concerns as important aspects of these orientations that can be easily detected in contemporary dialogue on educational policy. Surely, for example, the debate on multicultural education reflects the agenda of what Kliebard calls "the humanists," and certainly critical pedagogy is very much in the tradition of the "social meliorists." However, there are other forces in American cultures that influence the curriculum which are not so apparent in this formulation. For example, the persistence of the arts and athletics in the standard curriculum over time cannot be explained entirely or even largely by these four orientations. There is also the recurring phenomenon of using the curriculum as a vehicle for promoting nationalism (patriotism) and/or ideology (democracy), and the term "social efficiency" only begins to suggest the current obsession with competing in the global economy.

Underneath and cutting across these four approaches and their variations are what I would term fundamental educational imperatives, in which we are called upon, nay commanded, to earnestly and conscientiously pursue certain ideals. The most familiar and enduring cultural formulation of such imperatives urges us to seek "the True, the Good, and the Beautiful." Others would want to add to these commandments the injunction to pursue Meaning. These commandments are so profoundly revered and have become so powerfully internalized that they have come to constitute the spiritual foundations of education. Put another way, no matter what the specific educational goals may be, there is the underlying demand that we reach these goals without violating the canons of these fundamental imperatives.

Today, perhaps the single most powerful and pervasive of these educational commandments is "Thou Shalt Seek the Truth." In modern times, truth has come to be typically defined as accurate and precise knowledge; information that can be verified through empirical and/or logical processes. The triumph of Enlightenment thought is testimony to the primacy of this imperative, with its basically unchallenged demands for precision, proof, reason, analysis, detachment, and skepticism. We are enjoined to seek this kind of Truth, however difficult and unsettling it may be and regardless of the consequences, presumably in the faith that the Truth will make us free. Not only is this pursuit presented as a moral and aesthetic imperative, but as a pragmatically essential dimension of creating a progressive civilization. If nothing else, American education is about preserving and enhancing the intellectual and aesthetic processes of pursuing this kind of Truth. Critics and defenders of the educational status quo unite in their dedication to the values of critical rationality insofar as they give us valid information and knowledge that at least approaches the Truth. Our schools and universities constantly test for accuracy and precision, for right answers, and for the presence of compelling evidence. Indeed, the mottoes of two of our oldest and most prestigious universities—Harvard and Yale—are simply and boldly translated as "*Truth.*"

This is surely not to say that the school curriculum centers on the acquisition of knowledge for its own sake or that universities are singularly committed to the search for Truth. What I am saying is that whatever the social and cultural goals may be (job training, national solidarity, human development, social change, personal fulfillment, etc.), we are deeply committed to pursuing them within a context of intellectual integrity—that is, we all want to be sure to be accurate, precise, rational, and knowledgeable. Indeed, at the cost of appearing to be gratuitous, I want to reaffirm my own strong commitment to an education strongly rooted in reason and rationality.

Having said all that, it is also clear that such an education is not without criticism. There are those who insist on the validity and significance of other ultimate goals such as wisdom or goodness. It is also clear that although knowledge and intellectual acuity may be necessary, they are surely not sufficient conditions for wisdom and goodness. Our history has made it painfully clear that smart people can do hateful things and that the impulse to be cruel and callous is not significantly mitigated by acquiring knowledge or analytical skills. Even more troubling is the phenomenon of people deliberately utilizing knowledge (truth) for destructive purposes. The design and production of Zyklon B, napalm, and land mines requires the same degree of intellectual mastery as the design and production of antibiotics and computers. Manipulation requires as much insight as does enlightenment; knowledge of how people learn is as useful to the wizards of Madison Avenue as it is to the gurus of Sesame Street.

There is, of course, another strong educational tradition that seeks to go beyond the pursuit of information and knowledge, namely that of the pursuit of meaning. In this tradition, knowledge is an important dimension of this pursuit and Truth is thought to be metaphysical in nature. Abraham Joshua Heschel expresses this orientation eloquently: "Socrates taught us that a life without thinking is not worth living. . . .Thinking is a noble effort, but the finest thinking may end in futility. . . .The Bible taught us that life without commitment is not worth living; that thinking without roots will bear flowers but no fruit. . . . Our systems of education stress the importance of enabling the student to exploit the power aspect of reality. . . . We teach the children how to measure, how to weigh: We fail to teach to revere, how to sense wonder and awe . . . the sense of the sublime, [and] the sign of the inward greatness of the human soul" (Heschel 1955, 36; 216).

Postmodernism: The Worm in the Apple

It is surely not for me to enter into the seemingly interminable and torturous scholarly debate about the meaning and significance of this concept except to be clear on what I make of all this hullabaloo. Beyond all the smoke of battle and prolixity is the harsh reality of a very serious crisis of authority. We have come to see more and more clearly how much of our understanding of the world is contingent on such matters as history, culture, gender, class, and above all, language, and how much we have been confusing universal truth with particularist interpretation. The very tools of Enlightenment thinking itself have, ironically enough, undermined its most basic and profound project—that of affording human liberation through reason, objectivity, science, technology, and detachment, a project now described by many postmodernists as delusional.

This critique goes beyond eroding our epistemological grounding (as fundamental as that is) and extends to questioning the nature of and commitment to our core moral aspirations. It would appear that not only have we committed the sin of being wrong about the nature of truth, but to make things worse, we have compounded that sin by utilizing these errors in such a way as to provide privilege and advantage to some. What is involved are not only the sin of intellectual arrogance, but also the evil of political oppression. Walter Brueggemann puts it this way:

> "The practice of modernity . . . has given us a world imagined through the privilege of white, male, Western, colonial hegemony with all its pluses and minuses. It is a world that we have come to trust and take for granted. It is a world that has wrought great good, but also has accomplished enormous mischief against some for the sake of others. The simple truth is that this constructed world can no longer be sustained, is no longer persuasive or viable, and we are able to discern no larger image to put in its place. . . . The imagined world of privilege and disparity is treasured by all who live in the advantaged West. It is treasured more by men than women, more by whites than blacks, but all of us in the West have enormous advantage." (1994, 18–20)

The notions of the social construction of knowledge, the close relationships between power arrangements and constructions of reality, and the problematics of essentialist formulations, although surely not new, have had a profound effect on all cultural institutions, including education. What we face amounts to an intellectual and moral crisis that comes in a most importune time. In this time of enormous peril from the forces of greed, divisiveness, and hatred, what we urgently need is a common understanding of our plight and a common vision that saves us from ourselves. In a time when we seek community, we are confronted with the realities of its ambiguities and problematics; at a time when we long for authentic identity, we are required to face the indictment of essentialism; in a time when we feel impelled to speak out at the injustices inflicted on marginal groups, we must deal with the ways in which the definitions of these groups has been deconstructed; and in a time when we search for the moral vision to sustain us through despair and cynicism, we must confront new insights on how ideology impinges on our moral quests.

The implications for education are deeply troubling, for as we have indicated, underlying the various curricular approaches has been the profound commitment to the pursuit of truth in the more restricted sense of critical rationality and/or the metaphysical sense of ultimate meaning. Much of postmodern thought would seem to undermine both of these quests. If truth is an illusion and meaning a delusion, then what are we to teach, other than basic literacy, numeracy, and the conversation-ending assertions of postmodernism? How do we make a rational and coherent plan for education when many brilliant theorists make a compelling case that rationality and moral coherence are no more than charming fictions?

Enter Spirituality

It is hardly surprising that in an atmosphere of political, moral, and intellectual crisis that we as a culture would look to the spiritual as a path toward sanity and hope. The extraordinary surge of interest in matters religious and spiritual is as deep as it is broad, expressing itself not only in religious fundamentalism and New Age spiritualism, but in such movements as liberation theology, feminist theology, and Jewish renewal, as well as in such phenomena as alternative approaches to healing and to organizational management.

This interest has also manifested itself in education, as reflected in the recent publication and popularity of a growing number of articles and books on spirituality and education. There are a growing number of authors like Dwayne Huebner, Jeffrey Kane, Kathleen Kesson, James Moffett, Ron Miller, Parker Palmer, and Douglas Sloan who are writing directly on issues on the intersection of education and spirituality. There are also other major curriculum theorists whose work surely is spiritual in nature, even though they do not necessarily use religious or spiritual language as their primary form of discourse. For example, Nel Noddings's daring and challenging work on caring and compassion speaks to matters of the spirit and to the centrality of human connectiveness, while Jane Roland Martin's focus on nurturance, relationship, and responsibility is a powerful affirmation of the deep inner impulses for love and intimacy.

However, proclaiming the bond between education and spirituality does not begin to resolve our problems since that only begs further questions. Whose spirituality? Which spirituality? How are we to accept the authority of particular spiritual orientations? In other words, the same critiques that have rendered other educational formulations problematic require us to critically examine the claims for a spiritually grounded education. Indeed, the history of religious and spiritual expression requires us to be especially alert to its particular problematics, such as the possibilities of dogmatism, zealotry, authoritarianism, and irrelevance. The whole notion of an education based on spiritual beliefs goes totally counter to what we have learned about the danger and implausibility of visions that emerge from "grand narratives."

And yet, the power of the spirit is the very energy we need lest we fall into the paralysis and cynicism that are the consequences of moral despair and intellectual confusion. Even as intellectuals scoff at facts as fiction, reform efforts as self-serving, and moral visions as pretentious, there is vast and needless human suffering in our midst. Millions of human beings are malnourished and maltreated; millions of people do not have adequate housing, medical care, and education; and the gap between rich and poor has grown to obscene proportions. Even more disheartening is the way that we as a people, nation, and profession have failed to begin to fully accept the depth and gravity of this human suffering, never mind take responsibility for it. The problem is surely not rooted in a lack of understanding, knowledge, and information. There can be no doubt whatsoever that we know about the suffering and that we have the material and intellectual resources to significantly relieve, if not eliminate it. However, the great irony and shame is that we cannot utilize the extraordinary knowledge and expertise that we have accumulated to meet our most profound moral commitments. This is largely, but not entirely, because of the spirits of greed, suspicion, hate, and the divisions which are so pervasive and dominant in our culture.

The reality of immense human suffering is made even more unspeakable by its origins in human stupidity and cupidity, as our failure to redress these sins provides proof enough of our capacity to do evil. Surely we have enough understanding of the intellectual underpinnings of our efforts at creating a just and loving society to make some judgments about them. As far as modernism is concerned, all I have to say is that the misery and suffering of millions of people is not a socially constructed metaphor, but is as real and certain as misery and suffering.

How then do we go on with our commitments in a time when we have clear responsibilities and fuzzy authority and how do we generate hope and vision in an era of uncertainty, despair, and disenchantment? This is not merely a challenge that educators must address, but one that requires creative and thoughtful responses from all aspects of our society and culture. One very helpful response has been presented by Walter Brueggemann in his book, *Texts Under Negotiation,* in which he struggles with the implications of postmodernism for another influential cultural institution, the Christian church. After acknowledging the power and influence of postmodern thinking, he goes on to offer some suggestions on how the Church can sustain its efforts in the light of this disquieting critique without in any way loosening its commitment to a worldview based on divine creation and ultimate redemption:

> It is not, in my judgment, the work of the church . . . to construct as preemptively and imperialistically as all those old construals and impositions. Rather, the task is a more modest one, [namely]. . . to fund—to provide the pieces, materials, and resources, out of which a New World can be imagined. Our responsibility, then, is not a grand scheme or a coherent system, but the voicing of a lot of little pieces out of which people can put life together in fresh configurations. (Brueggemann 1994, 22)

He goes on to urge his colleagues to create places of meeting where people can come together to share their "funds," but not to make "claims that are so large and comprehensive that they ring hollow in a context of our general failure, demise, and disease. It is, rather, a place where people come to receive new materials, or old materials freshly voiced, that will fund, feed, nurture, legitimatize, and authorize a *counter-imagination of the world* . . . an imagination that is not at all congenial to dominant intellectual or political modes" (Brueggemann 1994, 23).

Modest Funding Proposal

I want to move past all the postmodern handwringing about the nature of reality and truth as a troubling, interesting, and useful critique, but one that is marginally relevant and fundamentally distracting to our moral responsibilities. Surely, the suffering and the pain are real enough and there is no great mystery about what is required to ease that suffering. In spite of this, one of the horrible ironies of the past few decades is serious erosion in concern for social justice, such as concern for the poor and the homeless. Much of the responsibility for this erosion lies with those who have chosen to see the poor as irresponsible, unskilled, and/or an impediment to the demands of a highly competitive global economy. However, the erosion has been heightened by the neglect of many of those who have traditionally been active in drawing attention to the plight of the poor, a neglect that is not so much the result of a change in moral conviction, as it is a consequence of being distracted by other important concerns. Among such concerns are postmodern thought, cybernetics, and the ecological crisis, all matters of enormous import and significance. There are undoubtedly important connections among issues of social justice, computers, ecology, and postmodernism, but my view is that priority for social justice has significantly eroded, if not superseded. I reject the notion that we cannot pursue social justice until we get our epistemology right, as well as the notion that issues of social justice must be seen only in the perspective of the fate of the universe. My point is not to discount the importance of such powerfully significant issues as the nature of truth, the impact of technology, or the preservation of the planet, but only to argue that we not be held hostage to them or not allow ourselves to be distracted from our nonnegotiable, permanent, and solemn responsibility to work for the elimination of unnecessary human suffering.

At the same time, and in spite of the devastating postmodern critique, the commitment in the academy and among educators (conservatives, as well as radicals) to the pursuit of knowledge and critical rationality seems as passionate and relentless as ever. The dedication to being rational, precise, accurate, perceptive; the solemn vows to conduct careful research and thoughtful inquiry; and the devotion to creating new knowledge and discovering the laws of nature constitute the ultimate raison d'être of contemporary formal education. One way or another, educators pay homage to this Holiest of Grails, for whether it's vocational education or critical pedagogy, a book report or a dissertation, a manifesto or a monograph, we want it to be grounded in the name of the spirits of rationality, knowledge, and inquiry and meet their demands for accuracy, precision, and reliability.

My intention is by no means to reject these spirits as false gods, only to put them in perspective and in their proper place. Let us begin with an examination of the aesthetic values of pursuing knowledge and understanding—that is, the idea of knowledge for its own sake. My sense is that even as educators and scholars embrace pragmatism and functionalism and make eloquent and poetic claims for the benefits of increased knowledge and understanding (e.g., as necessary for citizenship or for personal meaning), there remains an abiding love and passion for the search and accumulation of knowledge and understanding per se. This seems reasonable enough for an educational goal for the relatively limited number of people with that highly specialized sensibility, but hardly plausible as the Ground Zero of all curriculum being.

There is also the problematic nature of the pragmatic claims for knowledge since it has become eminently clear that even though highly knowledgeable and understanding people tend to be richer, more powerful, and more famous, they are also among the most dangerous and evil. This is certainly and emphatically not to say that smart equals bad, but only to say that it is often the case that people use their smarts to do bad things. Power in the United States is not in the hands of the illiterate and intellectually dense; I dare say that we would find a disproportionate number of highly educated (or at a minimum, highly schooled) among the movers and shakers of Wall Street, Madison Avenue, Capitol Hill, Hollywood, and all the other power centers of our society and culture. It must also be said that many of the people who genuinely do serious good are also very knowledgeable and understanding. And that, my friends, is the whole point.

At the very least, the persistence of such claims suggests that increasing knowledge and understanding is supposed to have some consequence over and above the fun and profit of simply finding and having it. The very simple and obvious "truth of the matter" is that education for increased knowledge and understanding should be grounded in a deeper commitment to pursue a larger good than studying for its own sake. My own explanation as to why heightened understanding and knowledge continues to be used for bad things is that we have not demanded that if and when it is to be used, it be used *only* for good things. I believe that there are three basic reasons why we haven't made such demands:

1. Some of us genuinely like finding truth for its own sake.
2. Some of us really want to do bad things.
3. Some of us don't know the difference between good and bad.

To those in Group One, I offer respectful tolerance; to those in Group Two, I have only contempt, but to those in Group Three, I offer some suggestions.

My most basic recommendation is that we ground our education *not* in the pursuit and adoration of truth, knowledge, understanding, insight, critical rationality, interpretive scheme, or analytic tools, but rather in a relentless and wholehearted quest for the attitude formerly known as *agape*. I say this because I have the wisdom in that all-time, oldest, and corniest of all clichés that it is only unconditional and dispassionate love that can truly overcome unnecessary human suffering. It is a wisdom that persists across time and space in spite of vulgarization and oversimplification and in the face of scorn, ridicule, and cynicism, including more than my fair share. I am convinced that a people grounded in a consciousness of *agape* would end most misery even as I realize that such a statement is somewhat tautological, as it can also be said that human misery is rooted in lack of human caring and compassion. I am also very much aware that a project for an education based on nourishing a human consciousness of *agape* is incredibly ambitious if not outrageously pretentious or just plain impossible. However, I do not see such a project as any less ambitious, impractical, pretentious, or possible than the Enlightenment project of human freedom through increased knowledge, understanding, and insight. Indeed, I believe that developing the capacity for understanding and insight alongside a commitment to nourishing the capacity for love is a whole lot more practical than teaching people only to be critical and thoughtful.

Mary Daly has defined *agape* as:

> "In the fullest sense, *agape* is God's love. It is generous love, not appetitive in the sense that there is the need to satisfy that in oneself that is incomplete, not stimulated by or dependent upon that which is loved. It is indifferent to value, seeking to confer good, rather than to obtain it. It is, therefore, spontaneous and creative, and it is rooted in abundance rather than in poverty." (1973, 210)

The idea that we as a people could attain such a consciousness seems remote, if not the stuff of delusion and fantasy. However, the idea that all people have the capacity for the development of an equally intense critical consciousness seems no less daunting and improbable. A major difference is that most educators, as a matter of faith, readily accept the call to work as if people have both the need and the potential to develop a critical consciousness, continually pressing students to stretch and expand their critical skills. Indeed, the educational project for the development of a critical consciousness is deeply embedded in the whole array of our curricular and instructional repertoire. It has been well organized and its elements subdivided into any number of categories, such as literacy and numeracy; the sciences and the humanities; writing skills, analytic and interpretive skills; research skills; reliance on theories of cognitive development; and the use of laboratories for experiments. The point here is that schools and universities approach the task of developing intellectual acumen not as a special program, but as a Spirit that is to energize and permeate all aspects of its academic program with at least the implicit understanding that the effect that all the particular intellectual skills adds up to something more than the sum of its parts—that is, a critical consciousness.

What I am suggesting here is parallel to that approach—that is, not a special program or course in moral education or caring (although these are not unreasonable possibilities), but a larger, deeper, and more endemic commitment to the project of nourishing and demanding the enhancement of the human capacity to love. In doing so, we also encounter problematics parallel to that of the commitment to develop critical consciousness, such as issues of definition, resistance, and complexity. As educators and citizens, we have the responsibility to continue to engage these issues and problems, as difficult and perplexing as they are. It surely is not that we are without resources in such an endeavor, for one of the marvels of human life is that people, over time and across space, have seriously and profoundly involved themselves with the question of how we are to live with each other with justice and love. As a result, we have an extraordinary heritage of powerfully enduring ideas, images, and visions of love and social justice, as well as the legacy of remarkable children, men, women, and groups who have endeavored to embody them.

It is easy enough to realize that many of these visions have been betrayed, that many of these formulations conflict with each other, and that much misery has been inflicted in their names. This is a reality that we must not ever deny or rationalize and which represents a human potential for stupidity and cruelty that we dare not discount nor minimize. At the same time, and without blinking from the horrors of some of our best intentions, it must also be acknowledged that, in spite of all the turmoil and divisiveness, there really does exist an important space of common moral affirmation in which there is a very large degree of consensus, even if some of this is limited to rhetoric. It is a space worthy of passionate embrace and zealous protection that is no less real, but one that is perhaps more vulnerable than the privilege, domination, and greed which occupy the space of human conflict. These items of consensus are admittedly general, perhaps ambiguous and even vague; yet their very persistence, in spite of the intellectual and empirical battering they have taken, is nothing short of miraculous.

Perhaps the most basic and most profound element in this consensus is our belief in the preciousness of life itself and, in that context, our affirmation of the right of every person to a life of dignity and respect. I really do believe that we believe this even though there are reservations to this commitment. For example, there are those who say that certain people like serial killers, child molesters, and rapists should be excluded from this affirmation by virtue of the unforgivable nature of their crimes. I admit to my own deep ambivalence about forgiving and affirming such people, but I am clear that we should not let the worst of the world shape our moral visions, and I am equally certain that the vast majority of us are not vicious and hateful criminals. As educators, we can surely affirm the dignity of children, even if we are perplexed and grieved when some of them act out in anger and violence. At the very least, we can reaffirm our commitment to enhance the dignity of those students who are not hateful and to continue to struggle with how to respond to those who are.

These reservations notwithstanding, the roots for the affirmation of life with dignity run very deep and wide in our history and in our religious, spiritual, and moral traditions. People of all faiths, colors, denominations, classes, genders, ethnicities, creeds, and epistemological preferences embrace them, surely in a variety of discourses. Such affirmation is reflected in the Bible, the Koran, the Declaration of Independence, the U.S. Constitution, the Gettysburg Address, and the Pledge of Allegiance, although regretfully, they are not exactly prominent in Goals 2000. Indeed, the United Nations' Universal Declaration of Human Rights (which all member nations are required to uphold) begins with this assertion: "*Whereas,* recognition of the inherent dignity and of the equal and inalienable rights of all members of the human family is the foundation of freedom, justice, and peace in the world . . ." Later on, in the preamble, the statement goes on to require that "every individual and every organ of society, keeping this declaration constantly in mind, shall strive by teaching and education to promote respect for these rights and freedoms and by progressive measures, national and international, to secure their universal and effective recognition and observance. . . ."

However, educators bent on connecting curriculum making with such stirring discourse need to be reminded of the dangers of grand narratives and magisterial programs. As Walter Brueggemann points out in support of his notion of "funding the pieces, materials, and resources out of which a new world can be imagined,"

> What is yearned for among us is not new doctrine or new morality, but new world, new self, new future. The New World is not given whole, any more than the new self is given abruptly in psychotherapy. It is given only a little at a time, one miracle at a time, one poem at a time, one healing, one promise, and one commandment. Over time, these pieces are stitched together into a sensible collage, stitched together, all in concert, but each of us idiosyncratically, stitched together in a new whole—all things new. (1994, 24–25)

I would like to suggest a few such pieces of the collage that certainly can give us direction and an agenda. First, the concepts of *agape,* or unconditional love, are at once daunting and controversial, laden with so much baggage that it can be a nonstarter. We might begin more modestly, and perhaps more realistically, by taking Charity James's suggestion of substituting the concept of "respect" for the notion of *agape* as a goal of education. She has this to say:

> Swami Muktananda teaches that the true *dharma* (way, path, religion in the nondogmatic sense) is to "welcome one another with great respect and love." I find this helpful because respect is more difficult for the ego to fool around with than is love or compassion. It seems to be a truly manageable proposition to build an institution and a process on an ethic of uncompromised mutual respect. And, of course, if we make (and encourage) the steady practice of respecting others, the privilege, the great attainment of loving will increasingly flow toward us. (1980)

This adds up to respect for life itself and for the affirmation of human dignity for all. In order to move such an affirmation beyond more rhetoric, I suggest that we can agree on some minimum standards of what it means concretely to affirm human dignity. These standards not only help to define basic human dignity, but they also serve as part of the conditions under which individuals can find meaning and fulfillment. I want to suggest standards that are not only consistent and resonant with our consensual moral commitments, but are also eminently and immediately doable technologically, logistically, and materially. They are simultaneously simple and profound, traditional and radical, spiritual and material.

Every person should have enough to eat. Every person should have adequate shelter. Every person should have proper health care. Every person should be afforded dignity and respect. Every person has the responsibility to participate in efforts to ensure that these requirements are met.

Notice that I have *not* said every person should have the opportunity to *pursue* adequate diet, shelter, and health—these are not areas that are to be left to chance or the market, nor are they to be rationed as scarce commodities or awarded as prizes, but instead are the inherent and inviolable rights afforded by membership in our community. There are important questions, of course, as to what constitutes adequate diet, shelter, and medical care, and there are legitimate questions concerning the conditions under which individuals can be said to forfeit these rights. Important as these questions are, they are still marginal ones and are no excuse to put everything else on hold. The uncontested dignity of the vast majority of human beings should not be held hostage to the very few who try our patience. In summary then, we can, at least partially, fund what Brueggemann calls "that which can help us to imagine a new world" by grounding our educational program in the commitment to respect human life by ensuring adequate food, shelter, and health care for all, with the understanding that there are unsettled questions, problems, and policies that need to be debated within that commitment.

For educators, generally speaking, this would mean that the spirit of this commitment would pervade the rhetoric, consciousness, and energy of the schools to the point that it would be as taken for granted and assimilated as much as the spirits of critical rationality and the accumulation of knowledge are. Indeed, the decisions on content selection and instructional emphases would be largely driven by the concern for which bodies of knowledge, which research skills, which resources, and which attitudes are most likely to further the commitment to human dignity.

More particularly, schools would be required to examine their policies, rules, and regulations on the basis of their consonance with this commitment. To make them consonant would surely mean drastic changes in these policies and rules, which, by itself, tells us a great deal. For example, what does it mean to have a grading system at all in a situation where we are endeavoring to promote deep and profound respect and dignity for all? Imagine the impact on the schools if all students, faculty, and staff were required to treat each other with utmost respect. Imagine what the effect would be if that policy was considered as vital and enforced as firmly as the policies forbidding violence and drugs in the school. How affirming this would be for those educators who have devoted their lives to honoring their students as precious and unique beings.

This is surely not to say that such a process is without controversy and difficulty, since it would certainly and very quickly generate any number of torturous and anguishing dilemmas, since we would have to constantly consider what most deeply and truly constitutes and enhances human dignity. However, this is not essentially different from the complex and contradictory problems that educators face currently; the difference being one of focus and priority. Moreover, it cannot be but enormously beneficial that educational discourse be driven by the heuristic of vigorous dispute and argument over which educational policies are most likely to enhance human dignity!

Further, we should need an educational psychology less concerned with instruction, measurement, and evaluation and more with the conditions under which people can learn to love and respect themselves and each other. We would need to have more research that delves into the human impulses for community, compassion, and social justice, and there would need to be more analysis and understanding of the forces that disrupt those impulses. Our history needs to be enriched with more of the language, stories, and images of the costly and courageous struggles for social justice that sanctify our past, give energy to the present, and provide hope for the future. Our art can be the vehicle not only for self-expression and the evocation of form, but also for the creative and imaginative processes that can give voice, shape, and image to the community of justice, love, and joy for which we so ache. Indeed, our failure to create communities of justice and love is not so much a reflection of the failure of the intellect, but of the failure of the imagination to envision a life where both freedom and equality can flourish.

The commandments to seek Truth and the processes that facilitate it would be replaced by the commandments to seek Justice and the arts and sciences that yield it. To pursue the pleasures of the mind, while there are bodies in pain, is to be seen as aberrational rather than quaint, more as an indication of self-indulgence than as a sign of grace. However, we must be mindful that both minds and bodies are terrible things to waste. The capacity for love can only mature when it is nurtured and enhanced by the enormous powers of human rationality, imagination, and creativity. In this way, education becomes the integration of body, mind, and spirit.

A Last Word

I accept, as a matter of course, that life is extremely complicated, contradictory, and messy, and I have spent a great deal of my career learning, teaching, and writing about the incredible tangle of ambivalence, uncertainty, and perplexity that is involved in dealing with educational issues. I have, inevitably, also come to learn about the problematics of problematics, particularly in their capacity to obscure and paralyze, and so I come not to praise complexity, but to give it a rest. Some very important issues are quite clear and eminently simple.

No person should have to go hungry, homeless, or without health care. We have the material and logistical capacity to make this possible. In spite of this, millions endure the pain and humiliation of hunger, homelessness, and poor health.

I would submit that these facts be the dominant and underlying elements of *all* discussions and debates on educational policies and practices. The realities of widespread unnecessary human suffering should replace issues of competing in the global economy, of accountability, of computer instruction, of school-based management, of multicultural education, even of critical pedagogy, ecofeminism, and spirituality as the starting and ending points of any and all educational dialogue. It is inconceivable to me that we could do otherwise than be constantly aware of and attentive to the shameful way we have reneged on our most profound commitments and responsibilities to our brothers and sisters.

Let us not ask how the problems of human misery illumine and demonstrate the importance of our favorite specialized projects like success in the global economy, accountability, computer instruction, school-based management, multicultural education, critical pedagogy, ecofeminism, or spirituality. Let us, instead, insist that before anything else, all people should have enough to eat, adequate shelter, and proper health care. I believe very strongly that there are educational processes that can significantly contribute to these goals and that we should concentrate our energies on them as our number one priority. There is no number two.

It may be useful to see this task and responsibility as "spiritual" rather than "educational," since it does raise and reflect the most profound questions of existence. What is the origin of this intense impulse for social justice that is so pervasive across time and space? Why do we have this urge to seek meaning and to link the details of our everyday world with visions of the sacred? Asking and responding to such questions are spiritual acts in themselves. When we sense the pain of suffering, the ache of responsibility, and the joy of justice, we are surely in the presence of Mystery.

Heschel (1955) helps us to clarify this phenomenon:

> To the speculative mind, the world is an enigma; to the religious mind, the world is a challenge. The speculative problem is impersonal; the religious problem is a problem addressed to the person. The first is concerned with finding an answer to the question: What is the cause of being? The second, with giving an answer to the question: What is asked of us? . . . In spite of our pride, in spite of our acquisitiveness, we are driven by an awareness that something is asked of us; that we are asked to wonder, to revere, to think, and to live in a way that is compatible with the grandeur and mystery of living. What gives birth to religion is not intellectual curiosity, but the fact and experience of our being asked. (111–112)

Within this Mystery is an astonishing truth: we are asked to regard each other as our sisters and brothers, to be their keepers, to strive to respect, if not love them, at a minimum not to hurt them, and surely to provide for them. An education grounded in that Mystery and truth is light years away from the mean-spirited and vulgar spirit of our operating educational model. Nor, it must be said, does this educational vision guarantee a cosmic consciousness. Yet, it provides a perspective that is both practical in its application and idealistic in its hopes; doable in its possibilities and daring in its aspirations; traditional in its roots and radical in its critique.

The opportunity to develop a pedagogy of human dignity is an awesome one, for it goes beyond our professional obligations to our human responsibilities as co-creators of our world. What makes it so exhilarating is its very awesomeness—that is, the opportunity to match human capacities with a sacred vision, to engage in a task that is grand *and* realizable, and to make the educational process truly redemptive, not merely profitable.

References

Brueggemann, W. (1994). *Texts Under Negotiation: The Bible and Post-modern Imagination*. Minneapolis: Fortress Press.
Daly, M. (1973). "Love" in *Dictionary of History of Ideas, vol. 2*. New York: Scribner.
Heschel, A. J. (1955). *God in Search of Man*. New York: Farrar, Straus, and Giroux.
James, C. (1980). "Spirituality and Education." Unpublished manuscript.
Kliebard, H. (1986). *The Struggle for the American Curriculum*. Boston: Routledge and Kegan Paul.

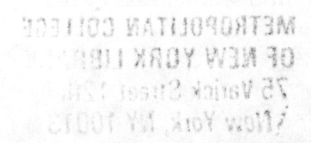

CHAPTER SIX

Engaging "Mind"fulness: Spirituality and Curriculum Connections

Elaine Riley

Watching from my cabin window, the stark, cold January morning stands in silent relief against refrains from earlier seasons. Humming sounds of summer insects skirt along the bayou separating a grassy apron below from the lush, Louisiana woodland beyond. Green summer tangles of vines and leaves are cast into colors of gold-to-orange-to-brown with autumn's rustling, cooling winds. Angles of light shift with the seasons. Shadows move and dance in a play of particularities, relational nexus of light-to-object in time and space. Life is cyclic, staccato, moving and ceasing to move, birthing-living-dying-birthing-ever-again. Commingling processes shape and are shaped by their interconnections, evoking a complexity of forms rich beyond belief. But the wondrous quality of this richness can be invisible, also, within its own continuity, within the ways that it is ever with us, ever changing, but ever present. We often cease to see it, to hear it, to feel it. We grow numb to it. I know that this is true for me. I often fail to perceive my own connection within that complexity, as if my sensibilities were clouded over and I was separate from the immediacy of experience. Herein lies my personal longing for an engagement with the "spirit" of life, a recognition and acknowledgment of my own embeddedness within the dynamic process of living. But, then there are times when I do feel my place within that process—I seldom look out on the bayou behind my house without a sudden awareness, a breathing in, a connection felt with my surroundings, the larger biosphere of which I am a part.

I want to speak of this connection, because I feel it must be spoken—our children, our people, our planet and its peace. I feel its call is one worth hearing and see it mirrored on the pages of our culture, both as a bleak absence as well as an "embodied presence." Both are our inheritance—the empty and the full; both and all that is in between. We have come into a world where we must find our way over landscapes mired with anguish, assaults, and assignations, inspired to keep moving toward some unnamable pull, a draw toward some perceived fulfillment; some final quenching of thirst. But, from where do we draw our water? How do we answer the question "What will bring peace and contentment?" Is it money? Is it health? Is it power and control? Is it relationship, or beauty, or status and image? We race ahead to fill the longing, but does the water we drink quench the desert of our inner thirst?

Here is a call that yearns for what has been separated and one that also rings with a joy at the resounding rhythm of life. Both possibilities are real—both are present, both and all—the choices among them are ours, a choice to wake up, a choice to hear the call of our own heartbeat. Surely we recognize the rhythm, the spirit which animates our deepest places and pulsates through every present moment, that rhythm which vitalizes our being from its prison of numbness. But do we feel that rhythm? Do we hear that call? As often as not, a numbness overtakes us. Although each person's experience is unique to their circumstance, I would venture to say that within western culture, many are well-acquainted with feelings of numbness, of separation. We live in a mechanistic world that has taught us to think in terms of separation: inner self from outer self; self from others; self from nature and the planet. We have replaced inner rhythms with routines in many ways. We wake to an "alarm," live our lives according to the hands on a clock, spend most of every week at a job which, in many cases, is disconnected from an internal desire to create, or to engage, in a task for its own sake. So often, the meaning within our work is disconnected from the immediacy of experience, or is even unknown to us. Extrinsic motivators such as output requirements and job security replace intrinsic motivation. The American system based on capitalism—coupled with industrial and technological growth—keeps us running on a wheel of overescalating production and consumption. Erich Fromm (1986, 20) reminds us that in this society a person's self-worth is more often based on *having* than on *being*. What has come to drive the day-to-day routine for many Americans is a desire for immediate gratification of material wants so to increase prestige or personal standing on a scale weighed hierarchically against others.

Advances in technology have likewise increased our capacities to exploit and destroy the natural world. We pollute the rivers, the air, and the soil with chemicals, pesticides, and toxic waste. We level forest lands to provide paper products for our "disposable" society. Eco-feminist author Starhawk (1994) tells us that, as humans, we see ourselves "as the 'Crown of Creation' for whom the rest of nature exists," and we wastefully plunder our resources all the while (Weaver 1994, 250). She has described the western consciousness as one of estrangement, in that we do not see ourselves as part of the world—we are strangers to nature, to other human beings, to parts of ourselves (176).

This sense of estrangement and alienation characterizes so many aspects of our culture, indeed of our lives. Perhaps we numb our consciousness in defense against the context in which we live. As if, in order not to feel the pain of separation, we cloud over the sense of lived experience itself.

With Susan Griffin (1990), I feel that:

> whether we want to or not, we share a social and biological matrix. We are connected. When we violate others or simply fail to feel this connection, we feel, instead, an emptiness, a mourning, an undefined grief. (95)

Drawing on contemporary anthropology, Juanita Weaver notes that it is the function of every culture to establish the "individual's relationship to the self, the individual's relationship to others, and the individual's relationship to the universe" (1994, 250). With this in mind, we might locate the numbing pain of separation within the inner longing to experience more fully the larger complexity of connections in which we are a part.

It is this sense of estrangement, of alienation, that I lament in our schooling. What could a deeper sense of inner connection lend to curriculum theory and its application to living life in the classroom and beyond? If there is any social context that could benefit from an exploration of what it means to be awake and aware as human beings, it is the American system of public education. If there is a place where we might seek to foster a sense of relationality—with our own inner presence, with those who are around us, with the larger community, the country, and the world—it is here with the children. The future of our planet is in their hands.

Scenarios of Separation

Many have attempted to generate discussions (Pinar et al., 1995) which could lend much to a conversation concerning how to widen and deepen our ways of educating children more holistically—as physical, emotional, mental, and spiritual beings. Unfortunately, the fruitfulness of these discussions has been limited, in part, by the subsequent imposition of western frames of relationality, which have been hierarchically ordered according to patriarchal worldviews framed in dualistic thinking. Through Cartesian method, the rational mind has become a "subject" in juxtaposition to that which is not of mind, an "object" existing as separate from, indeed, "other." In a similar way, separation of mind from *body,* mind from *emotion,* and mind from *spirit* has been transferred from its broad cultural use into the specific ways that we regard education and curriculum. Body, emotion, and spirit have each been dualistically opposed to the more highly regarded rational mind and, thus, have been considered less important, or even dismissed out of hand as being irrational, even, at times, pathological (Fox 1988). Meanwhile, there has been within schooling an overreliance on developing the rational mind, to the neglectful omission of other important aspects of the human character (54).

The American system of public education has been constituted by a mindset which has opted for the "education for efficiency" model (Tyler 1949), strongly framed by industrial principles of the early twentieth century (Doll 1993; Pinar et al. 1995). This view of schooling has led to the compartmentalization of knowledge, the fragmentation of content areas, and the separation of teacher from student in vertical relation hierarchically for the maintenance of control. Knowledge is seen as being easily separated into component parts. This "observer consciousness" frames curriculum along very narrow lines (Kesson 1994) in order to verify learning through "objective" evaluative methods. The testing machine, so deeply entrenched, increasingly drives the way that curriculum is conceived (measurability) and the way that it is taught (transmitted). This assumption renders the student as object and contributes to, what Fromm (1986) describes as a "necrophilia" a "propensity for death," characterizing much of our culture (112–114). He contrasts this with the term "biophilia," described as a "propensity for life" (112) and says that:

> The necrophilous person loves all that does not grow; all that is mechanical. [This person] is driven by the desire to transform the organic into the inorganic, to approach life mechanically, as if all living persons were things . . . [The necrophiliac] loves control, and in the act of controlling . . . kills life. (quoted in Freire 1970, 58)

Kesson (1994) encourages movement away from "isolated, atomized 'observer' consciousness into relational thinking and being, or 'participating' consciousness" (2) and questions "how might we begin to think differently" about curriculum. Could we bring it to the fulfillment of what she describes as a spiritual function, adapting to the unpredictability, the idiosyncrasies, the dynamic process implied in such a model? She distinguishes between the spiritual and the religious by saying that there is a need for an invigoration and infusion of the human spirit into secular life and a reappropriation of the notion of the "spiritual" without the baggage and institutionalized assumptions which surround the idea of "religion."

In contrast to the controlling, mechanistic frame of fragmentary school practices, a more holistic view of schooling would suggest Thich Nhat Hanh's (1992) philosophy of engaged Buddhism that would see students "as whole human beings with complex lives and experiences rather than simply as seekers after compartmentalized bits of knowledge (15)." Kesson (1994) notes that unlike the term "religion," which tends to "stress the ultimacy of categories such as 'matter' and 'creator,'" the term "spirituality" is used here to "emphasize the actuality of process and self-creativity" (3) within both curriculum and classrooms. I would suggest that such a view of spirituality is ecological, in a broad sense, in that it recognizes the human relation within the environment as mutually sustaining and honors an organic, deeply felt connection between microcosm and macrocosm. Not so much in terms of environmental management—which is typically human-centered and often ascribes only "use-value" to nature—but more akin to what some have called "deep ecology" which recognizes the intrinsic value of all living beings. I am interested in exploring the notion of spirituality as a practice of "mindfulness"—which draws on and emphasizes our connection within a larger matrix of planetary life and seeks to foster a sense of human "engagement" within that living process (Nhat Hanh 1992). Mindfulness is an attempt to live in a state of "full appreciation of each moment." It is reminiscent of what David G. Smith (1996) describes as "living awake to the way that sustains us" (9), and would emphasize an intentionality toward caring for the myriad forms of "others" cohabiting the planet. Nhat Hanh (1996) tells a story of a man who asked the Buddha:

> "Sir, what do you and your monks practice?" He replied, "We sit, we walk, and we eat." The questioner continued, "But sir, everyone sits, walks, and eats," the Buddha told him, "When we sit, we *know* we are sitting. When we walk, we *know* we are walking. When we eat, we *know* we are eating. This is the difference." (19)

Mindfulness suggests an attempt to enter deeply into the present moment and recognize its significance. As Nhat Hanh says, "the miracle is not to walk on water . . . the miracle is to walk on the green earth, dwelling deeply in the present moment and feeling truly alive" (20).

I agree with Thomas Berry (1988) that "what is needed is the deeper meaning of the relationship between the human community and the earth process" (10) so that we may cultivate "our sense of gratitude, our willingness to recognize the sacred character of habitat, our capacity for the awesome, for the numinous quality of every earthly reality" (2). An awareness of the human's place within a larger cosmological order can be cultivated, in part, through attention to increasing the individual's powers of personal reflection and action toward change, a personal praxis which attends to the ways we go about living life. This actively engaged spiritual praxis places the individual as a responsible participant within the experience of his/her own "becoming," as a never-ending process.

Engaging the "spirit" of living within the social milieu of human classrooms might imply a fostering of awareness within children. Such a view is very different from long-held notions of curriculum influenced by scientific, rationalistic models of schooling with curriculum framed along linear and deterministic lines. Even though there is a tradition which has questioned the ways that technorational thinking has dominated education, the characterization of schools as institutionalized knowledge factories remains the prevalent paradigm today.

Dharma Consciousness and Eco-emergence

In order to move toward a more holistic view of education, some scholars are looking for a "paradigmatic" curriculum shift from a linear, deterministic view to a "systems-based," process view (Doll 1993; Kesson 1994). Some are drawing from a variety of religious traditions or cultural beliefs and practices in eclectic and creative ways that blur the boundaries long dividing human understanding into categories framed in absolute terms. In seeking to heal the Cartesian split between the secular and the spiritual, there are many who would navigate that "middlespace" between the "intellectual and cultural binaries that . . . ensnare creative thinking in the contemporary context" (Smith 1996, 6).

Increasingly, Buddhism, for example, is proving useful for scholars interested in making a shift toward a dynamic, systemic, process view of reality. Smith draws on the notion of Buddha-dharma, which, in the original Sanskrit, means "one who is awake" and also "carrying" or "holding," respectively. He says that: "studying the Buddha-dharma, then, refers to the action of being awake to, or attending to what carries, upholds or sustains us as human beings" (1996, 8). Implicit within the idea of Buddha-dharma is the systemic nature of life, a cosmological view that all reality is "dependently co-arising" within a web of relationships, which are multidimensional (Macy 1991b, xv). It is a recognition of the deep sustenance which can result from a recognition of the human connection within a larger web of relationship extending from within the self (the personal) to "the other" (the community) to the wider planet and its universal framework of connection. Such a view has corollaries within quantum physics, which depicts the universal not as a collection of physical objects, but rather as a complicated web of relations between the various parts of a unified whole (Capra 1975, 138). This view of an "interconnected cosmic web," as described within atomic physics, has been used in the east, according to Capra, to "convey the mystical experience of nature" (139).

Joanna Macy (1991b) is an ecofeminist whose worldview is one which includes "interrelatedness, transformation, embodiment, and love" (187) congruent with the Buddhist doctrine of "dependent co-arising" (xi). She describes a systemic framework for living wherein

> each and every act is understood to have an effect on the larger web of life, and the process of development is perceived as multidimensional . . . Being interdependent, these developments do not occur sequentially, in a linear fashion, but synchronously . . . reinforcing the other through multiplicities of context in which other events occur. (xv)

She draws on the scientific notion of "systems theory" to intersect some of the fundamentals of Buddha-dharma consciousness with postmodern process theory. Process theory is a worldview which, unlike the rigidly deterministic view of Newton's mechanical world, "stresses the openness and indeterminism of nature" leading to an "organismic or ecological view of the universe" (Davies 1992, 182–183). A process view of reality is increasingly applied to the ways that scholars are envisioning curriculum, not meant as a model or a methodology, but rather a heuristic for thinking about how curriculum might be reconceived (Doll 1993). A process view of curriculum would move from the personal and social to the ecological and cosmological and would require a more holistic view of schooling—valuing and making connections between the body, emotion, mind, and spirit. Such an educational frame would be ecological, in its broadest sense, recognizing and evoking a deep respect within children for the larger organic and cosmic processes so vital to our existence. Such a vision would be a departure from the cause-effect, linear models put forth by behaviorists and social efficiency educators, which have traditionally separated and isolated the disciplines. This open-systems, ecocosmic view of curriculum would allow for a "complex interplay between openness and closure at a number of levels" providing structure, but also leaving space for possibilities beyond the dualistic framework of an "open-closed dichotomy" for new levels of complexity and dynamic interaction to emerge (Doll 1993, 58–68). Quantum mechanics has taught us that all of the things in the universe which appear to exist independently are actually parts of one "all-encompassing organic pattern, and that no parts of that pattern are ever really separate from it or from each other" (Zukav 1979, 48). Systems theory (Macy 1991b; Lazlo 1972) is a useful tool for analysis in viewing organizations and people as being embedded within multiple and interlocking systems, each system as unique and complete, but also affecting one another in a causal interrelationship. For example, the American education system would be one system, an individual classroom might be another, and individual acting within that classroom would be still another subsystem affected by that group (St. Julian, personal communication 1995). All systems have boundaries. If there are no boundaries, what you have is not a system, but rather, randomness. Since a system typically self-regulates and seeks a balance, it will always include constraint factors, or the system would fall apart. Systems have their own integrity, their own "gravity," if you will, which provides for some cohesion as a whole, yet boundaries are never fixed or static. A shift in gaze across boundaries reveals wider dimensions of combination or intersection within other systems (Lazlo 1972) in broader and more all-inclusive ways.

As well as systems theory, a process view of reality, consonant with the Buddha's teachings, would include the notion of an inherent order exemplified by patterning seen across diverse dimension or scale. Salient to this notion of multidimensionality as Gregory Bateson describes is the "pattern which connects" (1979, 8), the thesis of his book *Mind and Nature*. To view all phenomena through a relational frame of connecting patterns is a fascinating heuristic that can be applied at multiple levels. An example of such a pattern is the one of planetary bodies being held in orbit by some constraining force or gravity. Planets orbiting the sun, for example, exemplify a pattern that is replicated in a very similar form, but at quite a different scale, through the lens of a microscopic camera inside the human cell. Such self-similarities can be seen repeated across many levels of life, much in the way that serial homology repeats itself across different classes of animals. When one begins to look for the patterns that connect, one will find no thing in isolation.

In human terms, this cosmological view would recognize that we are dependent on more than ourselves. Indeed, we are

> conditioned by and coexist . . . in dynamic interdependence with all things. Such a cosmology . . . would reinvigorate the human in an ethic of reflection upon and care for life in its entirety, as the species which can identify the integrity of the whole in the richness of its diverse particularities. (Brown 1993, 136)

The idea of coemergence (Macy 1991b; Bateson 1979) is useful in reconceiving a linear mindset of a Newtonian worldview. Along Newtonian lines, Darwin's theory of evolution has long been viewed as a linear progression of the straight-ahead, ordered advancement of biological change. For example, as the strong, the smart, the agile is selected, the species differentiates and improves. But more and more is being said of the other side of the coin and the context in which the mutations occur. The receiver of the action/change is as vital to this process as that which does the action/changing. Mutations never occur in a vacuum, but as an action or result arising out of some interchange, some negotiation of difference. And mutation occurs because there is something in its environment which is ready for it, which receives it, and which is vital to what it becomes. Without the receiver, it may have become something altogether different. As Bateson puts it, the

> messages cease being messages when nobody can read them. The power to create context is the recipient's skill . . .[this] genesis of the skill to respond to the message is the obverse, the other side of the process of evolution. It is co-evolution . . . [because] it is the recipient of the message who creates the context. (1979, 48)

The cosmology of relations suggests, rather than a cause-effect linearity of relations, where B is the receiver of—and determined by—A's action, a relational view would recognize that B is codetermining A's action—that is, idea and context are mutually emergent. A hierarchical worldview, which perceives the active force as determining its effect, is softening into one which recognizes the infinite possibilities of relations and their capacity for combination. As well, it is one where the recipient of the action is as significant in determining an outcome as is its cause. In this regard, it could be said that the receiver is as important as the sender is, thereby countering hierarchical positions exemplary of Newton's cause-effect determinism, as well as certain "power-over" frames of patriarchy.

Eco-linkages: The Matrilineal Spirit

A cosmological view of nonlinear systemic interrelations and coemergence is a very different epistemological frame from that of the dualistic, "observer consciousness" described earlier. Deeply rooted in what has been characterized as the western worldview is the hierarchical notion of power, control, and dominion over typically labeled as the "patriarchal" mindset (King 1990). Deep ecologist Thomas Berry (1988) says that a

> sense of *patriarchy* has now evolved as the archetypal pattern of oppressive governance by men with little regard for the well being or personal fulfillment of women, for the more significant human values, or for the destiny of the earth itself. (143)

Ecofeminist scholars have offered much in the way of rethinking our understanding of human relationship. There are those who are suggesting that the dualistic models of the patriarchal mindset are limiting our ways of thinking about relations among people. Charlene Spretnak (1993, 1990) shows how the spiritual dimension of ecofeminism provides an alternative to the western patriarchal worldview of fragmentation, alienation, agonistic dualism, and exploitive dynamics. Fromm (1986) says that the salience of analogies describing patri (versus matri) focal views is in its metaphorical value, and that such a discussion is less about particularities of women versus men, per se, than it is a naming of worldviews as being relationally based or those which are hierarchical (104). Shifting from a vertical frame to a more horizontal one in which to view "the other" is a "revisioning" which carries with it seeds toward more egalitarian social relations (Sky 1993, 10). One result could be a "significant lessening of human-caused abuse" (10) often justified as "God's will," or for others' "own good," or that it is "biologically ordained"—which are all examples of the "doctrines of patriarchy" (10). Riane Eisler (1987) calls for relations between men and women based on "linking," not "ranking." She says the latter "dominator model" would be found in a

> patriarchy or matriarchy—[as] the *ranking* of one-half of humanity over the other, whereas, the former principal eliminates notions of rank and is characteristic of what she calls the *partnership* model. (xvii)

A partnership model is thought by many (Eisler 1987; Goodrich 1989) to be the prevalent frame within prehistoric matrilineal societies, which recognize human relations as more horizontal than vertical, and one in which a sense of communal sharing was the model for living. Matthew Fox (1983) has described a cosmological view which does not privilege one gender over another, but which evokes, instead, "a sense of balance, of harmony, and, therefore, of justice" (70). He explains that

> the word "cosmos" is in fact the Greek word for "order." A cosmic spirituality is a justice spirituality, for it cares with a heartfelt caring for harmony, balance and justice. (70)

Lack of "separation" is a key line of thought in cosmological writings and is a theme which recurs throughout many ancient traditions. Fox (1988, 1983) locates the idea of separation as analogous to the word "sin" within the tradition he refers to as creation-centered spirituality" (1988). He says

> [F]rom Meister Eckhart to Mary Daly, the sin behind all sin is seen as dualism. Separation. Subject/object relationships. Take any sin: war, burglary, rape, and thievery. Every such action is treating another as an object outside oneself. This is dualism. This is behind all sin. (1983, 49)

This view concurs with the Buddhist notion that "all sins are modifications of the basic sin, the only sin in the ultimate analysis, is the sin of separateness" (Iyer, quoted in Fox 1983, 4).

The idea of interconnection follows naturally from the view that we are all part of a living cosmos. And finally, as part of this web of interconnections, we are part of a community, earth, and what we do and how we live affect the community, just as the community affects each of us as individuals (Fox 1983, 74). Lydon (1995) speaks of an awareness of our cosmological embeddedness within an infinitely creative universal order predicated on complexity constituted by subjectivity, difference, and interrelation (78). Such an awareness would imply a different way of "seeing," wherein we "leave behind our preoccupation" with an abstracted view which sees chiefly through the lenses of profit, exploiting planetary resources for personal gain (79). Rather, such a paradigm shift implies an awakening within of a conscious awareness of place, seeing the world through an awe-filled knowing of humanity's place in the universe, moving curriculum beyond a static, institutionalized form of knowledge of how the world is.

The "Natural" Woman and Other Critiques of Cohesion

The dualistic thinking of patriarchy has objectified nature much in the same way that it has objectified women. Spretnak (1993) says that the social construction of the term "masculine" has been

> associated with rationality, spirit, culture, autonomy, assertiveness, and the public sphere, while the "feminine" is associated with emotion, body, nature, connectedness, receptivity, and the private sphere. (183)

The tendency to essentialize male and female roles is problematic. Ynestra King (1990), for example, points out how many feminists are in disagreement as to whether the "woman/nature connection is potentially emancipatory, or whether it provides a rationale for the continued subordination of women" (110). On the one hand, radical cultural feminists" would ask for a "separate feminist culture and philosophy from the vantage point of identification with nature and a celebration of the woman/nature connection" (110). Conversely, there are "radical rationalist feminists" who see the woman/nature connection as "imprisoning" women in a "primordial realm" which is "bound to reinforce sex-role stereotyping [and] gender differences" (110). The latter feel that regressions into what they see as mythologies, such as a woman being more prone to traditional roles, such as a nurturer, or as maternalistic, or as more peace-loving, are essentialisms we cannot afford (110).

Such contradictory positions are not unusual to philosophical perspectives of ecofeminism, which, like feminism from which it derives, is no unitary construct. There are multiple versions and particularized positions, which lend richness and complexity, as well as divergent tensions, to ecofeminist philosophical, political, and spiritual positions. Resisting univocality is seen as a strength by many ecofeminists (Quinby 1990) who would recognize the coexistence of conflicting viewpoints rather than seeking to flatten differences into a unitary story.

Further, the idea of a cosmology based on an inherent universal connection in a meaningful and ordered way is not without its problems. Many poststructuralists, and also feminists, would seek to disrupt modernist notions which frame "how things are" within essentializing and absolute categories comprising an all-inclusive metanarrative "ordering" the universe (Lyotard 1979). They point to the contingent nature of life and question whether the idea of a cosmology is not just presenting a new metanarrative to replace the modernist "story"—a Eurocentric, rationalist view with its roots in Enlightenment Europe. Some poststructuralist thinkers would critique any metanarratives which attempt to predefine who is human, in terms of a discourse of universals, and would resist any cohesive, unitary doctrine or essentializing metaphysic as either naive or arrogant.

Poststructuralisms and feminisms are informing one another in important ways. Poststructuralists' disavowal of any fixed or determinate framework (Foucault 1978; Quinby 1990) and feminists' attention to the particularities of contextualized embeddedness (Munro 1996) work to undergird one another's positioning with points of intersection. Neither would posit a unitary discourse, since contingency and particularity are common themes throughout their discussions, ruling out a reliance on cohesion.

The "impulse" toward a unitary discourse is a critique leveled against ecofeminist and deep ecology discourses extolling a cosmological view. Quinby (1990) warns against

> essentialist tendencies within eco-feminism [to] speak of a monovocal subject, Woman; of a pure essence, Femininity; of a fixed place, Nature; of a deterministic system, Holism; and of a static materiality, Body. (126)

She uses Foucauldian critique to argue against "calls for coherence" on the basis that resistance movements which become orthodoxy are

> complicitous with the tendency of power to totalize, to demand consensus, to authorize certain alliances and to exclude others—in short, to limit political creativity. (122)

She sees ecofeminism as "sites of struggle" in that power is dispersed and circulating through culture and there is no one "source" from which power emanates; likewise, "there is a plurality of resistance . . . in a multiplicity of places" (123–124). She cautions against totalizing theories and centralized practices which tend to make social movements "irrelevant . . . vulnerable . . .[or] participatory with forces of domination" (123).

Ecological Considerations: Can Healing Happen

Matthew Fox (1988) views calls for cohesion and unification very differently. He sees "embracing the world as a whole" as an affirmation, "not [of] the world laid waste by human neglect, sin, and greed, but as a source of "sustenance, challenge, and power from the whole" (51). He would work to heal the "psychic injustice" of separation between the "inner and the outer" as a training ground "for more effective struggle against social injustice" (62). He doesn't see goals of those engaged in emancipatory struggles as counter to or undermining those advocating a cosmological view. In his words

> [p]olitical movements for justice are part of the fuller development of the cosmos, and nature is the matrix in which humans come to their self-awareness and their awareness of their power to transform. Liberation movements are a fuller development of the cosmos' sense of harmony, balance, justice, and celebration. (1983, 18)

Indeed, historically, domination and hierarchical control have often been justified in the name of what is "natural" or "the order of things." For example, the widespread domination of women as naturally being the weaker sex; the discrimination against gays and lesbians in accordance with what is normal and natural; the perception of blacks or ethnic groups with a skin color other than white as being inherently inferior—these are among countless examples of people having been systematically excluded or devalued according to the rationale of natural law.

Feminists, poststructuralists, and critical theorists have questioned a cosmological reliance on nature from a myriad of positions. Some questions for consideration might include the following: when we cast people/cultures/societies onto the template of "natural order," what does that mean for legislation, for justice, for equality? Will there be those who are left out? Who are pushed aside? Who are not "naturally selected?" We have seen how it is possible for the "free hand of the market place" to exclude and dispose of human life without conscience. Where does human agency come in—to counter misogyny, homophobia, racial prejudice, and the accompanying violence committed in the name of eliminating difference? Was not the idea of unification all too often used to rationalize the colonialist appropriation of life, liberty, and resources from third-world peoples lacking strength and number to resist? Would the argument for unification flatten difference to the extent that the richness, which flavors diverse cultures, be dissolved into the mix, or worse, erased due to acts of violence? Are we to assume that as we move into "being" that some natural ethic will emerge? Do we trust the self-regulation of a "system" to replace ethics?

There are, indeed, no easy answers to these and countless problems raised by the consideration of an ecological framework for living. Fears of metanarratives and totalizing discourses are understandable in light of feminist and poststructuralist critiques of their use historically to exclude and to marginalize. And it is true that the disruption of hegemonic foundations, such as patriarchy or dualistic thinking, is paramount to a reenvisioning of who we want to become as a people. But disruption could well be brought forward within the spirit of hope. Not disruption for disruption's sake, rather disruption, desedimenting, challenging assumptions with the proactive intention of reframing and reworking the structure—proactive in the dictionary sense of "acting in anticipation of future problems, needs, or changes."

Many do not see a cosmological view as counter to emancipatory practices of liberation strategies (Macy 1991a), since it questions the traditional paradigm of a closed, determined worldview and provides for other, more open structures which may be used as points of departure, with openings—windows for unimagined possibilities and, as yet, unmanifest potentialities. It is a worldview with no final frame, no absolute determinacy, no Archimedean point, but rather as perpetually unfinished as the living of life itself. It is here that I see relevance for the cyclic idea of contingent frames acting as independent units with specific constraints and parameters, while they are also permeable and interdependent among other interconnected, interlocking systems of both broader and narrower base. Such a worlds-within-worlds view as an epistemological matrix for our knowing offers relative certainties contingent on the particular, the context-bound with an acknowledgment of openings onto other views, other frames, wherein the rules of certainty might shift with the relative dimension.

If there is any hope toward transforming our world from the dualistic, power-over frame of fragmentary thinking, to a more inclusive and relationally framed view, it will lie in the hands of individuals-in-community working at local sites. Susie Gablik (1991) has said that

> the source of creativity in society is the person.... Both the problem and the level at which the solution emerges are manifested initially in the individual, who is also an organ of the collective. What happens in the individual is typical of the total situation and is the place where future solutions emerge. (22–23)

Once again, commitment comes to mind. What is commitment? What is it that moves us toward a decision, a centering on, and a grounding into some goal, some reality, and some desired-for dream? Where does commitment come from? Is it a choice we can make or does it happen to us when we become caught up in some frenzy of momentum going on in our environment? Are there not times of agency? Decision for change? Decision to create? Is not commitment somehow a fuel toward that realization of agency? Is it not a buoyancy that keeps us afloat to be moved in the stream in which we place ourselves? Lisa Delpit (1997) has suggested that commitment comes from the recognition that we have a place, indeed, a purpose within something that is larger than ourselves: a relationship, a family, a community, and an ecosystem.

Bell Hooks says that "teachers must be actively committed to a process of self-actualization that promotes their own well being, if they are to teach in a manner that empowers students" (1994, 15). She uses the term "sacred" when she speaks of teaching as going beyond merely sharing information, but also sharing in "the intellectual and spiritual growth of our students . . . in a manner that respects and cares for [their] souls . . . where learning can most deeply and intimately begin" (13).

To ever think that the work of spiritual praxis can affect children in schools, we must begin within ourselves as teachers, as human beings. This work is no formula, or recipe, or method, but is a path, a journey that can only be one's own. By living this journey toward what Smith (1996) calls "being awake to the way that sustains us, we face ourselves" (9–11) and work for our own understandings of what is important to enrich and fulfill us along the way. It is a constant mode of reflecting and acting to continue the generation of new and more interesting ways of seeing, of thinking, of being, so that we are the journey and the journey is us. Alive in the moment of it, engaged to the 'present' of it. So that when we are sitting, we know we are sitting—when we are working, we *know* we are working—because we are *engaged* within the present moment of the experience. And as teachers, it is in learning to reflect, to become aware, to become engaged to life, that we may mirror these things for those whose lives we affect and whose lives affect our own.

Toward a Radical Re-cognition of Life

So, why do we resist the movement toward "life?" It happens all around us. It is February, the threshold of spring here in the south. There is a rejuvenation all around. I can feel it as I walk back from the mailbox—down the hill along the line of brown twiggy elderberries. There is no green as yet, but there is a feel in the air of freshness, an inherent seed of knowing what is to be. One can almost "feel" the movement toward life, toward renewal; recognize a stirring, a circulation begins within the stubby branches—a gathering, a rising, and a burgeoning forth. It will come from the ends, at first, a popping out of green. And then, it will spread into a profusion of burgeoning and budding, into an array of every shade of green imaginable. This is our life—this is all around, it comes to us regardless, of times unaware. We do not create it nor do we control it, rather we are it and it is we. We are a part of it. As a species, we too are sustained within the cyclical movements, which living affords, and we experience, also, this freshening and this renewal. Is there no way to allow this movement toward life, also, into our institutions? How do we build communities of learning, which could bring in a sense of the spiritual without systematizing "magic" into mechanization? How do we give voice within schools to an acknowledgment of the awe and wonder, which mark our connection with some larger sense of order? How do we suggest to young people that life has meaning, has purpose, that there is some context for their lives which has worth and value? How do we show them what it means to live a commitment? In the spirit of hope, these are questions to consider toward enhancing what it could mean to school. I believe within the ideas of relationality, connection making, and integration, that there is much that could be of use toward this end for curriculum theory and practice.

References

Bateson, G. (1979). *Mind and Nature: A Necessary Unity*. New York: Dutton.
Berry, T. (1988). *The Dream of the Earth*. San Francisco: Sierra Club.
Brown, B. (1993). "Toward a Buddhist Ecological Cosmology." In M. E. Tucker and J. A. Grim (Eds.), *Worldviews and Ecology*, pp. 124–137. Lewisburg: Bucknell.
Capra, F. (1975). *The Tao of Physics*. Boulder: Shambala.
Davies, P. (1992). *The Mind of God: The Scientific Basis for a Rational World*. New York: Simon & Schuster.
Delpit, L. (1997). Public lecture. Louisiana State University. April 7, 1997.
Doll, W. (1993). *A Post-modern Perspective on Curriculum*. New York: Teachers College.
Eisler, R. (1987). *The Chalice and the Blade*. San Francisco: Harper & Row.
Foucault, M. (1978). *The History of Sexuality*. New York: Random House.
Fox, M. (1983). *Original Blessing*. Santa Fe, NM: Bear & Co.
—— (1988). *The Coming of the Cosmic Christ: The Healing of Mother Earth and the Birth of a Global Renaissance*. San Francisco: Harper & Row.
—— (1995). *Wrestling with the Prophets: Essays on Creation Spirituality and Everyday Life*. San Francisco: Harper.
Freire, P. (1970). *Pedagogy of the Oppressed*. New York: Continuum.
Fromm, E. (1986). *For the Love of Life*. New York: Macmillan.
Gablik, S. (1991). *The Re-enchantment of Art*. New York: Thames and Hudson.
Goodrich, N. L. (1989). *Priestesses*. New York: Franklin Watts.

Griffin, S. (1990). "Curves along the Road." In I. Diamond and G. F. Orenstein (Eds.), *Reweaving the World: The Emergence of Eco-feminism.* San Francisco: Sierra Club.

Hooks, B. (1994). *Teaching to Transgress.* New York: Routledge.

Kesson, K. (1994). "Recollections: An Introduction to the Spiritual Dimensions of Curriculum." *Holistic Education Review* 7 (3): 2–6.

King, Y. (1990). "Healing the Wounds: Feminism, Ecology, and the Nature/Culture Dualism." In I. Diamond and G. F. Orenstein (Eds.), *Reweaving the World: The Emergence of Eco-feminism,* pp. 106–121. San Francisco: Sierra Club.

Lazlo, E. (1972). *The Systems View of the World.* New York: Braziller.

Lydon, A. (1995). "An Eco-zoic Cosmology of Curriculum and Spirituality." *Journal Curriculum Theorizing: An Interdisciplinary Journal of Curriculum Studies* 11(2): 67–86.

Lyotard, J. (1979). *The Post-modern Condition: A Report on Knowledge.* Minneapolis: University of Minnesota Press.

Macy, J. (1991a). *World as Lover, World as Self.* Berkeley, CA: Parallax Press.

——— (1991b). *Mutual Causality in Buddhism and General Systems Theory.* Albany: SUNY Press.

Macdonald, J. B. (1995). Theory as a Prayerful Act: *The Collected Essays of James B. Macdonald.* New York: Peter Lang.

Munro, P. (1996, April). Catching the "True" History: Post-structuralism, Gender and Curriculum History. Paper presented at the American Educational Research Association Conference. New York.

Nhat Hahn, T. (1992). *Touching Peace: Practicing the Art of Mindful Living.* Berkeley: Parallax.

——— (1996). *Be Still and Know: Reflections from Living Buddha, Living Christ.* New York: Riverhead.

Pinar, W. F., W. M. Reynolds, P. Slattery, and P. M. Tauban. (1995). *Understanding Curriculum: An Introduction to the Study of Historical and Contemporary Curriculum Discourses.* New York: Peter Lang.

Quinby, L. (1990). "Eco-feminism and the Politics of Resistance." In I. Diamond and G. F. Orenstein (Eds.). *Reweaving the World: The Emergence of Eco-feminism.* (pp. 122–127). San Francisco: Sierra Club.

Sky, M. (1993). *Sexual Peace: Beyond the Dominator Virus.* Santa Fe, NM: Bear & Co.

Smith, D. (1996). "Identity, Self, and Other in the Conduct of Pedagogical Action: An East/West Inquiry." *Journal of Curriculum Theorizing: An Interdisciplinary Journal of Curriculum Studies,* 12(3): 6–12.

Spretnak, C. (1990). "Eco-feminism: Our Roots and our Flowering." In I. Diamond and G. F. Orenstein (Eds.). *Reweaving the World: The Emergence of Eco-feminism,* pp. 3–14. San Francisco: Sierra Club.

——— (1993). "Critical and Constructive Contributions of Eco-feminism." In M. E. Tucker and J. A. Grim (Eds.), *Worldviews and Ecology.* Lewisburg, PA: Bucknell University Press.

Starhawk (1994). "Consciousness, Politics, and Magic." In C. Spretnak (Ed.), *The Politics of Women's Spirituality: Essays by Founding Mothers of the Women's Movement,* pp. 172–184. New York: Doubleday.

Tyler, R. (1949). *Basic Principles of Curriculum and Instruction.* Chicago: Chicago University Press.

Weaver, J. (1994). "Images and Models—in Process." In C. Spretnak (Ed.), *The Politics of Women's Spirituality: Essays by Founding Mothers of the Women's Movement,* pp. 249–257. New York: Doubleday.

Zukav, G. (1979). *The Dancing Wu Li Masters: An Overview of the New Physics.* New York: Bantam.

CHAPTER SEVEN

Feminist Ethics and Educational Reform: Education for Compassion and Social Justice

Jeanne F. Brady

> Until we ask schools to prepare our fellow citizens, until we view schooling for all of the nation's youth as an essential element in the preparation of the next generation of active and engaged participants in the common life of the nation, all debates about schooling will be trivialized and ultimately will miss the point
> —J. Fraser,
> *Reading, Writing, and Justice:*
> *School Reform as If Democracy Matters* (1997)

When Bill Clinton won the presidential election and took office in 1993, it appeared that a sense of hope had surfaced on the horizon. His administration was laying the groundwork for important steps in the progress of social reform in this country including an educational reform agenda that could possibly provide the foundation to cultivate vital and self-critical citizens. In the spring of 1994, the Clinton Administration passed Goals 2000: Educate America Act, a version of America 2000, Bush's reform agenda (which was a document that Clinton had co-authored during his governorship) with numerous modifications. An immediate $105 million was appropriated to initiate this new reform package (Pitsch 1994). In addition, a number of key provisions had been added. Goals 2000: Educate America Act included parent participation and teacher education and professional development. In addition, a number of new forums were established. Furthermore, $400 million had been appropriated for state and local systemic improvement grants, while additional funds were secured for programs that included safe school grants, parental assistance centers, international education, and minority-focused civics education programs.

Such ambitious goals to systematically improve the quality of schooling and academic performance were admirable. Clinton's educational reform acknowledged the need for a federal policy to reduce the grossly disproportionate discrepancies between the rich and poor districts (Kozol 1991). Within this framework, there was recognition of the disparate distribution of resources and opportunities, as well as the unequal distribution of educational services for our nation's children. The reform strategy of the "opportunity to learn standards," coupled with federal monies that were needed to address these inequities, was moving in the right direction. In this case, Clinton had incorporated the principles of social justice to the sphere of economic life. The compassion for children was clearly stated in these principles, yet as the time passed, the quality of life for children in our country did not improve.

Four years later, Bill Clinton was voted in for a second term. In the First State of the Union Address of his second term, President Clinton provided the American people with his new education reform proposals. Quick to act, he called for education to prepare Americans for the twenty-first century, pledging that all Americans would receive the best education in the world. Acknowledgment for more funding was articulated, although not directly related to programs, but rather supporting scholarships and needed school repairs. Unfortunately, however, his practical, "take action" agenda was devoid of the modest social justice components of the past. As McEwan (1997) points out:

> Questions of culture and morality do not appear on his agenda. On the issue of equality, Clinton advocates mild amelioration, hoping that a little more money for college scholarships and some funds to repair the most deteriorated schools will keep the peace and allow public education to perform its important role of providing legitimacy to the U.S. economic and political system. At the same time, the public schools must prepare their students to enter the work force, to provide the foundations for the profitability and growth of U.S. business. (2)

Although the previous Republican Administration's attacks on public education are abandoned from Clinton's most recent reform agenda, the corporate ideology that informs educational reform is not dissimilar to the Republican agenda of the past.

In this chapter, I want to briefly analyze how the language of educational leadership and reform are framed within the logic of bureaucratic rationality and how they relate to economic and cultural discrimination. Following, I will highlight the literature on multicultural education that attempts to provide inclusive education, which, in some instances, addresses injustices for children. Furthermore, I will attempt to provide empowering alternatives, using the language of feminist social ethics, that can invite active forms of intervention in educational leadership that engages a discourse of feminist ethics and democracy theorized from a postmodern position. Lastly, I will attempt to shift from the practice of theory to a "theory of lived practice," making this discourse of feminist ethics relevant to education for compassion and social justice.

Prevailing theories of schooling have been debated over many decades (Kliebard 1995), yet this still remains a difficult and heated dispute as American schooling continues to be defined by a dominant discourse of the marketplace and individualism so clearly stated in Clinton's call for educational reform. What business wants from the schools are an educated populace that blindly accepts the status quo and a work force that will unquestionably meet its needs. Although Bill Clinton understood clearly and efficiently the needs of the U.S. business, with regards to the school system, he did not discern the needs of the children within those schools to eliminate poverty or other concerns that would lead to substantial social change. It is evident that issues of social justice cannot be met when schools are defined and reforms determined based on U.S. business, or expert approaches deemed necessary by mandated state, local, and accredited agencies to provide what is considered a quality education for all children separated from its ethical justifications. Unfortunately, these present reforms only propose a severely confined agenda devoid of any perception of what is needed to provide an active and critical citizenry.

Education in our country is in trouble and drastic changes are needed. Approached from the perspective of a feminist postmodern position, I call into question the present philosophy of educational reform and school culture modeled on the logic and principles of economic and individual competitiveness by exploring the specificity of how inequity permeates its framework. Part of the dilemma is the gross inequities that so many of our children face every day. Conditions of poverty, racism, sexism, and alienation are embedded in the lives of children that fill many of the classrooms in which teachers work. Female and minority students and children of poverty have been victims far too long of educational and intellectual oppression within both curriculum and theories of schooling. And, it is at the very core of this debate that we must address the age-old question—what are schools for in our democracy? The answer is an honest one—a commitment to equality and justice—yet the solutions are not so simple because much of what has been laid out continues to be framed within a traditional modernist paradigm. These issues in and of themselves have evolved because of the changing structures of society, yet have not been explored through a postmodern lens applied to educational reform (McCarthy 1998; Kanpol and Brady 1998; Brady 1995).

Feminist Postmodern Perspective

Drawing on emerging feminist postmodern perspectives theorized in the work of Benhabib et al. (1995), Flax (1990), Fraser (1997), and Nicholson (1990), among others, this position attempts to deconstruct what is discernible and expose what is concealed. In other words, this perspective "takes a critical attitude toward everything, including particular ideas or social injustices, as well as the structures upon which they are based, the language in which they are thought, and the systems in which they are safe guarded" (Tong 1989, 219). In this sense, a postmodern feminism does more than deconstruct. It rejects "traditional" assumptions about reason, objectivity, and universal truths, stretching beyond modernism without rejecting modernist values of freedom, justice, emancipation, and love. Furthermore, a postmodern feminism is dialectal with modernism, but situates itself within the specificity of place, challenging the objectives of freedom and justice, examining lived conditions of a postmodern feminism, and exploring the very way in which this discourse gets carried out.

Peering through the lens of a postmodern feminist perception, what is being articulated in the language of educational leadership and reform is a notion of the subject and citizenship that is both patriarchal and narrowly defined within a sphere of material and cultural inequality. We are entangled between contradictory discourse and ambiguous structures associated with dominant theories of educational leadership and reform that continue to reproduce hierarchical relationships, excessive individualism, and bureaucratic rationality, devoid of all its ethical components. Much of this entanglement is situated within the realm of the multicultural debate, to which I will now turn.

Multicultural Literature Highlights

Although many strides have been made toward addressing cultural inequities within the multicultural movement, it is important to discern the varied and conflicting renditions of multiculturalism, for multiculturalism has become all-encompassing, utilized as a remedy for injustice, while supporting, as well as exploiting, the many it affects. Although there are numerous distinctions made in the research on multiculturalism (Kanpol 1994; McLaren 1997; Sleeter and Grant 1994; Nieto 1994; Darder 1995; Taylor 1994), I will limit my discussion to an overview of three general categories: conservative, liberal, and critical.

To the conservatives, multiculturalism poses a dilemma. Within the conservative position in schools, multiculturalism is developed around a view of pluralism that supports a "common culture." Assuming that justice already exists within our democracy, the conservative view conceives the call for cultural difference as being equated with a threat to national identity against a unified American society. Put differently, the conservative position on multiculturalism first labels, and then extinguishes, difference as an undemocratic approach to social authority and constitutes a movement to restabilize American life within the parameters of patriarchy and Eurocentrism. Less blatant, however, are the many conservative intellectuals who define multiculturalism in ways that produce and legitimate a discourse of management and efficiency within a highly stratified economy. In both cases, multiculturalism, from a conservative framework, maintains the status quo in such a way as to perpetuate the economic and cultural inequities that presently interfuse our schools.

A liberal position on multiculturalism is, for the most part, inclusive and respectful of diversity, yet reduces difference to equivalence. By stripping the core substance of difference and confining diversity issues to a set of neutral procedures and regulations, it erases the possibilities to further democratize our present institutions. Within the liberal configuration of diversity, consensus on procedural rules are considered to be enough to regulate and control the majority of interests in society (Mouffe 1996). In this sense, a liberal view of multiculturalism often means inclusion into the marketplace and consumer culture. In summation, the political philosophy of conservative and liberal discourses does not advance beyond a public morality to regulate the basic cultural, economic, and social structure of society. Rather than expanding on the notion of democracy and social justice, these ideologies attend to the logic and force of the marketplace generated by the language of management, accountability and efficiency, as the primary platform from which public education must serve its democratic function.

A critical multiculturalism pushes much further by understanding the politics of difference and challenging the conception that any one specific culture has a monopoly on virtues or insights. Differences in this sense do not always speak to consensus (like the liberal and conservative discourses), but rather to incommeasurability (Kanpol and Brady 1998). A politics of difference also offers students the opportunity for raising questions about how categories of race, class, gender, and ethnicity get shaped within the margins and center of power. The important questions explored in a critical multiculturalism address the gaps between principles and practices, promise and action, and discourse and agency. By placing the politics of difference within the language of educational reform, it is hoped that teachers and students and the community will be given the opportunity to engage with problems that construct the different, diverse, and, at times, contradictory, experiences they face everyday.

I realize that no one theoretical position on multiculturalism is without problems. And, I am also reminded that progressive thought, both critical and feminist, can be used against itself by creating its own repressive structures when viewed as fixed or final. This is the postmodern challenge for educational reform requiring each of us to live within the realms of uncertainty. I will now proceed to a critical feminist ethics that I believe can further progressive education within the critical multicultural position.

A Critical Feminist Politics of Ethics

As there are multiple feminist positions, there are equally diverse feminist ethical theories (Held 1995; Jaggar 1995; Robb 1981). A critical feminist ethics is multilayered. It is an ethics of neither relativism nor essentialism. It is not defined as equality founded on the principle of morality within an established set of rules that govern the principles and practices of universal actions which argue right from wrong. In this sense, it is not a positivist, paternalistic project. Nor does a critical feminist ethics rely exclusively on caring. Certainly, a critical feminist ethics is infused with commitment and caring, but it is also steeped within the principles of social justice.

Carol Robb (1981) provides nine general principles of feminist ethical reflection which establish a general basis of the discipline of social ethics and allow for the new and diverse voices to challenge its traditional practices.

1. The starting point for feminist ethics reflects upon concrete situations.
2. All relevant data about the historical situation must be taken into account in ethical decisions.
3. The location of the roots of oppression informs all aspects of ethical reflection.
4. With some exceptions, feminist ethics are loyal to women in a way that is concurrent to a loyalty to all of humanity.
5. Commitment to social justice is shared among others with commitment to racial and economic justice.
6. Feminist ethics is oriented toward the liberation of women and weighs the value of acts of policy in those terms.

7. Lived experience is the source of ethical claims that always ask whose experiences, under what conditions, for whose benefit.
8. The moral agent requires both autonomy and the understanding of the powerful forces that limit it.
9. Understanding feminist ethics is a broadened form of social ethics. (49–53)

Embedded in a language that integrates care and justice, a critical feminist ethics provides a democratic vision that takes up the struggle against inequality in both the public and private domains and opens a discourse for expanding basic human rights. In this sense, a critical feminist ethics focuses on economic and social structures and is taken up in personal experiences and in all social arenas, with concrete specificity. However, it would be a mistake to assume that moral and political issues can be resolved through a simple application of general ethical principles. Jaggar (1994) points out the limitations in applying principles to general situations when she states that "one reason for this failure is that to cover a wide range of cases, ethical principles are typically formulated at a high level of abstraction and consequently leave much room for individual discretion—and, therefore, disagreement—in determining how to apply them" (9). Within the concrete specificity of the historical moment, contradictions arise, rationality and reason do not always win out, and solutions are never final. In this sense, a critical feminist ethics presents endless challenges to the imagination and ethical action through a postmodern lens. It keeps us grounded on concrete historical experiences while providing us with outrage to get us off the ground.

A Feminist Ethical Discourse on Schooling

A feminist ethical discourse taken up as part of a critical philosophy of education encourages a language embedded in a political imagination that invites and encourages compassion and possibility, a language informed by a discourse of social justice, critical democratic principles, and economic and social equity. It is a discourse that challenges our institutions to become more humane, not only for children, but for all of us who grow up through them and exit their doors as young adults. This is a counter-language that can rupture the dominant discourse of schools and fundamentally oppose the present conservative and liberal philosophies of educational reform in favor of one that unites social ethics and citizenship with cultural recognition and economic redistribution.

A critical theory of recognition and redistribution (Fraser 1997) must take seriously questions regarding how the production of knowledge needs to be extended to the voices, histories, socioeconomic configurations, and forms of learning that students already possess when they enter the classroom. Yet, even within this struggle for recognition among group identity and collective unity, there is a missing component. Fraser challenges us with

> a new intellectual and practical task: that of developing a critical theory of recognition, one that identifies and defends only those versions of the cultural politics of difference that can be coherently combined with the social politics of equality. (12)

When cultural recognition displaces socioeconomic redistribution as the remedy for injustice and as the goal of political struggle, we can easily slide into a form of liberal politics which reinforces the notion of false consciousness that celebrates difference as the easily identified remedy for injustice (Fraser 1995). Similarly, when socioeconomic redistribution becomes the center of appeal, cultural difference can be forfeited. My point here is not to dismiss identity politics as a form of address, or limit the challenge for a critical democracy to economic injustice alone, but rather to assert the need to speak to a critical theory of feminist ethics that combines a cultural politics of difference with the social politics of equality. In other words, a theory of recognition allows for diversity as a framework for cultural recognition and unity as a form of social collectivity, while simultaneously challenging the unequal distribution of wealth and power. In this sense, for justice to be imagined, we must address the gaps between discourse and action around recognition (cultural injustice) and redistribution (socioeconomic injustice), both of which are deeply intertwined in the political structure of society (Fraser 1997). Within the politics of recognition, the cultural and symbolic patterns of representation, interpretation, and communication must be explored for their complexities within the categories of race, class, gender, and so on. Yet, the issue of a politics of difference mobilized under the rubric of race, gender, ethnicity, and sexuality is inadequate. Any form of difference, in isolation, or without the understanding of each complex configuration inherent within these differences, gives us an incomplete reading of multiple issues, which coexist within cultural and economic realms. Furthermore, each category, in and of itself, has multiple dimensions that demand explorations of each within itself. It is beyond the scope of this essay to develop, in detail, the intricacies of each category and the need for both recognition and redistribution inherent within them, but an acknowledgment of this complexity is required.

It is within the discourse of socioeconomic injustice that we can address our nation's poorest—our children. The statistics are staggering: approximately 45 percent of children under the age of six are living in poverty or near poverty (NCCP 1997). And, contrary to general belief, most children of poverty live in working families (NCCP 1997). As Reed and Sautter (1990) point out: "Poverty in America knows no racial boundaries, no geographic borders. The only common denominator for the children of poverty is that they are brought up under desperate conditions beyond their control—and, for them, the rhetoric of equal opportunity seems a cruel hoax, an impossible dream" (4).

How do we as educators respond to these problems aside from providing school breakfasts and lunches? The challenge is to develop a plan of action that addresses the root causes—a critical theory of recognition and redistribution (Fraser 1997) that seriously addresses both critical multicultural education and economic and social inequities.

This project is a complex undertaking. Restructuring the very discourse of organizations, including aspects of that discourse which address educational leadership, is a difficult process. But it is through the relationship among ideologies, official policies, grassroots movements, and everyday experiences that a discourse needs to be reconstructed and put into practice. If educators and other critical citizens believe schools are important public institutions that provide a social site of entrance for developing a critical democracy, then they must address questions that bridge, rather than rupture, issues concerning cultural differences and social inequities. We do not have to wait for Clinton! This does not have to happen as top-down reform, but rather, should be attempted daily within the cracks and crevices of prevalent injustices. Understanding the principles of feminist ethics provides the groundwork to engage in the act of personal and institutional disclosure. Personal disclosure is the first step in translating theory into lived practice. An internal critical dialogue reflecting on our own personal routines and practices in reproducing and manifesting racial, class, homophobic, and gender prejudices and understanding how we are a part of these occurrences must take place. Expanding this notion onto institutional disclosure allows us to build community through shared dialogues with others around compassion, acceptance, and understanding of the oppressive social structures that exist, while challenging those structures in some form of action. In her book, *Crazy for Democracy*, Temma Kaplan (1997) provides examples of grassroots movements that reveal how democratic political ideas and practices can develop through everyday encounters. In this sense, coalition building is a needed strategy to help find approaches that can, even in the smallest way, rupture the reprehensible actions that reinforce cultural and economic subordination.

In the section following, I look more specifically at how we might translate into educational reform and implement the theoretical framework of a feminist ethics and a critical multiculturalism that addresses recognition and redistribution.

Feminist Ethics and Educational Reform

Classroom Praxis

> Either public education will be part of the solution to this fundamental crisis in our nation's life, or our schools will continue to perpetuate the inequality and separation which has been too much a part of our land. Meaningful school reform—and the development of a strong public commitment to the institution of schooling—must have at the heart of its agenda, a commitment to building an American democracy in which the contribution of all citizens is valued and in which the potential of all citizens is developed if democracy itself is to survive and flourish. (Fraser 1987, 49)

A critical multicultural pedagogy that incorporates a feminist politics of ethics should emphasize a number of issues as a form of classroom praxis. First, it should give teachers and students the opportunity to discover their hidden histories and to reclaim them. This means that the identity of any group or individual cannot be grounded in a notion of history that is unchanging, monolithic, or static, nor in the conservative stance, named so as to be assimilated into a "common culture." Rather, a critical multicultural education is committed to both the process of narrating genuine histories, and also to the dynamics of cultural recovery, which involves a rewriting of history and identity through a resurrection of the historical past (Hall 1990).

Second, critical multicultural pedagogy that incorporates a feminist politics of ethics must reject an empty pluralism that has often served to contain and reproduce cultural differences and economic stratification. Generally, naming differences becomes the first step in policing them so that they can be integrated into the dominant culture. Within this conservative discourse, differences are abstracted from the discourse of power and history. Cultural and economic difference must be taken up as a relational issue and not as one that serves to isolate and mark particular groups. Therefore, critical educators need to understand a conception of cultural differences that makes power and struggle central to any discourse about multiculturalism.

Third, critical multicultural pedagogy that incorporates a feminist politics of ethics needs to understand more clearly how social forms and language signify, how they inscribe meaning within the relations of power that offer images and representations of the identities of others (Shannon 1998). But more is demanded here than an understanding of the new technologies of representation and how they are used to fix identities within relations of domination and subordination. Critical educators also need to use these technologies as part of a counter-narrative of emancipation in which new visions, spaces, and discourses can be developed that offer students the opportunity for rewriting their own histories within, rather than outside of, the discourse of critical citizenship and democracy.

Fourth, critical multicultural pedagogy that incorporates a feminist politics of ethics would elaborate on the issue of educating students to be leaders in the broad sense of being able to govern themselves in a critical democracy. Moreover, such a view would incorporate a specifically feminist conception of the subject as multiple, shifting, contradictory, and gendered. Even the concept of work would be enlarged. This would not simply challenge existing capitalist assumptions about hierarchy, white supremacy, economic discrimination, racial injustice, and labor, but would also include questions concerning the role of women in the workplace, the related issue of reproduction as domestic and specifically gendered and racial, and the division of labor within the workplace. Clearly, these issues would not be taken up only as questions concerning production, efficiency, and capital accumulation within a white, hierarchical framework, but rather, and more radically, transform the discourse to a network of multiple and intersecting differences and shared positions around gender and race (inclusive of other forms of oppression), merging the dialogue and action between recognition and redistribution.

Finally, a critical multiculturalism informed by the imperatives of a feminist politics of ethics is not merely about difference and equity. It engages passionately with reality in an attempt to respond to the undeserved harm and unmerited pain experienced by children every day of their lives (Kozol 1995, 1991; Sidel 1996).

Conclusion: Theory as "Lived Practice"

Beyond the institutions of schools, communities need also to become a site of struggle over meaning and values, a locale that engages and contributes to discourses of recognition and redistribution. As educators, our work must go beyond the classrooms and into the lived communities of the schools in which children play, parents work, and everyday life continues. We must participate in grassroots movements that challenge the economic and cultural inequities that exist in our communities. This would entail intervention by critical, ethical people; to raise questions of justice and ethics in everyday life and take action to unmask ways that patriarchy depends on acceptance of its values. As a political project, it must address real-life issues to minimize unjust suffering and sorrow: unemployment, homophobia, illiteracy, overcrowded and dilapidated schools, youth gangs, homeless children and their parents, violence against women, people living in poverty, and the elderly. In this sense, critical public discourses can emerge in the gaps of patriarchal hegemony created in moments of struggle, disruption, and rebellion (Kaplan 1997; Giroux 1992).

While a critical feminist politics of ethics attempts to take on the issues of redistribution and recognition, it doesn't automatically lead to significant changes in critical priorities and institutional discourses of power. However, it does offer opportunities for critical discussions to take place, finding approaches that can be pursued and allowing for the process to begin by unraveling dominant discourses as one goal of education for compassion and social justice.

References

Benhabib, S., J. Butler, D., Cornel, and N. Fraser (1995). *Feminist Contentions.* New York: Routledge.
Brady, J. (1995). *Schooling Young Children: A Feminist Pedagogy for Liberatory Learning.* Albany, NY: SUNY Press.
Darder, A. (1995). *Culture and Difference.* Westport, CT: Bergin & Garvey.
Flax, J. (1990). *Thinking Fragments: Psychoanalysis, Feminism, and Postmodernism in the Contemporary West.* Los Angeles: University of California Press.
Fraser, J. (1997). *Reading, Writing, and Justice: School Reform as If Democracy Matters.* Albany, NY: SUNY Press.
Fraser, N. (1995). "From Redistribution to Recognition? Dilemmas of Justice in a Post-Socialist Age," *New Left Review* 212 (July/August) 68–93.
Giroux, H. (1992). *Border Crossings: Cultural Workers and the Politics of Education.* New York: Routledge.
Hall, S. (1990). "Cultural Identity and Diaspora." In Jonathan Rutherford (Ed.), *Identity, Community, Culture, Difference,* p. 225. London: Lawrence.
Held, V., Ed. (1995). *Justice and Care.* Boulder, CO: Westview Press.
Jaggar, A. (1995). "Caring as a Practice of Moral Reason." In Virginia Held (Ed.), *Justice and Care.* pp. 179–202. Boulder, CO: Westview Press.
——— (1994). *Living with Contradictions: Controversies in Feminist Social Ethics.* Boulder, CO: Westview Press.
Kanpol, B. (1994). *Critical Pedagogy: An Introduction.* Westport, CT: Bergin & Garvey.
Kanpol, B., and J., Brady (1998). "Teacher Education and the Multicultural Dilemma: A "Critical" Thinking Response." *Journal of Critical Pedagogy.*
Kaplan, T. (1997). *Crazy for Democracy: Women in Grassroots Movements.* New York: Routledge.
Kliebard, H. (1995). *The Struggle for the American Curriculum, 1893–1958* (2nd ed). New York: Routledge.
Kozol, J. (1991). *Savage Inequalities.* New York: Crown.
——— (1995). *Amazing Grace.* New York: Crown.
McCarthy, C. (1998). *The Uses of Culture.* New York: Routledge.
McEwan, A. (1997). "Bill Clinton's Practical Approach to Public Education." *Radical Teacher.* (Summer).
McLaren, P. (1997). *Revolutionary Multi-culturalism: Pedagogy of Dissent for the New Millennium.* Boulder, CO: Westview Press.

Mouffe, C. (1996). "Radical Democracy and Liberal Democracy?" In D. Trend (Ed.), *Radical Democracy*, pp. 19–26. New York: Routledge.

National Center for Children of Poverty (Winter, 1996–1997). Vol. 6, No. 2.

Neito, S. (1994). *Affirming Diversity: The Sociopolitical Context of Multicultural Education*. White Plains, NY: Longman.

Nicholson, L. (Ed.) (1990). *Feminism/Postmodernism*. New York: Routledge.

Pitsch, J. (1994). "Stage Set for Senate Showdown on Goals 2000." *Education Week*.

Reed, S., and R. C. Sautter. (June 1990). "Children of Poverty." *Phi Delta Kappan*. p. K4.

Robb, C. (1981). "A Framework for Feminist Ethics." *Journal of Religious Studies*. 9:(1) 48–68.

Shannon, P. (1998). *Reading Poverty*. Portsmouth, NH: Heinemann.

Sidel, R. (1996). *Keeping Women and Children Last*. New York: Penguin Books.

Sleeter, C., and C. Grant (1994). *Making Choices for Multicultural Education*. New York: Macmillan.

Taylor, C. (1994). "The Politics of Recognition." In A. Gutmann (Ed.), *Multi-culturalism,* pp. 25–74. Princeton, NJ: Princeton University Press.

Tong, R. (1989). *Feminist Thought*. Boulder, CO: Westview Press.

CHAPTER EIGHT

The Critical Discourses of Liberation Theology and Critical Pedagogy

Thomas Oldenski

> One of the most exciting theoretical accomplishments that has emerged in critical theory is the development of a discourse that links certain strands of radical feminist theory with selected aspects of liberation theology.
> —Henry Giroux, *Schooling and the Struggle for Public Life* (1988)

> [Postmodernism] posits instead a faith in forms of social transformation that are attentive to the historical, structural, and ideological limits that shape the possibility for self-reflection and action. It points to solidarity, community, and compassion as essential aspects of how we develop and understand the capacities we have for how we experience the world and ourselves in a meaningful way.
> —Henry Giroux, *Border Crossings* (1992)

As part of the dialogue on the role of spirituality within the learning community, I believe that it is important to consider the discourses of liberation theology and critical pedagogy as a possible "method" to assist students and teachers with the search and yearnings of the heart. In this chapter, I will explore the relationship or the themes common to these two discourses, while acknowledging their many differences. Immersed in the literature of the discourse of critical pedagogy, one at first wonders whether this could be the language of an educational or theological discourse like liberation theology. One is continually reminded that both critical pedagogy and liberation theology provide a language of possibility and transformation, and both have implications for what transpires in schools and what purpose schools serve. Both discourses challenge the current practices in most schools, both public and private. Pamela Smith (1989) concluded her work on democratic education in public schools by stating that "a discussion of democratic education could be strengthened by a clear, theoretical explication of hope and how it can be supported by re-conceptualized understandings of power and voice. Liberation theology might be a focal point in this area" (254).

While these critical discourses share similarities, however, each continues to maintain its uniqueness. Critical pedagogy has evolved from the democratic discourses in education originally articulated by John Dewey, George Counts, Harold Rugg, and other social re-constructionists, by neo-Marxist discourses of liberation and transformation, and by the Frankfurt School of Critical Theory. Liberation theology is rooted in the Christian scriptures and has evolved from a political-critical theology. While drawing from a variety of different sources, the two come together in the work and writings of the renowned Brazilian educator, Paulo Freire.

I intend to elaborate on Freire's "pedagogy of conscientization" as a common source for liberation theology and critical pedagogy, along with the theory and method of liberation theology as articulated by Latin American theologians Leonardo Boff and his brother Clodivis, feminist theologians Sharon Welch and Rebecca Chopp, and the discourse of critical pedagogy associated with Henry Giroux and Peter McLaren. I conclude by presenting a generalizable model of the common themes or elements of the discourses of liberation theology and critical pedagogy that posits liberation theology and critical pedagogy as discourses of praxis and transformation.

I developed this model as the result of synthesizing these two discourses, and I intend that it be understood less as a reified or static model of what liberation theology or critical pedagogy is than as a heuristic model helpful in understanding the similarities between these two discourses.

Paulo Freire's Influence on Liberation Theology and Critical Pedagogy

Paulo Freire wrote his classic work, *Pedagogy of the Oppressed*, in 1968, and it first appeared in English and Spanish in 1970. John Medcalf (1995) claims that "no book on the philosophy of education has received so many garlands" and that the pages devoted to the importance of dialogue deserve unreserved support" (801). Patrick Slattery (1995) points out that Freire's classic work is "an important early example of critical theory in practice" (198). Certainly Freire's work has inspired "hundreds of scholars worldwide to link literacy, culture and politics" (Pinar et al. 1995, 230). Gadotti (1994) called *Pedagogy of the Oppressed* "Freire's most important and extensive work" (43).

The Critical Discourses of Liberation Theology and Critical Pedagogy

In *Pedagogy of the Oppressed* (1989), Freire begins the development of his pedagogy by acknowledging that humanity's central problem is achieving humanization, since the effort leads to the recognition of dehumanization. In his view, "the great humanistic and historical task of the oppressed is to liberate themselves and their oppressors as well" (28). He presented the pedagogy of the oppressed as:

> A pedagogy which must be forged with, not for, the oppressed (whether individuals or peoples) in the incessant struggle to regain their humanity. This pedagogy makes oppression and its causes objects of reflection by the oppressed, and from that reflection will come their necessary engagement on the struggle for their liberation. And in the struggle this pedagogy will be made and remade. (33)

This pedagogy produces solidarity with the oppressed and then the oppressed with each other. This solidarity—this entering into the experience of the oppressed—is a radical posture, defined as "fighting at their side to transform the objective reality which has made them 'beings for another'" (Freire 1989, 34). It is an act of love, existential and praxis, a "reflection and action upon the world to transform it" (36).

The method of this pedagogy is dialogue, or problem posing, as opposed to a "banking" methodology; it values the voices and experiences of the students in the process of developing knowledge. This process of dialogue is also characterized as an act of love and commitment to other persons; as intense faith in humanity's "power to make and remake, to create and re-create, faith in its vocation to be more fully human" (Freire 1989, 79); and also as mutual trust between persons and hope for the "encounter of seeking to be more fully human" (80).

Critical reflection on one's situation of being oppressed begins the dialogue. By "critical thinking" Freire meant "a thinking which discerns an indivisible solidarity between the world and people and admits of no dichotomy between them—thinking which perceives reality as process, as transformation, rather than as a static entity—thinking which does not separate itself from action, but constantly immerses itself in temporality without fear of the risks involved" (Freire 1989, 81).

In *Education for Critical Consciousness* (1990), first published in 1978, Freire continued these themes, but developed the concepts of the process of human agency and "conscientization." He is clear there that "to be human is to engage in relationships with others and with the world . . . [and that] people relate to their world in a critical way" (3). Education is the process that helps individuals understand themselves and their world with a view toward transforming it. Freire stated that "the important thing is to help men and nations help themselves, to place them in consciously critical confrontation with their problems, to make them agents of their own recuperation" (16). Education then helps people "reflect on themselves, their responsibilities, and their role in a new cultural climate—indeed to reflect on their very power of reflection" (16).

Freire identified this process of critical awareness as "conscientization." It involves the process of dialogue and "a critical education which could help to form critical attitudes" (Freire 1990, 32). Thus, education becomes an act of love and courage, since education "cannot fear the analysis of reality or, under pain of revealing itself as a farce, avoid creative discussion" (38).

In some of his later essays, Freire (1985) described the process of conscientization as acts of denunciation and annunciation in a specific historical context (58–59). He identified it with theological language as an experience of Easter (122–123) and as the role of the prophetic church (137–140). He also defined conscientization as "the effort to enlighten men about the obstacles preventing them from a clear perception of reality. In this role, conscientization effects the ejection of cultural myths that confuse people's awareness and make them ambiguous beings" (89). Concerning the process of conscientization, Freire stated that:

> The word "conscientization," the process, by which human beings participate critically in a transforming action, should not be understood as an idealist manipulation. Even if our vision in conscientization is dialogical, not subjective or mechanistic, we cannot attribute to this consciousness a role it does not have—that of transforming reality. Yet we also must not reduce consciousness to a mere reflection of reality. One of the important points in conscientization is to provoke recognition of the world, not as a "given" world, but as a world dynamically "in the making.". . . It is precisely this creation of a new reality, prefigured in the revolutionary criticism of the old one, that cannot exhaust the conscientization process, a process as permanent as any real revolution. (106–107)

Freire (1987, 1989) continued to expand on his pedagogy of the oppressed, putting it into practice as head of the education department of the World Council of Churches and with adult literacy programs in Guinea, Bissau, and São Tomé. In 1987, Freire began to speak of his own work and pedagogy as an "emancipatory and critical pedagogy." Ira Shor and Paulo Freire (1987) identified Freire's pedagogy of the oppressed as potentially a viable pedagogy for the United States. Freire understood the process of schooling to involve the development of a critical awareness of one's world and the injustices and oppressions that exist in that world, and he hoped this critical awareness could lead to political actions that would help to transform it.

Peter McLaren and Tomaz Tadeu da Silva (1993) offered this brief summary of Freire's pedagogy, as well as the effects of Freire's work:

> Freire's move away from the pseudo-equality of liberal pluralism is evident in his challenge to deepen our understanding of how individuals can gain a greater purchase on social agency through a critical narrativization of their desire, through the naming of their own histories, and through claiming the necessary power to resist their imposed subalternity and the deforming effects of social power. For nearly two decades, Freire's work has been employed by teachers, social workers, literacy workers, theologians, and others to construct an educational vision in which self-development and social transformation go hand in hand in the struggle for social justice. (52)

Freire's experiences as secretary of education of São Paulo informed his *Pedagogy of the City* (1993). Beyond narrating these experiences, Freire expressed the need to integrate theory with practice as a teacher and educational leader, amid hopes for what schools could be. We must, he said, "change the face of schools" (32). This progressive struggle requires a vision of schools that generate happiness rather than torpor. Freire characterized the new face of schools as "serious, competent, fair, joyous, and curious—a school system that transforms the space where children, rich or poor, are able to learn, to create, to take risks, to question, and to grow" (37).

Freire went on to characterize the teacher in this new school as integrating theory with practice. He stated that "one of the indispensable virtues of a progressive educator has to do with the coherence between discourse and practice" (Freire 1993, 119). In addition, Freire observed that the role of teachers is "to testify constantly to his or her students his or her competence, love, political clarity, the coherence between what he or she says and does, his or her tolerance, his or her ability to live with the different and to fight against the antagonistic" (50). He urged that teachers discover education as possibility and a source of liberation.

Again, Freire affirmed the pedagogy of dialogue rather than the pedagogy of banking; his school is "one where there is great emphasis on the critical apprehension of meaningful knowledge through the dialogical relation. It is the school that stimulates the student to ask questions to critique, to create" (Freire 1993, 77).

Meanwhile, Freire shared some of his hopes for a democratic school with the interests of underprivileged children at heart. As he said, "[T]he utopian dream that always served as the impetus for all my political and pedagogical adventures . . . has to do with a society that is less unjust, less cruel, more democratic, less discriminatory, less racist, less sexist" (Freire 1993, 115).

Paulo Freire augmented his classic work with *Pedagogy of Hope: Reliving Pedagogy of the Oppressed* (1994), in which he focused less upon what he had previously written and more on the need for hope. Guided by his own considerable experience, Freire nevertheless stated that "I do not intend to wallow in nostalgia. Instead, my reencounter with *Pedagogy of the Oppressed* will have the tone of one who speaks not of what has been, but of what is" (11).

As Freire explained the context in which he wrote his classic work and those that followed, he reemphasized the principles of his pedagogy of dialogue and conscientization, as well as the necessity of confidence in this process. "Things have not changed a great deal between 1973 and 1994," Freire observed, "when it comes to an all but systematic refusal on the part of the antiracist and antisexist movements . . . and the same is true for the struggle against the thesis of unity in diversity" (Freire 1994, 158).

Concerning hope, he makes it clear that "without a minimum of hope, we cannot so much as start the struggle," and that "the progressive educator, through a serious and correct political analysis, can unveil opportunities for hope, no matter what the obstacles may be" (Freire 1994, 9). This element of hope lives at the heart of critical discourses as one becomes more and more concerned with the poor and the oppressed. Hope offers a way of coping with the discouraging situations that exist in today's schools and world. Progressive educators cannot afford to abandon efforts to change school practices or the world.

Freire also emphasized dialogue and conscientization as the key elements of his educational pedagogy, suggesting that "teaching is a creative act, a critical act" in conveying hope. He reaffirmed that "one of the tasks of democratic popular education, a pedagogy of hope, [is] that of enabling the popular classes to develop their own language—which emerges from and returns upon their own reality, sketches out the conjectures, the designs, the anticipations of their new world" (Freire 1994, 39). Freire could not "resist repeating [that] teaching is not the pure mechanical transfer of the contour of a content from the teacher to passive, docile students" (69), and he emphasized that the role of the progressive educator "is to bring out the fact that there are other readings of the world, different from the one being offered as the educator's own, and at times antagonistic to it" (112). This process of teaching and learning through dialogue would "while respecting the educands' understanding of the world, challenge them to think critically, [then] refuse to separate the teaching of content from the teaching of thinking precisely" (169).

Freire continued to describe the process as pedagogy of both denunciation and annunciation:

> There is no authentic utopia apart from the tension between the denunciation of a present becoming more and more intolerable, and the annunciation, announcement of a future to be created, built—politically, esthetically, and ethically—by us women and men. Utopia implies the denunciation and proclamation, but it does not permit the tension between the two to die away with the production of the future previously announced. (1994, 91)

I have already suggested the indebtedness of both liberation theology and critical pedagogy to Freire's work, and Medcalf (1995) points out that liberation theology was "influenced by [Freire's] thought and, in turn, influenced him" (801). Freire rooted his pedagogy of the oppressed and liberation theology in Brazilian experiences of the 1960s. As Freire developed the practice and theory of a liberating pedagogy, while instilling literacy among the poor of Brazil, numerous church leaders in Brazil were developing the pedagogy of Christian-based communities. Freire based his articulation of a pedagogy of the oppressed upon what he saw happening in his own work with indigenous people. At the same time, liberation theologians began to articulate what was happening among these same people from a theological and spiritual perspective.

Henry Giroux (1988a) acknowledged Freire's relationship with liberation theology, as well as his influence upon liberation theology, this way:

> Freire's own philosophy of hope and struggle is rooted in a language of possibility that draws extensively from the tradition of liberation theology. It is from the merging of these two traditions that Freire has produced a discourse that not only gives meaning and theoretical coherence to his work, but also provides the basis for a more comprehensive and critical theory of pedagogical struggle. . . . Freire's opposition to all forms of oppression, his call to link ideology critique with collective action, and the prophetic vision central to his politics are heavily indebted to the spirit and the ideological dynamics that have both informed and characterized the Liberation Theology Movement that has emerged primarily out of Latin America. (110–113)

Alfred Hennelly (1990) began his documentary history of liberation theology with a talk, which Freire delivered in Rome in 1970. He noted that the church appeared to follow something resembling "conscientization" in Latin America (2), and similar principles informed the discussions and documents of the 1968 Medellín Conference of Latin American Bishops (103–105).

The Medellín Documents represent the first official Catholic Church articulation of, and commitment to, liberation theology; in fact, they "serve as the founding documents of Latin American liberation theology; they determine, as well, a direction of solidarity and liberation through the creation of grassroots communities" (Chopp 1989, 15).

Anticipating Hennelly, Rebecca Chopp (1989) acknowledged Freire's influence upon and relationship with liberation theology: "Latin American liberation theology draws upon the resources of Paulo Freire, Marxism, and modern theology to demand that theology be grounded in a concrete praxis of commitment to social justice" (5). Chopp argued that liberation theologians had borrowed Freire's concept and method and that "Latin American liberation theologians revise conscientization to name the activity of faith: becoming human in solidarity with God and with the poor" (21).

Still earlier, Leonardo Boff and Clodivis Boff (1984, 1989) also noted that liberation theology borrows from Freire's conscientization. They presented the strategy of liberation as "the oppressed come together, come to understand their situation through the process of conscientization, discover the causes of their oppression, organize themselves into movements, and act in a coordinated fashion" (1989, 5).

Clodivis Boff (1987) mentioned Freire's influences upon his own understanding of theology as dialectic of theory and praxis similar to Freire's development of conscience and revolution. He also related his development of relevant themes of theology to Freire's use of generative themes as part of the process of popular education.

According to Leonardo Boff (1991a), the popular pedagogy of liberation theology "extensively uses the contributions of Brazilian educator, Paulo Freire." He went on to describe this pedagogy as helping people "to discover the pathways of their own liberation—techniques that begin with their values, cultures and practices" (68). The influence of Freire, moreover, extends beyond liberation theology to a whole new sense of evangelization. Boff (1991b) described this new evangelization as a "new way of being church" and employing

> new methods, along the lines of the pedagogy of the oppressed, and of education as a practice of freedom, of the famous Christian educator Paulo Freire, according to whom educand and educator, catechized and catechist, enter into a process of mutual apprenticeship and exchange of learning, on the basis of accumulated experience, which is criticized and broadened in an integral perspective that attends to the various dimensions of personal, social, intellectual, affective, cultural, and religious human existence. (116–117)

Freire (1985) himself developed a sense of the relationship between the role of theologians and the Church and the role of education. He wrote of the Church as a prophetic institution that understands itself as having a political and an emancipatory project involved with education as an "instrument of transforming action." In regards to liberation theology as a part of his process of transformation, involving both critique and possibility, Freire (1985) observed that

> this prophetic attitude, which emerges in the praxis of numerous Christians in the challenging historical situation of Latin America, is accompanied by rich and very necessary theological reflection. The theology of so-called development gives way to the theology of liberation—a prophetic, utopian theology, full of hope. Little does it matter that this theology is not yet well systematized. Its content arises from the hopeless situation of dependent, exploited, invaded societies. It is stimulated by the need to rise above the contradictions that explain and produce that dependence. Since it is prophetic, this theology of liberation cannot attempt to reconcile the irreconcilable. (139)

Freire is clearly familiar with liberation theology and recognizes its relationship with his own work and writings, and this relationship between his discourse of a liberatory or critical pedagogy and liberation theology gains continual recognition. Stanley Aronowitz (1993) found Freire's pedagogy "grounded in a fully developed philosophical anthropology, that is, a theory of human nature, one might say a secular liberation theology" (12).

Carlos Torres (1993) described Freire's early involvement with the Catholic Church in Brazil, concentrating on the development and influence of liberation theology. In so doing, he observed that "one of the main reasons for Freire's success was the close relation between Freire's early philosophy of education and Catholic thinking. [In 1963], Freire's method of literacy was given official approval by the national Bishop's Conference in Brazil and was adopted by the Movement of Education from the Bases as its own method of attaining literacy" (121–122). Freire's thought influenced the document on education among the Documents of Medellín that emerged from the Latin American Bishops Conference in 1968. Until his death in 1997, Freire maintained close contact with liberation theology and the Catholic Church in Brazil. Torres also described some of Freire's activities in Brazil since 1980; among these he mentioned that Freire was a professor in the faculty of education at the Catholic University of São Paulo and that he remained involved in a project of popular education sponsored by the Archdiocese of São Paulo (136, 142).

Freire's work and writing developed in dialogue with liberation theology, and his contributions to the discourse of critical pedagogy continue in dialogue with liberation theology. Liberation theologians acknowledge that Freire influenced both their theology and their praxis of liberation, and he both provides a source for liberation theology and critical pedagogy and demonstrates the communality between these two critical discourses.

Educational theorists also acknowledge the relationship between critical pedagogy and Freire's work, and they acknowledge, as well, that Freire has become a reliable reference for the critical discourses of schooling (Bennett and LeCompte 1990; Spring 1991; Slattery 1995; Pinar et al. 1995). In his book on urban school reform and the teachers' work in these schools, Dennis Carlson (1992) acknowledged that "critical pedagogy, as Giroux and others have developed it within an American context, owes much to the work of the Brazilian educator, Paulo Freire" (274). David Purpel (1989) advocated that educators in public schools become aware of Freire's writing and start to analyze schooling from his perspective. He also admitted that "the writings and life of Paulo Freire have had a profound influence on [my] ideas" (156), in that they address "a cultural, political, and moral crisis and hence, ipso facto, an educational crisis" (1). Freire and Giroux jointly contributed the introduction to Purpel's book.

Repeatedly, Giroux (1981a, 1983, 1988a, 1988b, 1992) acknowledged the relationship between his development of the discourse of critical pedagogy and Freire's work, and Aronowitz and Giroux (1985) dedicated their book, *Education under Siege,* to him: "This book is dedicated to Paulo Freire who is a living embodiment of the principle that underlies this work: that pedagogy should become more political and that the political should become more pedagogical."

Freire wrote the foreword to Giroux's *Theory and Resistance in Education: A Pedagogy for the Opposition* (1983) and Giroux also included Freire in his dedication. The mutual admiration continued: Freire wrote the introduction to *Teachers as Intellectuals: Toward a Critical Pedagogy of Learning* (1988b), and Giroux wrote the introduction for Freire's book (1985) and for Freire's and Macedo's book (1987). Within these forewords and introductions, Freire and Giroux acknowledged their influence and thought upon each other. In Giroux (1992), moreover, David Trend acknowledged Freire's influence upon critical pedagogy in the introduction of his interview with Giroux: "Giroux has emerged as one of the most outspoken proponents of the 'critical pedagogy' movement, an amalgam of educational philosophies that first gained wide public recognition in the 1960s through the writings of Brazilian expatriate Paulo Freire" (149).

A decade before, Giroux (1981b) wrote that he was already "indebted to Paulo Freire for the insight he provides and the courage he displays in fighting for social justice." Giroux proceeded to develop Freire's approach to radical educational theory and practice, and with regard to Freire's pedagogy being utilized by educators, Giroux stated that

> Freire's work demonstrates that the dynamic of progressive change stems, in part, from working with people rather than on them. It is in the latter spirit of respect for human struggle and hope, that an emancipatory pedagogy can be forged, one in which radical educators can consolidate and use the insights of Freire within the context of our own historical experience in order to give new shape to the meaning of radical praxis. (139)

Giroux (1983) next developed Freire's concept of critical literacy as a radical theory of literacy and pedagogy. He pointed out that when addressing literacy, "Freire moves from critique to cultural production to social action linking these notions of culture and power within the context of a radically informed pedagogy" (226).

Freire's model of emancipatory literacy, his conception of cultural politics, and his languages of critique and possibility helped him develop critical pedagogy, and Giroux (1988a) declared that Freire "has provided one of the few practical models upon which to develop a radical philosophy of literacy and pedagogy" (153). About Freire's work and influence on critical pedagogy, Giroux (1988b) stated that

> Freire's work provides a view of pedagogy and praxis that is partisan to its core; in its origins and intentions it is for "choosing life." Moreover, Freire demonstrates, once again, that he is not only a man of the present, he is also a man of the future. His speech, actions, warmth, and vision represent a way of acknowledging and criticizing a world that lives perilously close to destruction. In one sense, Freire's presence is there to remind us not simply about what we are, but also to suggest what we might become. (120)

Meanwhile, over and over again, Peter McLaren (1986a, 1986b, 1987, 1989, 1991a, 1993, 1994, 1995) has acknowledged Freire's influence upon his work with the discourse of critical pedagogy. McLaren's book on critical pedagogy, *Life in Schools: An Introduction to Critical Pedagogy in the Foundations of Education* (1989), identified Freire as a critical educator and presented his writing as an important part of critical pedagogy. McLaren observed there that "the work of Brazilian educator Paulo Freire places him in the front ranks of that 'dying class' of educational revolutionaries who march behind the banner of liberation to fight for social justice and educational reform" (194).

McLaren further pointed out that "Freire's work, cited by educators throughout the world, constitutes an important contribution to critical pedagogy not simply because of its theoretical refinement, but because of Freire's success at putting theory into practice" (1989, 194). Likewise, throughout his 1989 book, McLaren included Freire and Giroux as sources for his discussion of critical pedagogy: "This book draws primarily on radical perspectives exemplified in the works of such theorists as Paulo Freire and Henry Giroux, who make an important distinction between schooling and education" (165). These same sentiments appear in the second edition of *Life in Schools* (1994).

Peter McLaren and Peter Leonard (1993) introduced their book, *Paulo Freire: A Critical Encounter,* celebrating Freire's contribution to critical pedagogy, this way:

> This volume of chapters on the work of Paulo Freire is an intellectual contribution to the central political project of our time: how to struggle for the social transformation of our post-modern and post-colonial world in the interests of the liberation of subordinate populations and cultures from the structures and ideologies which dominate them. . . . Today, Freire's influence extends far beyond the area of literacy and includes developments in social work education, economics, sociology, liberation theology, participatory research, and critical pedagogy, developments of concern to the authors of this book. (1–2)

In the foreword, Freire wrote that "more than a testament to my work alone, however, this volume attempts to grapple with a number of pivotal issues currently engaged by critical scholars who have set out to refine and develop a critical pedagogy attentive to the changing face of social, cultural, gender and global relations" (ix).

In *Politics of Liberation: Paths from Freire* (1994), Peter McLaren and Colin Lankshear collected essays that reflect Freire's influences on educational practices in both developed and developing countries. In his Afterword, Joe Kincheloe observed that "this book is a testament to Freire's critical pedagogy—it is an example of what happens when students are empowered" (216).

Thus, one can easily see Freire's influence upon the development of critical pedagogy, and his work still influences critical pedagogy as it conducts a dialogue with such current theoretical discourses as feminism, postmodernism, and postcolonialism. Particularly, Freire's concept of conscientization—of valuing the voices and experiences of the poor, the marginalized, and the "other"—has influenced critical pedagogy from the beginning. Critical pedagogy aims to apply Freire's concepts to schooling in our own country, and Giroux and McLaren have expanded his concept of literacy in relationship to curricular issues and pedagogical practices.

I have shown here how Paulo Freire's work influences the critical discourses of liberation theology and critical pedagogy, because Freire's influences account for the fact that these two discourses share themes and elements. Both begin with a concern for the amelioration of society and focus upon the economically poor and marginalized. Now I turn to a description of each of these critical discourses and an explanation of their importance.

Liberation Theology: A Critical Discourse and Method

Liberation theology appears, at first, to be Freire's process of conscientization expressed in the language of religion. But it is more than that, since liberation theologians require that liberation take place before theology begins. They view liberation theology less as a theological movement and more as a theology within a movement.

One can understand the link between liberation theology and the pedagogy of the oppressed from the perspective of Robert Ackermann's understanding of religion as criticism. As Purpel (1989) pointed out, "Ackermann's position is that religion has played an important role in providing critical criteria for judging the moral adequacy of a culture, in participating in the active change of protest and organization, and in offering a set of alternatives.

Ackermann goes on to assert that only those religions that engage in social and cultural criticism can retain their legitimacy and vitality" (79).

Like Freire's conscientization, liberation theology begins with reflection upon experience. It is also a consequential ethics, its aims being part of the process itself. Its goal includes the amelioration of society, especially for those who experience oppressions like classism, racism, and sexism. Boff and Boff (1989) stated that:

> liberation theology is far from being an inclusive theology. It starts from action and leads to action, a journey wholly impregnated by and bound up with the atmosphere of faith. From analysis of the reality of the oppressed, it passes through the word of God to arrive finally at a specific action. "Back to action" is a characteristic call of this theology. It seeks to be a militant, committed and liberating theology. (39)

Liberation theology attempts to integrate both theory and praxis from the perspective of a faith community. Like Freire's pedagogy of the oppressed, it is more than simply aid or reformism: It is a process of seeing, judging, and acting. Boff and Boff define liberation theology as "reflecting on the basis of practice, within the ambit of the vast efforts made by the poor and their allies, seeking inspiration in faith and the Gospel for commitment to fight against poverty and for integral liberation of all persons and the whole person" (8).

Sharon Welch (1985) noted that the integration of theory and praxis of liberation theology also includes an integration of the political with the spiritual: "Liberating communities of faith show no separation between the spiritual and the political. The worth of human life is undivided; spiritual transformation is inextricably tied to social and political transformation. These claims are radical; the practice they reflect and enhance is revolutionary" (51).

Liberation theology has its roots in the experiences and the actions of those who resist oppression in the attempt to integrate theory with praxis. Welch saw that the uniqueness of liberation theology is "its reconceptualization of theology in light of a particular experience of the relation between theory and practice" (Welch 1985, 25).

Welch (1990) set forth a feminist ethic of risk in dialogue with liberation theology and in opposition to a patriarchal ethic of control. In developing the ethic of risk, Welch used the voices of African American women (Paule Marshall, Toni Morrison, Mildred Taylor, and Toni Cade Bambara) as expressed in their novels to develop a sense of memory and accountability. These African American writers, she perceived, are the bearers of "dangerous memories" and demonstrate an ethic of risk in action; they present a "rich heritage of empowerment, resistance, and renewal, offering models of how

Euro-Americans who resist oppression can find courage to face the long struggle for justice" (19).

The feminist ethic of risk is a communicative ethic "characterized by three elements: (1) a redefinition of responsible action (2) a grounding in community, and (3) strategic risk taking" (Welch 1990, 20). Significantly, Welch developed this ethic as part of the discourse of liberation theology:

> In the past 25 years many theologians have turned to an analysis of the theological dimensions of movements for political liberation. Liberation theologians (African American, feminist, and Third World) join poets and singers in a celebrative retelling of stories of solidarity and defiance. We name the divinity at work in our people's histories. . . . A critical theology of liberation can do much to motivate and sustain us in our work for social transformation. Communicative ethics can lead to a critical theology of liberation, a theology that begins with an acknowledgment of the cultural and the political matrix of our thought, as well as our particular location within a tradition. (155–156)

One immediately notices common elements in the feminist ethic of risk and an ethic of liberation theology. In developing her feminist ethics of risk, Welch demonstrated how liberation theology represents an integration of theory and praxis based upon the experiences of those marginalized or silenced by dominant others.

Liberation theology also demands a radical commitment of the victims of oppression while it gives a voice to the oppressed. It is not a theology conducted by others for others; it rallies the victims of oppression, and points them toward "the transformation of present society in the direction of a new society characterized by widespread participation, a better and more just balance among social classes and more worthy ways of life" (Boff and Boff 1989, 5). It also demands of those who are poor and oppressed a commitment of solidarity. As Gustavo Gutierrez, one of the leaders of liberation theology, said: "We will have an authentic theology of liberation only when the oppressed themselves can freely raise their voice and express themselves directly and creatively in society" (cited in Welch 1985, 44).

Boff and Boff (1989) are adamant about this commitment to and solidarity with the poor as main characteristics of liberation theology, and they formulated this commitment to the poor as existing at three distinct levels: visiting the poor, conducting scholarly work in regards to the poor, and living permanently among the poor. Even the pretheological stage, Boff and Boff insisted, demands an effective solidarity with the oppressed and their liberation: "One point is paramount. Anyone who wants to elaborate relevant liberation theology must be prepared to go into the "examination hall" of the poor. Only after sitting on the benches of the humble will he or she be entitled to enter a school of higher learning" (24).

Chopp (1989) also understands liberation theology as an ethical discourse of theory and praxis—a discourse, which like Freire's conscientization, includes critical reflection, action, and solidarity with the oppressed. She compared the work of such Latin American liberation theologians as Gustavo Gutierrez (a Roman Catholic from Peru) and Jose Miguez Bonino (a United Methodist from Argentina) with the German political theology developed by Johann Metz (a Roman Catholic) and Jurgen Moltmann (a Lutheran). She called these theologies "two distinct voices within the paradigm of liberation theology" (4). Utilizing the work of these four theologians, Chopp constructed two models: "Christ Liberating Culture" and "Toward Praxis: a Method for Liberation Theology":

> The first model of Christ liberating culture considers the fundamental claims of liberation theology to relocate human existence in praxis and to reinterpret Christianity as a praxis of solidarity with those who suffer.... The second model, a model of critical praxis correlation, investigates the methodological claims of liberation theology. Through the identification of six theses, this formal model sketches the new nature and process of theological reflection through the use of practical hermeneutics, ideology critique, and social theory. (6)

The six theses of liberation theology Chopp developed are as follow:

1. The two sources for Liberation Theology are human existence and Christian tradition.
2. Liberation Theology interprets the source of human existence politically, using, among other disciplines, the social sciences to reflect on the full concreteness of historical existence.
3. Theology employs a hermeneutics of liberation, including a project of deideologization in relation to the source of Christian tradition.
4. The method of Liberation Theology can be characterized as a critical praxis correlation, wherein praxis is both the foundation and the aim of theological hermeneutics.
5. Liberation Theology's method of critical praxis correlation is, by its nature, a form of ideology critique.
6. Liberation Theology must develop an adequate social theory to attend to the full meaning of praxis. (Chopp 1989, 134–148)

This author (Oldenski 1995) suggested that liberation theology—as developed by Boff and Boff, Chopp, and Welch—appears to be the religious version of the language of critique and possibility of critical pedagogy, or the language of denunciation and annunciation in Freire's process of conscientization. Liberation theologians acknowledge Christian faith and human experiences as its two sources; however, they realize that liberation, through critique and possibility, must first take place before they can construct a theology. Liberation theology is not just a new theology or a new theory or metanarrative; it is, to repeat, a theology in movement characterized by praxis and a commitment to the oppressed and the marginalized. Like critical pedagogy, its main project is ethical and political, and that project aims to develop a more just and democratic society for all. But liberation theology views and understands this ethical and political project as being integrated with the practices of one's religious faith and commitment.

Understanding theology as a source of knowledge thus leads liberation theology, like critical pedagogy, to raise similar critical questions (Clodivis Boff 1987; Segundo 1976, 1992). Whose God is known in this knowledge? Whose interests does this theological knowledge serve? What values and assumptions form the foundation for such theological knowledge? Who are the marginalized and silenced people excluded from these theological discourses? Why do they continue to be excluded?

Liberation theology moves directly into a language of possibility by offering a radical commitment to the poor, the oppressed, and the silenced (Boff and Boff 1984, 1989; Gutierrez 1988, 1991). Liberation theology values the memories and everyday experiences of these "others" as the source of a new theology: a new way of constructing an understanding of and a relationship with God. Liberation theology rejects the dominating theological discourses of a pervasively Eurocentric cultural experience of religion, spirituality, and even church, in attempting to reconstruct these theological concepts and religious practices.

Liberation theology criticizes how the Eurocentric churches historically used and currently use power. It sees how this history can perpetuate the oppression and marginalization of those who have been excluded from the Eurocentric metanarratives. Liberation theology aims to convey power to the people whose histories and situations include them among the victims of poverty or other forms of oppression. Liberation theology values their everyday experiences as a source of power, theology, and spirituality. Liberation theology is also a process of conscientization of individual identities, rights, and freedoms so as to rid society of social injustice.

Liberation theology presents a new understanding of what it means to be Christian in a transformative way. It suggests that the act of believing in Jesus includes a belief in social justice as a prime virtue and in the reality of evil as the social injustice that dominates and marginalizes oppressed people. One exercises Christian faith by participating in the transformation of society towards a more just and democratic society and establishing a solidarity with other people, including a commitment to the poor and the victims of gender, class, and race oppression. Liberation theology understands theology in a multicultural perspective and values diversity as opposed to a monocultural religious practice and theological discourse.

Boff (1991a) characterized one of the results of liberation theology as a new understanding of evangelization, which he called "popular Catholicism." He supposed that this new evangelization requires the Church to relinquish any "option, but the option for the cultures of the oppressed and the marginalized, with a view to their liberation" (116).

Boff further characterized this new evangelization as

> based on the Gospel rather than on the pure and simple propagation of church doctrine. . . . [I]ts principal subject and agent are the poor themselves. . . . [I]t has new addresses such as popular culture and piety, blacks, marginalized women, street children, the chronically sick, the landless, the homeless, slum dwellers, and so on. It is new in that it employs new methods, along the lines of the pedagogy of the oppressed, and of education as a practice of freedom, of the famous Christian educator Paulo Freire. . . . [I]t communicates a new content, derived from an interrelationship between the discourse of faith and the discourse of the world of the oppressed. . . . [I]t inaugurates a new way of being Church. . . . [I]t generates a new spirituality, which appears in celebrations not only of the mysteries of faith, but of the struggles and joys of community. It appears in the manner of its political commitment to collective causes concerned with the poor and outcast. . . . [I]t forges a new relation of church to world. (1991a, 116–117)

Thus, liberation theology echoes the pedagogy of the oppressed of Paulo Freire as a process of conscientization which leads to transformation. Seeing in liberation faith themes and language similar to those that Freire used, Welch (1985) concluded

> Liberation faith is conversion to the other, the resistance to oppression, the attempt to live as though the lives of others matter. . . . To live honestly and believe as universal the imperative of love and freedom is to hope that suffering can be ended, to hope that all lives without liberation in history were not meaningless, but it is to work for this hope without the guarantee that such meaning is possible. (87)

Meanwhile, we can find this process of transformation and hope echoed in critical pedagogy.

Critical Pedagogy: A Discourse of Critique and Possibility

Many individuals working in diverse fields have become associated with the discourse of critical pedagogy—for example, Michael Apple, Ira Shor, Patti

Lather, Jennifer Gore, and Carmen Luke. In developing an understanding of critical pedagogy, however, I chose to focus on the work of McLaren and Giroux, who have directly influenced my own thinking and understanding of critical pedagogy.

The origin of critical pedagogy can be located in the work of the social reconstructionists of the 1930s and 1940s, and particularly, the work of John Dewey and George Counts, both of whom sought to assimilate democracy into education so as "to redefine the meaning and purpose of schooling around an emancipatory view of citizenship" (Giroux 1988b, 8).

The development of critical pedagogy is characterized by "the categories of social and cultural critique" developed by the Frankfurt School as critical pedagogy meets reproduction theory (Giroux 1983, 42). These neo-Marxist theorists focused on the role of "cultural capital" and the idea that schools and forms of knowledge exist in the interests of dominant power blocs or classes to maintain a skilled and unskilled labor force. These social and cultural reproduction theories provide a valuable commentary on what transpires in schools. But, critical pedagogy struggled both with how schools reproduce cultural capital and with how schools resolve the contradictions between class, race, and gender that exist within the dominant culture. Critical pedagogy suggests that a need exists for understanding schools as political sites that produce meaning in opposition to dominant cultural values and practices, while understanding students and teachers as social agents of change.

Critical pedagogy developed along with the influence of the theories of conflict and resistance as expressed in such ethnographic studies as Willis's *Learning to Labour* (1977). These theories of resistance acknowledge that students produce and act as agents within the process of schooling and within the wider society. Students insert themselves into school and do resist if they do not like what they experience. Resistance theories helped students use their experiences as impetus for change.

While recognizing the contributions of resistance theories, critical pedagogy began to focus on the relationship between the hidden curriculum on the one hand, and, on the other, social classes and gender, the voices of oppressed men and women, and the role of student resistance as political action aimed at creating a new public sphere, which "represents a critical category that redefines literacy and citizenship as central elements in the struggle for self and social emancipation" (Giroux 1983, 116).

Critical pedagogy presently juxtaposes itself with various discourses of postmodernism and postcolonialism. Critical pedagogy is now viewed as a form of border pedagogy (Giroux 1991, 1992; Aronowitz and Giroux 1991; Giroux and McLaren 1994). As a critical discourse, it presents schooling less in a language of reproduction and resistance and more in terms of different ways of articulating one's identity from the perspective of social class, gender, race, and sexual preference, and in terms of developing a language of meaning as teachers and students address together the issues and struggles of critique and possibility. Issues of power and identity construction receive productive consideration in a language of the self and the other, acknowledging and accommodating differences with the hope of transforming society. The discourses of schooling and pedagogy derive from social and literary theories and various forms of popular culture that characterize present day postmodernism.

McLaren (1989) presented critical pedagogy as both a new theory and a sociology of education, and he noted that "critical pedagogy examines schools both in their historical context and as part of the existing social and political fabric that characterizes the dominant society" (159). In *Life in Schools: An Introduction to Critical Pedagogy in the Foundations of Education* (1989, 1994), McLaren presented both the major themes of critical pedagogy and some examples of its relevant educators, their work and their thinking: Jonathan Kozol, Paulo Freire, John Dewey, Michael Apple, and Henry Giroux. Kathleen Bennett and Margaret LeCompte (1990) discussed the historical roots of the work of Apple and Giroux, emphasizing not only the theories of reproduction and correspondence, but also the "Frankfurt School of critical theory, the writings of Italian Marxist Antonio Gramsci, and the work of Brazilian educator Paulo Freire" (24).

Giroux (1988a, 1988b, 1991, 1992, 1993) and McLaren (1986a, 1987, 1989, 1994, 1991a, 1991b, 1993, 1995) continue to develop critical pedagogy as a discourse for schooling responsive to the situation of today's educational practices. Giroux wrote that "the over-riding goal of education is to create the conditions for student self-empowerment and the self-constitution of students as political subjects" (1988b, 167). In the foreword to Giroux's (1988b) *Teachers as Intellectuals,* McLaren commented that "the major objective of critical pedagogy is to empower students to intervene in their own self-formation and to transform the oppressive features of the wider society that make such an intervention necessary" (xi).

Thus, the goal of critical pedagogy is to free students from those practices that now oppress them in their schooling. Giroux (1988b) concluded that the central question for schooling is "How can we make schooling meaningful so as to make it critical, and how can we make it critical so as to make it emancipatory?" (2). Students and teachers require mutual solidarity to resist those traditional elements that oppress them and deny their dignity as persons with valued lives and experiences. Meanwhile, schooling itself becomes a site for struggle leading to a structured transformation. Giroux (1993) pointed out that central to critical pedagogy is "the need to rewrite the relationship among cultural and pedagogical production as part of a broader vision that extends the principles and practices of human dignity, liberty and social justice" (79).

Giroux (1988a) also concluded that "radical educational theory needs to develop a moral discourse and theory of ethics [and that] educators should link a theory of ethics and morality to a politics in which community, difference, remembrance, and historical consciousness become foundational" (58). He envisioned this radical theory of ethics productive of emancipatory schooling as "based on norms of solidarity, sympathy, caring, friendship and love." In this regard, he drew upon both feminist theory and liberation theology "in order to redefine how authority and ethics can be formulated in order to reconstruct the role that teachers might play as intellectuals engaged in criticizing and transforming both the schools and wider society" (73).

Giroux acknowledged the contributions of both liberation theology and a feminist ethic of risk to the discourse of critical social theory:

> What is important to recognize here is that both feminists and religious critics have increasingly contributed to developing a new language of critique, and uncovering forms of knowledge generally removed from the dominant public sphere. Moreover, they have begun to redefine in critical and emancipatory terms the language of ethics, experience and community. (1988a, 92)

Like John Dewey, Giroux (1988a, 1988b) presented teachers as transformative intellectuals with the task of defining "schools as public spheres where the dynamics of popular engagement and democratic politics can be cultivated as part of a struggle for a radical democratic society" (1988a, 32). Teachers would thus take the responsibility for making the pedagogical more political. Teachers as transformative intellectuals must "speak out against economic, political and social injustices both within and outside of schools . . . must work to create the conditions that give students the opportunity to become citizens who have the knowledge and the courage to struggle in order to make despair unconvincing and hope practical" (1988b, 128). Giroux went further:

> As transformative intellectuals, educators can serve to uncover and excavate those forms of historical and subjugated knowledge that point to experiences of suffering, conflict, and collective struggle. In this sense, teachers, as intellectuals, can begin to link the notion of historical understanding to elements of critique and hope. Such memories keep alive the horror of needless exploitation as well as the constant need to intervene and to struggle collectively to eliminate the conditions that produce it. (220)

Giroux (1988b) went on to develop an emancipatory curriculum that would provide a critical understanding of social reality and individual experience. This transformative curriculum:

> Would be developed around knowledge forms that challenge and critically appropriate dominant ideologies, rather than simply rejecting them outright; it would also take the historical and social particularities of students' experiences as a starting point for developing a critical classroom pedagogy; that is, it would begin with popular experiences so as to make them meaningful in order to engage them critically. (184)

Thus, the curriculum would focus on democratic empowerment and provide a language of possibility, as well as a pedagogical basis "for teaching democracy while making schooling more democratic." This curriculum would include both basic skills for work and adult life and "knowledge about the social forms through which human beings live, become conscious, and sustain themselves, particularly with respect to the social and political demands of democratic citizenship." The starting point for such a curriculum would be the problems and needs of the students, and it would provide them "with a language through which they can analyze their own lived relations and experiences in a manner that is both affirmative and critical" (102–103).

McLaren (1989, 1994) developed, in one sense, a primer on critical pedagogy. As his preface stated, "This book represents an approach to schooling that is committed to the imperatives of empowering students and transforming the larger social order in the interests of justice and equality" (vii). He described there the current situation in public education as well as excerpts from his journal and field notes on his experience teaching in a suburban ghetto. He also developed the major concepts of critical pedagogy and summarized the thinking of the educators who had guided his thought. Its major concepts urge an attention to issues of hegemony and resistance; cultural capital and the reproduction of social capital; the construction and forms of knowledge, power, and culture; and the influence of race, class, and gender.

Critical pedagogy as formulated by Freire, McLaren, and Giroux subverts the canon of knowledge and the neutrality this knowledge claims. It pushes the purpose of schooling beyond the transmission of the knowledge and culture of Eurocentric metanarratives. It questions how knowledge is constructed, whose interests knowledge serves, whom knowledge excludes or silences, and what values and assumptions inform knowledge. Critical pedagogy draws upon postmodernism in rejecting the totalizing narratives of reason, science, and technology that emerged from the Enlightenment. Critical pedagogy values popular culture as part of understanding the milieu and rejects the positioning of high culture over and opposed to popular culture.

Thus critical pedagogy includes the memories and voices of those who have been rejected and marginalized by monocultural Eurocentrism.

Likewise, critical pedagogy questions the use of power from a base of knowledge and reason. The voices of those who have been silenced and excluded through the exercise of power must be included in reconstructing knowledge and in the process of schooling. This inclusion requires valuing the experiences of students, the marginalized, and the oppressed. Critical pedagogy begins with their experiences as a source of knowledge, including their everyday culture expressed in a variety of contemporary and familiar forms. Thus, schooling becomes less a "banking" process and more a process of "conscientization" as developed in the works of Freire and expanded by McLaren and Giroux.

Meanwhile, classroom teachers pass beyond performing as instruments of technical rationality or serving as sources of power and knowledge. This traditional expectation keeps them deskilled and driven by hegemonic mandates shaped by standardized testing, prepackaged curriculum units, a "national curriculum," and the like. Critical pedagogy, in short, cries out against how society understands and how universities prepare teachers—to be subservient to the hegemonic controls of government and business. Instead, teachers must become transformative intellectuals, and schools of education must prepare them for this new role.

In this new role, teachers must know how to act against social injustices and create conditions to help transform society, including changing their own working conditions. As teachers begin to realize that schooling includes the reality of being linked to society in a wider context of developing a just and democratic society, they become aware of social injustices created by monoculturalism, the current cynical structures of schooling like tracking and sorting students, and the authentic purpose of schooling as the transmission of culture and knowledge. Teachers must develop new belief systems in regards to themselves, their students, and the purposes of schooling, and they must realize that the curriculum itself bears changing and reconstructing once self, students, and "the others" of society become empowered.

Henry Giroux (1992) developed nine principles for recasting "the relationship between the pedagogical and the political as central to any social movement that attempts to effect emancipatory struggles and social transformations" (73). These nine principles echo some of the earlier themes and elements of critical pedagogy, but Giroux cast them in light of postmodern and feminist discourses:

1. Education needs to be reformulated so as to give as much attention to pedagogy as to traditional and alternative notions of scholarship.
2. Ethics must be seen as a central concern to critical pedagogy.

The Critical Discourses of Liberation Theology and Critical Pedagogy

3. Critical pedagogy must focus on the issue of difference in an ethically challenging and politically transformative way.
4. Critical pedagogy needs a language that accommodates competing solidarities and political vocabularies that do not reduce the issues of power, justice, struggle, and inequality to a single script, a master narrative that rejects the contingent, the historical, and the everyday as serious objects of study.
5. Critical pedagogy must create new forms of knowledge through its emphasis on breaking down disciplinary boundaries and creating new spheres in which knowledge can be produced. In this sense, critical pedagogy must be reclaimed as a cultural politics and a form of social memory.
6. The Enlightenment notion of reason must be reformulated within a critical pedagogy.
7. Critical pedagogy must regain a sense of alternatives by combining a language of critique and possibility.
8. Critical pedagogy must posit educators and cultural workers as transformative intellectuals who occupy specific political and social locations.
9. Central to the notion of critical pedagogy is a politics of voice that combines a postmodern notion of difference with a feminist emphasis on the primacy of the political. To engage issues regarding the construction of the self is to address questions of history, culture, community, language, gender, race, and class. (73–80)

Giroux continues to view pedagogy as a "technology of power, language, and practice that produces and legitimates forms of moral and political regulation, which construct and offer human beings particular views of themselves and the world" (81). This pedagogy invites attempts "to negotiate, accommodate, and transform the world in which we find ourselves" (81).

Since the early 1980s, Giroux and McLaren have expanded the discourse of critical pedagogy and refined their own thinking about this pedagogy. Freire influences them both, and one can easily recognize Freire's ideas in the language of critical pedagogy that Giroux and McLaren adopt. Critical pedagogy continues to challenge schools and educators to embrace an agenda of transformation and hope as a strategy to ameliorate the lives of students and society. Moreover, the demands and challenges of this discourse resemble those called for in liberation theology in that both are discourses of critique and possibility with the hope of transforming the lives of individuals and their worlds.

An Integrative Model of Liberation Theology and Critical Pedagogy

The similarity between liberation theology and critical pedagogy just noted is hardly accidental, both discourses being strongly influenced by Paulo

Freire. Thus, one naturally wonders whether their common elements could be developed into a model or a "constructed theory." As I struggled to explain the two discourses to my undergraduate students and my colleagues, who were unfamiliar with them, I found myself naturally talking in terms of models. At this point, therefore, I present the model formulated as I attempted to explain the elements these two critical discourses share.

Both liberation theology and critical pedagogy address any situation or anyone's experience so as to describe what is happening. One can call this reality "my present world"—that is, the worlds in which people find themselves, the living situation in which they now exist. As critical discourses, liberation theology and critical pedagogy assume that all is not well with the way things are and have been. These discourses animate individuals to identify and describe the precise problems with the hope of reducing them. Thus, an individual acknowledges that something is wrong with "my world" as I now perceive it to be. Freire identified this process as "conscientization"—that is, becoming aware of my world and my life in a whole new way and gaining a new perspective on it.

As an individual acknowledges that something is wrong with "my world," the critical discourses of liberation theology and critical pedagogy both urge that individual toward the realization that "I want to make my world better." The individual now takes the position that he or she does not want to go on experiencing reality as it is. He or she wants to make it different, to be an "agent of change." Thus, the individual takes on a political role. Both discourses encourage that individual to make his or her world more caring and just and thus eliminate or lessen that which oppresses or keeps the world from accommodating the individual and others in the same "state of existence." Drawing upon the ideas of Paulo Freire, therefore, critical pedagogy and liberation theology share the same model as critical discourses and discourses of possibility.

In liberation theology, however, becoming more humane and just through political action aimed at eliminating oppression also derives from the tradition of justice as expressed in the Scriptures, certain aspects of this tradition receiving emphasis in the struggle to affect a better, more caring, and just world. Some of these emphasized aspects include the prophetic tradition implicitly promising justice, the Book of Exodus and its themes of freedom and overcoming slavery, the teachings of Jesus about the Kingdom of God, the universal community as demonstrated by caring for others and sharing one's goods with others, and the writings of the apostles, who stress the themes of justice and generosity. This sense of willing self-sacrifice and love is presented as the Christian ideal known as *agape*. This love feast tradition specifies the

Kingdom of God as the place where one enjoys justice, freedom, peace, and love. Explicitly or by implication, all liberation theologians acknowledge the Christian scriptures as the starting point of their critiques. These Scriptures also provide a language of longing to make the world better, different, and more caring and just.

Critical pedagogy draws from various critical discourses for its sources, and these sources reside in "feminist literature, in literary theory and in liberation theology" (Giroux 1992, 13). Giroux recognized that his "referent is how we make this country a real critical democracy" (18). Schooling becomes the site of struggle for critical pedagogy, which proposes to make the world of schooling more humane and equitable and, in turn, make the world more humane and equitable. Giroux sees schooling in terms of "educating students for public life" (p. 18). We have already seen these ideas expressed repeatedly throughout Giroux's and McLaren's writings on critical pedagogy.

The Scriptures define being human as being a member (as a son or daughter of God and as a brother or sister to each other) of the community of the Kingdom of God. The membership subsumes the realities of this secular world, and one gains rights and privileges simply by becoming a member. Sometimes, the liberation theologians draw apart from those who neglect to acknowledge their membership in the Kingdom, behavior that presents a challenge to liberation theology both as a practice and as a discourse. How does this apartness affect those who are resolutely non-Christian or those who belong to different Christian communities from one's own? Can we extend our understanding of what it means to "be human" to include those who do not believe in the Christ or those who express their belief in the Christ differently? Thus, the challenge of making our world more humane and just also challenges liberation theology to espouse inclusivity for those beyond the Christian beliefs. This challenge requires the application of Christ's words as recorded in Scripture to the world as it now is.

The critical discourses of liberation theology and critical pedagogy provide a three-step method—that is, a way to change the reality of what is to what it can be. The practices one can infer from these discourses provide a methodology for changing "my world" and constructing "my new world." This methodology includes, first of all, becoming aware of those conditions that sicken the current world and, therefore, require treatment or cure. This part of the method I call "critical reflection upon my world."

The second part of the methodology involves proposing solutions for curing my current world. These solutions may include either large or modest efforts at improving or righting the current reality. Proposing solutions is also part of critical reflection, including as it does the realization that "what can be" emerges from "what is" and need not involve creating something totally new.

Third, this methodology includes implementing the proposed solutions—that is, putting into practice the products of reflection. These three steps together constitute praxis: the integration of critical reflection with practice and then continuing the process of critically reflecting upon the present practices, always with a view of improving world conditions.

Employing this methodology, both liberation theologians and critical pedagogues engage in a political and ethical discourse because each attempts to change the systems and establishments of political power or those realities that either afflict my world or oppress someone else.

The critical discourses of liberation theology and critical pedagogy start with a concern for the poor or oppressed, specifically, those individuals or groups that have been dominated in one way or another by those in power. This concern evolves into a commitment to the poor and oppressed to help them change their world through political action. One demonstrates this commitment in solidarity with the poor and oppressed and by helping to form a more humane community. Sometimes this commitment requires one to enter into experiences far different from one's own.

Hope and transformation are characteristics of both critical pedagogy and liberation theology and significant elements of each. Both imply that "my new world" does, in fact, exist and is, in fact, possible. This hope also presumes each person can be an agent of change, making a significant contribution to the construction of a new world better than the old.

Changes in how individuals see themselves and their worlds are also part of the hope and transformation these two discourses promote. The accompanying change in the language of theology develops as a process of conversion or transformation, a "change of heart" in the scriptural tradition. This personal change is also characterized by hope. In critical pedagogy it also demands a personal transformation and an understanding of self as an agent of change.

Meanwhile, liberation theology and critical pedagogy are both recursive—that is, they are ongoing and perpetuate themselves with change, modification, and refinement by repeating the steps of the methodology, an ongoing praxis of reflection and action. Thus, both discourses offer a methodology for change that is constantly in process itself. So in one sense—as discourse in praxis—both liberation theology and critical pedagogy remain unsatisfied with what is now and continually long for "more": a more just and caring world, a better world, a world different from what it is now.

Might the critical discourses of critical pedagogy and liberation theology be influencing those schooling practices that include the best of these two discourses as a language of critique and possibility during the learning process? Could the discourses of liberation theology and critical pedagogy benefit education in the United States? Can an integrative model of these two discourses help one to understand what occurs at a specific school site? My responses to these questions demonstrate that both liberation theology and critical pedagogy provide viable discourses for understanding schools. These two critical discourses appear to me to offer much in the dialogue on the identity, mission, and purposes of schools. These two critical discourses help establish meaning in the lives of students. The challenge before these two discourses is to start guiding school practices, thus making a more humane and just society in which all people enjoy democracy and emancipation.

I conclude with an outline of this integrative model of liberation theology and critical pedagogy. The intention is not to simplify the common elements and themes of the discourses of liberation theology and critical pedagogy. Nor do I contend that this model presents either a complete depiction of the contradictions within and between these discourses or the ongoing implications of these critical discourses as they meet other critical discourses and new social and cultural experiences. Rather, the model merely synopsizes schematically the main points of the foregoing discussion. My hope is that I am able to stimulate and continue the dialogue about how these two discourses can contribute to the lives of teachers and students as they struggle with issues of meaning within an emancipatory curriculum.

An Integrative Model of Liberation Theology and Critical Pedagogy

A. CRITICAL DISCOURSE describing my "present" world and its problems
  1. Something is wrong with my world.
  2. I want to make it:
     a. better;
     b. different; and
     c. more caring than it now is, thus more humane and just.
B. METHOD producing change
  1. A methodology for changing "my current world" to "my new world" would:
     a. develop an awareness of those conditions that spoil my current world and, therefore, require change; and
     b. propose solutions that could transform my current world.

2. That methodology would also suggest implementation for creating my new world.

C. Both Liberation Theology and Critical Pedagogy offer these benefits. They:
 1. begin with a concern for the poor and the oppressed;
 2. encourage solidarity with the poor and oppressed in developing a humane and just community;
 3. offer hope;
 4. offer change in how I see myself and my world; and
 5. perpetuate themselves even as they achieve change.

References

Aronowitz, Stanley (1993). Paulo Friere's *Radical Democratic Humanism*. In Peter McLaren and Peter Leonard (Eds.), *Paulo Friere: A Critical Encounter*, pp. 8–24. New York: Routledge.

Aronowitz, Stanley, and Henry A. Giroux (1985). *Education under Siege*. New York: Bergin & Garvey.

——— (1991). *Post-modern Education: Politics, Culture, and Social Criticism*. Minneapolis: University of Minnesota Press.

Bennett, Kathleen P., and Margaret D. LeCompte (1990). *The Way Schools Work: A Sociological Analysis of Education*. New York: Longman.

Boff, Clodovis (1987). *Theology and Praxis*. Maryknoll: Orbis Books.

Boff, Leonardo (1991a). *Faith on the Edge*. Maryknoll: Orbis Books.

——— (1991b). *New Evangelization: Good News to the Poor*. Maryknoll: Orbis Books.

Boff, Leonardo, and Clodivis Boff (1984). *Salvation and Liberation*. Maryknoll: Orbis Books.

——— (1989). *Introducing Liberation Theology*. Maryknoll: Orbis Books.

Carlson, Dennis (1992). *Teachers and Crisis: Urban School Reform and Teachers' Work Culture*. New York: Routledge.

Chopp, Rebecca S. (1989). *The Praxis of Suffering*. Maryknoll: Orbis Books.

Freire, Paulo (1985). *The Politics of Education*. New York: Bergin & Garvey.

——— (1989). *Pedagogy of the Oppressed*. New York: Continuum.

——— (1990). *Education for Critical Consciousness*. New York: Continuum.

——— (1993). *Pedagogy of the City*. New York: Continuum.

——— (1994). *Pedagogy of Hope: Reliving Pedagogy of the Oppressed*. New York: Continuum.

Freire, Paulo, and Donaldo Macedo (1987). *Literacy: Reading the Word and the World*. Granby, MA: Bergin & Garvey.

Gadotti, Moacir (1994). *Reading Paulo Freire: His Life and Work*. New York: State University of New York Press.

Giroux, Henry A. (1981a). "Resistance and the Paradox of Educational Reform." *Interchange on Educational Policy,* 12, 3–26.

——— (1981b). *Ideology, Culture, and the Process of Schooling*. Philadelphia: Temple University Press.

——— (1983). *Theory and Resistance in Education: A Pedagogy for the Opposition*. New York: Bergin & Garvey.

——— (1988a). *Schooling and the Struggle for Public Life; Critical Pedagogy in the Modern Age.* Minneapolis: University of Minnesota Press.
——— (1988b). *Teachers as Intellectuals: Toward a Critical Pedagogy of Learning.* New York: Bergin & Garvey.
——— (1991). *Post-modernism, Feminism, and Cultural Politics.* New York: State University of New York Press.
——— (1992). *Border Crossings: Cultural Workers and the Politics of Education.* New York: Routledge, Chapman and Hall.
——— (1993). *Living Dangerously: Multiculturalism and the Politics of Difference.* New York: Peter Lang.
Giroux, Henry A., and Peter McLaren (Eds.) (1994). *Between Borders: Pedagogy and the Politics of Cultural Studies.* New York: Routledge.
Gutierrez, Gustavo (1988). *A Theology of Liberation.* Maryknoll: Orbis Books.
——— (1990). *The Power of the Poor in History.* Maryknoll: Orbis Books.
——— (1991). *The God of Life.* Maryknoll: Orbis Books.
Hennelly, Alfred T. (Ed.) (1990). *Liberation Theology: A Documentary History.* Maryknoll: Orbis Books.
McLaren, Peter (1986a). *Schooling as a Ritual Performance.* Boston: Routledge and Kegan Paul.
——— (1986b). "Making Catholics: The Ritual Production of Conformity in a Catholic Junior High School." *Journal of Education,* 168, 55–77.
——— (1987). "The Anthropological Roots of Pedagogy: The Teacher as Liminal Servant." *Anthropology & Humanism Quarterly,* 12, 75–85.
——— (1989, 1994). *Life in Schools: An Introduction to Critical Pedagogy in the Foundations of Education.* New York: Longman.
——— (1991a). "Critical Pedagogy: Constructing an Arch of Social Dreaming and a Doorway to Hope." *Journal of Education,* 173,(1), 9–34.
——— (1991b). "Critical Pedagogy, Multiculturalism, and the Politics of Risk and Resistance: A Response to Kelly and Portelli." *Journal of Education,* 173 (3), 29–59.
——— (1993). "Multiculturalism and the Post-modern Critique: Towards a Pedagogy of Resistance and Transformation." *Cultural Studies,* 7, 118–146.
——— (1994). *Life in Schools: An Introduction to Critical Pedagogy in the Foundations of Education, Second Edition.* New York: Longman.
McLaren, Peter, and Tomaz Tadeu da Silva (1993). "Decentering Pedagogy: Critical Literacy, "Resistance and the Politics of Memory." In Peter McLaren and Peter Leonard (Eds.). *Paulo Freire: A Critical Encounter,* pp. 47–89. New York: Routledge.
McLaren, Peter, and Colin Lankshear (1994). *Politics of Liberation: Paths from Freire.* New York: Routledge.
McLaren, Peter, and Peter Leonard (Eds.) (1993). *Paulo Freire: A Critical Encounter.* New York: Routledge.
Medcalf, John (1995). "A Prophet's Lesson." *Tablet* (June 24) 801–802.
Oldenski, Thomas (1995). "Critical Pedagogy: A Union of Liberation Theology and Feminist Ethic of Risk?" *Journal of Curriculum Discourse and Dialogue* (Fall 1994/Spring 1995), 69–76.
Pinar, William F., William M. Reynolds, Patrick Slattery, and Peter M. Taubman (1995). *Understanding Curriculum: An Introduction to the Study of Historical and Contemporary Curriculum Discourses.* New York: Peter Lang.
Purpel, David E. (1989). *The Moral and Spiritual Crisis in Education.* Granby, MA: Bergin & Garvey.

Segundo, Juan Luis (1976). *The Liberation of Theology*. Maryknoll: Orbis Books.
—— (1992). *The Liberation of Dogma*. Maryknoll: Orbis Books.
Shor, Ira, and Paulo Freire (1987). *A Pedagogy for Liberation: Dialogues on Transforming Education*. New York: Bergin & Garvey.
Slattery, Patrick (1995). *Curriculum Development in the Post-modern Era*. New York: Garland Publishing.
Smith, Pamela K. (1989). In Search of Forms and Practices for Democratic Education. Unpublished doctoral dissertation. Miami University, Oxford, Ohio.
Spring, Joel (1991). *American Education: An Introduction to Social and Political Aspects*. New York: Longman.
Torres, Carlos Alberto (1993). "From the Pedagogy of the Oppressed to A Luta Continua: The Political Pedagogy of Paulo Freire." In Peter McLaren and Peter Leonard (Eds.). *Paulo Friere: A Critical Encounter,* pp. 119–145. New York: Routledge.
Welch, Sharon D. (1985). *Communities of Resistance and Solidarity*. Maryknoll: Orbis Books.
—— (1990). *A Feminist Ethic of Risk*. Minneapolis: Fortress Press.
Willis, Paul (1977). *Learning to Labour: How Working Class Kids Get Working Class Jobs*. Westmead: Saxon House.

CHAPTER NINE

Integrating Liberation Theology into Restructuring: Toward a Model for Urban Catholic Schools

Edward P. St. John

Introduction

In *Liberation Theology and Critical Pedagogy in Today's Catholic Schools: Social Justice in Action* (1997), Brother Thomas Oldenski offers a compelling portrait of a Catholic alternative high school in East St. Louis that had adapted aspects of liberation theology and critical pedagogy. He describes how critical pedagogy, coupled with the emphasis on social justice, transformed students and educators. He concludes these practices can be used to transform both public and Catholic schools, as well as the alternative high school he studied. This represents an important challenge for educators, especially those in urban Catholic schools.

However, while the beliefs of educators in Catholic schools help distinguish them from public schools (Bryk, Lee and Holland 1993), the process of transforming urban Catholic schools to meet the learning needs of inner-city youth involves more than adhering to traditional beliefs about education or Catholicism. Indeed, in the past few decades some urban Catholic schools have closed and many of those that had redirected themselves to service the inner-city poor have faced similar problems as inner-city public schools: the dominant theories of educational effectiveness simply do not work as well in inner cities as they do in the suburbs. Indeed, restructuring to meet the needs of inner-city children involves reflecting critically on beliefs, which is why liberation theology seems important, along with school restructuring.

I propose that integrating an orientation toward liberation theology into the Accelerated School Project (ASP), a successful restructuring methodology (Finnan et al. 1996), could provide a model for restructuring that is appropriate for urban Catholic schools. Liberation theology is important because it can enable those within the Catholic belief community to focus on the challenges facing the urban poor. The ASP is suggested because it is a systematic approach to restructuring (Hopfenberg, Levin, and Associates 1993; Finnan 1996) that is highly effective in transforming the urban public schools that serve poor families (St. John, Griffith, and Allen-Haynes 1997). First, I explore the compatibility between the underlying philosophies of liberation theology and the ASP, then review research evidence about the ASP in urban schools, and finally, suggest some steps that can be taken by those interested in integrating liberation theology into the ASP as part of the new wave of experiments in urban Catholic schools.

Liberation Theology

In the past three decades, there was a remarkable, mostly peaceful, transformation of political systems in Latin America from dictatorships to democracies. In the middle 1960s, leaders in education and the Catholic Church began to reflect on fundamental questions of oppression in Latin America. They critically examined the assumptions of both Marxism and Christianity. In the process, they built new understandings about both oppression in communities of poverty and the process of liberation within these communities. In his analysis of the emergence of liberation theology in Latin America, Edward L. Cleary (1985) observed: "Paulo Freire and Gustavo Gutierrez have been preeminent in the creation of liberation thought. Their contributions have allowed liberation theology to move along paths it might not have taken without them" (74). Given the central importance of Freire and Gutierrez to the emergence of liberation theology, this inquiry begins with a probe into some of their writings.

Freire on Conscientization

The central concept in Freire's writings is conscientization: "Conscientization refers to the process in which men, not as recipients, but as knowing subjects, achieve a deepening awareness both of the sociocultural reality that shapes their lives and of their capacity to transform that reality" (Freire 1985, 93). Thus, conscientization is: *situated,* in the sense that it involves understanding how the historical and cultural realities shape the individual's life; *transformational,* in the sense that it potentially involves the individual in a process of making fundamental changes in this reality; and involves building an inner awareness, or *consciousness.* Each of these aspects of conscientization merit consideration.

First, Freire linked his arguments about consciousness to the historical and cultural contexts in which they existed. He argued: "To understand the levels of consciousness, we must understand cultural-historical reality as superstructure in relation to an infrastructure. Therefore, we will try to discern, in relative rather than absolute terms, the fundamental characteristics of the historical-cultural configuration to which such levels correspond" (1985, 71). In Freire's experience in the 1960s, the dominant social force was the oppressive dictatorship in Latin America, and his arguments were situated in this context, in building an understanding of oppression. He argued: "There can be no conscientization without denunciation of unjust structures, a thing that cannot be expected of the right. Nor can there be popular conscientization for domination. The right invents new forms of cultural action only for domination" (1985, 85). Does this strong leftist position about the politics of oppression in Latin America mean that conscientization, by definition, requires taking a political position in opposition to the political right? This would imply liberation theology was a political ideology first and foremost. While Freire positioned himself on the political left, he also argued against the tacit acceptance of any political ideology.

Indeed, Friere argued that the fundamental role of those committed to cultural action for conscientization is "to invite people to grasp with their minds the truth of their reality" (1985, 85). Further, he argued that scientific knowledge could not be subordinated to beliefs:

> Those who use cultural action as a strategy for maintaining their domination over the people have no choice but to indoctrinate the people in a mythified version of reality. In doing so, the right subordinates science and technology to its own ideology, using them to disseminate information and prescriptions . . . By contrast, for those who undertake cultural action for freedom, science is the indispensable instrument for denouncing the myths created by the right, and philosophy is the matrix of proclamation of a new reality. Science and philosophy together provide the principles of action for conscientization. Cultural action for conscientization is always a utopian enterprise. This is why it needs philosophy, without which, instead of denouncing reality and announcing the future, it would fall into the "mystification of ideological knowledge." (86)

Freire originally made this argument while in exile. In essence, he took a position, based on reflection on his practice as an educator in Brazil, that: (1) the rightist dictatorships in Latin America were wrong when they claimed their regimes were essential in the cold war; and (2) tacitly accepting such arguments, the dominant American position during the cold war, represented a false consciousness. Further, he argued: (3) a true consciousness involved first and foremost an understanding of the experience of the poor in Latin America; (4) it was not sufficient to base this point of view on philosophy alone; and (5) scientific knowledge must be used to test the claims of these false points of view.

The second element of Freire's conscientization involves focusing on a vision of humanity in action. The ultimate aim of the process, he argues, is utopian:

> In this sense, the pedagogy that we defend, conceived in a significant area of the Third World, is itself a utopian pedagogy. By this very fact it is full of hope, for to be utopian is not to be merely idealistic or impractical, but rather to engage in denunciation and annunciation. Our pedagogy cannot do without a vision of man and of the world. It formulates praxis in which the teachers and learners together, in the act of analyzing a dehumanizing reality, denounce it while announcing its transformation in the name of the liberation of man. (1985, 57)

The very idea of education embedded in this construction is education for liberation, for the transformation from domination to freedom. In other words, the process involves both a critique of what is (denunciation) and a vision for what might be (annunciation). Freire further makes a link between this utopian vision for education and his arguments about cultural action:

> The utopian nature of cultural action for freedom is what distinguished it above all from cultural action for domination. Cultural action for domination, based on myths, cannot pose problems about reality to the people, nor orient the people to the unveiling of reality, since both of these projects would imply denunciation and annunciation. On the contrary, in problematizing and conscientizing cultural action for freedom, the annunciation of a new reality is the historical project proposed for men's achievement. (1985, 86)

Further, for Freire the political aspect of conscientization is inexorably linked to a politically situated understanding. This position becomes clear when he critiques attempts to remove his methodology from the intent of educating for liberation:

> Another dimension of the mythologizing of conscientization—whether by the shrewd or the naïve—is their attempt to convert the well-known education for liberation into a purely methodological problem, considering methods as something

purely neutral. This removes—or pretends to remove—all political content from education, so that the expression *education for liberation* no longer has meaning. (1985, 125)

This is an especially difficult challenge for urban educators. In particular, the challenge involves reflecting critically on educational practice as a process of social justice, educating for liberation of the child and family, rather than merely conveying a content. While holding that an authentic attitude toward the poor and their liberation is compatible with Jesus's teachings, it is not always central to the educational beliefs of urban Catholic educators. Thus, the centrality of the belief community in urban Catholic schools is a crucial foundation, just as the Catholic Church was a crucial foundation for the liberation of Latin America.

A third aspect of the definition of conscientization involves the individual's reflection on action and the relationship between theory and practice. Freire describes critical reflection as having a central role in conscientization:

> The reflectiveness and finality of men's relationships with the world would not be possible if these relationships did not occur in an historical, as well as physical context. Without critical reflection, this is not finality, nor does finality have meaning outside an uninterrupted temporal series of events. For men there is not a "here" relative to a "there" that is not connected to a "now," a "before," and an "after." Thus, men's relationships with the world are, *per se,* historical, as are men themselves. Not only do men make the history that makes them, but also they can recount the history of this mutual making. (1985, 70–71)

In an interview with Donaldo Macedo, a translator of his book, *The Politics of Education,* Freire (1985) describes the crucial role his own reflection played in his work while he was in exile:

> It was while in exile that I realized I was truly interested in learning. What I relearned in exile is what I would recommend to all readers of this book: each day be open to the world, be ready to think; each day be ready not to accept what is said just because it is said, be predisposed to re-read what is read; each day investigate, question, and doubt. I think it is most necessary to doubt. I feel it is always necessary not to be sure, that is, to be overly sure of "certainties." My exile was a long time of continuous learning. (1985, 181)

This statement captures the essence of critical reflection, which is the willingness to be critical and have doubt, even about one's own assumptions. By being able to question and critique one's own assumptions, one is capable of meaningful learning.

Thus, when we begin to probe the three constructs embedded in conscientization—viewing action as historically and culturally situated, having a vision of the transformation of practice, and being willing to reflect critically, especially on our own practices—an integrated way of viewing consciousness in practice emerges. For Freire, this view is embedded in a situated understanding of the political aspects of action, political aspects that are historically and culturally situated in an understanding of the politically oppressed.

Gutierrez on Critical Practice

While Paulo Freire was an educator who reflected on the political aspects of the journey toward liberation, Gustavo Gutierrez was a priest who reflected on the practice of theologians in their communities. In *A Theology of Liberation* (1988), Gutierrez outlines how reflection on the gospels led him to reject conventional notions of national development. He challenged church leaders to reflect on their own beliefs, their own attitudes toward the poor and toward social action. His writing helped stimulate a peaceful revolution.

In *We Drink from Our Own Wells: The Spiritual Journey of a People*, a book that reflected on changes in Latin America, Gutierrez (1984) focused on freedom of the individual in community:

> In search of this utopia, an entire people—with all its traditional values and the wealth of its recent experience—has taken a path of building a world in which persons are more important than things and in which all can live with dignity, a society that respects human freedom when it is in the service of a genuine common good, and exercises no kind of coercion, from whatever source. (27)

In this passage, Gutierrez places an emphasis both on the "genuine common good" and "human freedom," a freedom without the exercise of "coercion" of any kind. Thus, he exposes the delicate balance between the community and the common good of the community on the one hand, and the freedom of the individual to make choices within the community on the other.

This theme of *individual in community* is central to Gutierrez's concept of critical reflection in action. He argues that solitude is necessary for individuals to reflect on their experiences:

> When they find themselves alone—and there are many kinds of solitude—many persons would like to rewrite their lives; they wish they had not done or said this or that. Not all wishes at such a moment are dictated by healthy self-criticism; weariness plays a part, as does cowardice and even despair at the thought of the many obstacles and misunderstandings that must be overcome. (1984, 130)

The journey into self, then, is central to the construction of a new consciousness of practice. This solitude, with its accompanying loneliness and self-doubt, is essential to the emergence of consciousness: "The experience of solitude, on the other hand, gives rise to a hunger for communion. There is an aloneness with oneself and with God that, however, hard as it may be to endure at certain times, is a requirement for authentic community" (Gutierrez 1984, 132). Thus, Gutierrez argues that we must travel through our own uncertainties as we journey toward authentic community. Further, Gutierrez leaves us with no question that such an individual aspect of the journey is necessary: "There is, however, no question here of two stages: first solitude and *then* community. Rather, it is within community that one experiences solitude. The successive levels of depth prove baffling, even to the person who is experiencing them" (132). Herein lies a very interesting aspect of Gutierrez's view of liberation: it is within community that one experiences the solitude—and, indeed, the freedom—to ponder the inner aspect of the journey.

Gutierrez adds two new understandings to the constructs that emerged from the review of Freire's writing. The first is the importance of a sense of community in the individual's transformation process. The second is the complex argument that the individual's critical reflection both precedes the emergence of a deep sense of community and, paradoxically perhaps, happens within the community-building process.

Discerning Central Claims

From these reflections by two of the founding scholars in the liberation theology movement in Latin America, we can discern three central claims about liberating pedagogies which we can examine further in an examination of the experiences of practitioners in restructuring schools. The first claim is that the practice of liberation theology is historically and culturally situated. This is a political argument based on an historical-cultural understanding of context, an understanding that, Freire argues, necessitates taking a position in favor of liberation and freedom. Further, this issue represents a serious challenge to those, like myself, who might wish to abstract methodological aspects of liberation theology into a reconstructed way of viewing critical reflection in professional practice. To explore this first claim, I first examine reflections by Henry M. Levin, the founder of Accelerated Schools, as a means of exploring how he envisioned a methodology for school transformation. However, this represents only an initial litmus test as to whether the ASP is situated in a particular historical-cultural context, or moment. The more crucial question is whether the method can help urban Catholic educators situate themselves in their historical-cultural moments.

The second claim examined here is that liberation involves a change in individuals' consciousness about their practices. This central concern is with individuals' needs to recognize oppression within themselves, as a step toward re-envisioning their own practices. To explore this claim, I examine the ASP methodology, to see if analogous processes are evident, then review research on the educational practices of educators in accelerated schools, focusing on whether the ASP fosters this inner transformation for educators.

The third claim uncovered from this review is that the path toward liberation not only involves a journey through solitude in community, but also a transformation of the community. In other words, through the process of building an authentic sense of community, a freedom can be created that has the potential not only to heal the individual, but also to heal the community. To explore this claim, I examine findings from research in accelerated schools that focused on parent involvement and community building processes beyond the boundaries of the schools.

Accelerated Schools as a Liberation Process

Accelerated Schools is a comprehensive school restructuring process that has attracted more than 500 schools in more than 20 states (Finnan et al. 1996). The Accelerated Schools process was originally conceptualized by Henry Levin, a professor at Stanford University (now at Columbia University). This section explores the three claims emerging from the review as a measure of exploring the compatibility between liberation theology and the ASP.

A Situated Reform

In his reflections on the origins of the project, Levin (1996) recalls he began to reflect on disparities that persisted in education. In particular, he was concerned that the National Commission on Excellence in Education and other reform efforts made no mention of students who dropped out. He speculated that there were two possible hypotheses for this oversight: "One possibility was that we had won the war on poverty, but no one had noticed. The other possibility was that we had accepted a clandestine truce in that war. My curiosity won out, and I decided to turn my attention once again to the so-called educationally disadvantaged student to find out what happened" (7-8). When Levin began to explore the status of schooling for the so-called "educationally disadvantaged," he found that schools were not structured to serve the students who came without expected skills:

> If children arrive at school without the skills that schools expect, slowing their development through remediation will get them farther behind. If all the young are ultimately to enter successfully the academic mainstream, we must accelerate their growth and development, not retard it. This notion was further reinforced by the fact that the only educational stimulation and excitement that I saw in schools with high concentrations of at-risk students was in the few classrooms characterized as "gifted and talented" or "enrichment." In these classes, students were identified according to their strengths and provided with educational activities and projects that built on those strengths. Instead of being stigmatized with labels such as "slow learner," they were celebrated for their talents. And learning was palpable in those classrooms, as these highly valued and stimulated students were continually motivated and challenged to think, reflect, create, and master. (1996, 9–10)

Based on these reflections, Levin began to explore how schools that served at-risk students could be restructured to accelerate learning for all the students in these schools. Initially, he and a few graduate students worked with a few schools on testing his ideas in action. He envisioned a thirty-year movement and, during the first decade, the methodology has evolved and become more dynamic. The overall intent of the Accelerated Schools process is to transform schools from places that slow down the learning of students that the system identifies as being at risk—a culture of remediation—into organizations that accelerate the learning of all children. In this sense Accelerated Schools can be viewed as a process with an intent of liberating all students from the oppressive aspects of schools as they are currently structured.

Through this systematic process, a new school culture can be created (Finnan 1996), a culture that thrives on practitioner reflection. Levin (1996) describes the present status of the Accelerated Schools Project as follows:

> The Accelerated Schools Project is a 30-year experiment in creating a learning community. It is not a completed work, but a project that is always coming into being through continuous trial and error, theory and practice, inspiration and hard work. Acceleration necessitates the remaking of the school in order to advance the academic and social development of all children, including those in at-risk situations. This has meant creating a school in which all children are viewed as capable of benefiting from a rich instructional experience rather than delegating some to a watered-down one. It means a school that creates powerful learning situations for all children, integrating curriculum, instructional strategies, and context (climate and organization) rather than providing piecemeal changes limited to periodic changes in textbooks, training, and instructional packages. (13–14)

When we review Levin's statements about the origins of Accelerated Schools, in relation to Freire's arguments about historically and culturally situating revolutionary projects, it becomes evident that there is a parallel in thought, but not necessarily a consonance in intent. The parallel in the logical process is evident in that both Freire and Levin start with an orientation toward the poor. Levin focused on students diagnosed as being at risk of failure, while Freire focused on the domination of the poor by elite classes in dictatorial Latin American societies. Freire concludes that social transformation and utopian thinking were necessary. Levin concludes that the patterns in schools that reinforce the lower attainment of students in at-risk situations must be transformed, an idea with a utopian aspect.

A lack of consonance in their ultimate intent is also evident. While Freire's aim is social transformation and he views education as a means toward that end, Levin's explicit aim is transformation within schools, and he does not address larger social questions. However, we need to keep in mind that Levin is considering school transformation within a democratic society. And while there are inequities in American society, the discovery and transformation of those inequities is not Levin's explicit intent. Thus, while there are parallels—for example, both discuss their efforts to understand Marxism—Levin gives a perspective on utopian thinking about educational transformation that is situated within schools, while Freire views education in its larger social context, as a process of liberation.

Restructuring as Conscientization

In addition to being oriented toward bringing at-risk students into the educational mainstream, Accelerated Schools have other parallels to the constructs embedded in liberation theology. Four aspects of the Accelerated Schools process are important to gaining visibility as a potentially liberating process.

First, the ASP is built on three principles: *unity of purpose,* the process of striving toward a common set of goals for the school community; *empowerment coupled with responsibility,* a process enabling participants in the school community to take responsibility for important decisions, implement those decisions, and take responsibility for the outcomes; and *building on strengths,* which means using all of the learning resources that students, parents, school staff, and communities bring to schools (Hopfenberg, Levin, and Associates 1993; Finnan et al. 1996). When these principles are communicated and acted upon in schools, there is great potential for transformation of a school culture, beginning with the ways teachers view their own practices as educators (Finnan 1996; Keller and Soler 1996; St. John, Davidson, Meza, and Allen-Haynes 1996). It is this potential for transformation that is systematically examined below in relation to the second two claims discerned from the review of writings on liberation theology. Indeed, both Levin (1996) and Freire (1985) discuss their own efforts to build an understanding of Marxism.

Second, the ASP methodology includes a comprehensive, systematic restructuring process during the first year a school engages in the process. It involves all members of the school community in a process of *taking stock* of where the school is here and now, *developing and celebrating a vision for the school* as it might be, and *setting priorities* based on an understanding of challenges that emerge from taking stock juxtaposed to developing a vision (Hopfenberg, Levin, and Associates 1993; Finnan et al. 1996). These processes can be viewed from at least a couple of vantages: as a comprehensive process with elements similar to an accreditation process; or as a critical process with the potential of building consciousness. While the process itself has mechanical aspects that are similar to most mandated school change processes, it also contains within it the potential for conscientization, or enabling practitioners to become more conscious practitioners. This could explain a contradiction evident in the Accelerated Schools literature: virtually all schools can finish the first-year process, but only some Accelerated Schools seem to embrace change on a deep level (St. John, Griffith, and Allen-Haynes 1997). Part of our challenge then, if we attempt to view Accelerated Schools through the lens of liberation theology, is to untangle further these aspects of the getting-started process.

Third, once a school has completed the getting-started process, they begin a comprehensive change process aimed at creating a capacity for accelerating the learning of all students. A new governance structure is created, with the school as a whole making major decisions, a steering committee guiding the process, and, at the core of the process, cadres of school participants engaged in an inquiry process intended to transform educational practices in challenge areas. The inquiry process was initially intended as a collective process by teams of teachers, but "spin offs" in the form of individual teachers' inquiry were soon observed (Brunner and Hopfenberg 1996; Keller and Soler 1996). However, there is some question about whether this teacher-level inquiry is actually a "spin off." A few studies have found that teacher inquiry actually precedes the emergence of inquiry in cadres in Accelerated Schools that more rapidly realize the potential for transformation (Dell 1995; St. John, Davidson, Meza, and Allen-Haynes 1996). It is this process of practitioner-level inquiry versus inquiry in cadres that so closely parallels Gutierrez's claim (1984) that liberation involves solitude in community. This aspect of the emergence of Accelerated Schools merits further exploration.

Thus, there are several levels on which the ASP can be viewed as a liberating process for communities of educators and students. In Accelerated Schools, the process of reflecting on the meaning of the three principles—empowerment coupled with responsibility, building on strengths, and unity of purpose—provides an opportunity for practitioners to think critically about past practices, as well as to generate a will to transform them. The practitioner-inquiry process provides them with a method of moving toward the new practice they envision. Having longitudinal data on a small group of Accelerated Schools provides an information source to examine two aspects of this transformation process: (1) the emergence of practitioner inquiry in Accelerated Schools and the relationship between practitioner inquiry and educational practice; and (2) the emergence of a sense of community within Accelerated Schools.

Critical Reflection in the ASP

There is a substantial and growing body of research on Accelerated Schools that documents the profound influence the process has had on in the educational practices and reflection of educators. This research finds that teacher inquiry is central to the success of Accelerated Schools (Brunner and Hopfenberg 1996; Dell 1995; Keller and Soler 1996; St. John, Griffith, and Allen-Haynes 1997), and that open critical reflection by principals is crucial to fostering teacher inquiry (Dell 1995; St. John, Griffith, and Allen-Haynes 1997). Consider this finding from a study of four exemplary Accelerated Schools:

> The link between critical reflections and teacher empowerment was readily evident in our analysis of teachers' experiences in the school restructuring process. In schools where teachers were more willing to take risks—try out new instrumental approaches and to experiment with new approaches to curriculum—their principals had exhibited a capacity to reflect critically on their leadership practices. (St. John, Griffith, and Allen-Haynes 1997, 77).

By reflecting openly and collectively, educators can go down a path different from conventional school reform. Rather than overemphasizing test scores, as do most of the reforms of the past two decades, achievement tests were not the primary outcome of value in these Accelerated Schools:

> This criticism [of the conventional approach] is not meant as an excuse for low achievement in the target schools. There was, in fact, notable improvement in test scores in two of the target schools, and the other two held their ground while they contended with an array of more troubling issues. . . . Rather than replicating mandated curriculum and pedagogies, these schools attempted to create powerful learning environments as a means of challenging their students. (St. John, Griffith, and Allen-Haynes 1997, 79)

Educators in Catholic schools who had prior experience with the ASP also noted the central importance of the orientation toward powerful learning in the ASP. Indeed, powerful learning is consonant with the concept of critical pedagogy advocated by Oldenski (1997). In a study of first year Accelerated Schools in Louisiana, I interviewed three sisters (two teachers and a principal) in Louisiana's first Catholic school in the ASP. Each spoke to the ways the ASP had been consonant with their sense of "calling," their deeply held values that had led them into religious life (St. John, Dell, and Associates 1994). In the spring of 1997, I also had the chance to interview two principals in two other urban Catholic schools in New Orleans, both of whom had experience with the ASP. Both argued that the emphasis on teacher inquiry and powerful learning (in the ASP) was appropriate for their schools, for the students in their schools.

Remarkably, when the ASP takes root in schools, educators and parents begin to reflect critically and openly, as well as to take new forms of action (St. John, Grifflith, and Allen-Hayes 1997). There is a restructuring of power relationships within schools, involving parents and teachers in a more authentic dialogue about themselves and their care for children. This caring community also has ripple effects in neighborhoods surrounding schools.

Building Community

If we extend Gutierrez's insights into the domain of school reform, then we need to ponder how success with the ASP influences community building in schools and in neighborhoods surrounding schools. Several studies have documented the ways the ASP can help build community within schools and heal divisions between schools and their neighborhoods (Miron, St. John, and Davidson 1998; St. John 1995; St. John, Griffith, and Allen-Haynes 1997). This research reveals how the deep social divisions of race and class that divide urban communities also can divide educators in urban schools. Not only did educators reflect on their own educational practices and whether they were addressing the learning needs of the children in their classrooms, they also reflected on their relationships with each other and with parents. Indeed, a ripple effect has been observed in the neighborhoods surrounding Accelerated Schools. These studies indicate that schools must first heal divisions among educators, creating a deeper unity within the school and communities, before they can begin to be a force for community building in the neighborhood. However, once educators in the target schools reflected on the learning environments, they began to reinvent their relationships with parents (St. John, Grifflith, and Allen-Hayes 1997, 83). Thus, when educators reflected critically on their practices as educators, they became more welcoming toward parents.

In two Catholic schools I recently visited, the principals indicated that the dialogue about the faith community was central to their efforts to build unity within the schools and to reconstruct the power relationships with parents. When educators and parents reflected on their strengths and developed visions for their schools, they came back to the issue of the value of the belief community. Their vision statements, for example, emphasized both religious values and powerful learning opportunities. Thus, in Catholic schools, critical reflection in the restructuring process leads directly into issues of faith, which suggest a more direct linkage is durable.

Toward a New Model

When we compare the philosophy and origins of liberation theology to the Accelerated Schools Project, there appears to be a very basic compatibility. And there appears to be a need to deal with theology as an integral part of restructuring in Catholic schools. Thus, I conclude that deeper and more direct links between liberation theology and the ASP's systematic restructuring process could be crucial to restructuring in urban Catholic schools. Not only are the philosophic foundations for the two methods analogous, but the integration of a more explicit focus on reflections on the gospels, especially passages that relate to the call for social justice, seems crucial in Catholic schools located in inner cities.

The alternative of generating a new restructuring method, building on understandings reached from research on Accelerated Schools and from case studies like the one written by Oldenski (1997), could be used to generate an entirely new restructuring method, one tailored for Catholic schools and that integrated the fundamentals of liberation theology. Indeed, this may be a desirable long-term goal for urban Catholic educators. However, as the decade of experience with Accelerated Schools and other restructuring processes indicates, it can take a decade or more to refine a restructuring methodology. Therefore, in the near term, it makes sense to encourage urban Catholic schools to experiment with integration of liberation theology into the ASP.

Specifically, the experiments with the ASP should be encouraged among Catholic schools in inner cities. ASP training methods for these schools should be expanded to include reflection on key passages of the synoptic gospels, much as the priests in the early liberation theology movement began to reflect on the New Testament in new ways. Through reflection on the gospels, parents and educators alike can openly discuss issues of care and justice in their communities, a process that was central to the building of base communities among the poor in Latin America (Clearly 1985; Gutierrez 1984, 1988). This involves taking a step beyond seeing repression from outside, by reflecting how individuals and communities share responsibility for action (Freire 1989; Gutierrez 1984). It includes taking personal responsibility, through reflecting on the oppressor within. This process can help educators and parents to reflect on the issues of care and justice in their learning communities and the value of serving the poor, of using their talents and God-given strengths to build spirit and community. Public schools are constrained by the boundaries of secularism, well established by litigation, from engaging in this crucial discourse about faith in learning communities. However, Catholic schools have no such boundaries. They can be true centers for community development through learning in our urban communities.

The combination of liberation theology and the ASP offers a way to build learning communities in urban Catholic schools. Liberation theology offers a way to reflect on the plight of the urban poor, from a perspective that values the central beliefs of Catholicism. This approach explicitly values the sense of calling that attracts educators to work in Catholic schools. The ASP offers a way to move through critical reflection into new forms of action, to restructure schools to meet the learning needs of children. The combination seems to fit with the challenge facing urban Catholic schools that have chosen to work with lower-income families.

References

Brunner, I. V., and W. Hopfenberg (1996). "Growth and Learning Big Wheels and Little Wheels Interacting." In Finnan, et. al. *Accelerated Schools in Action: Lessons Learned from the Field*, pp. 24–46. Thousand Oaks, CA: Corwin.
Bryk, A. S., V. E. Lee, and P. B. Holland (1993). *Catholic Schools and the Common Good*. Cambridge, MA: Harvard University Press.
Clearly, E. L. (1985). *Crisis and Change: The Church in Latin America*. New York: Orbis.
Dell, G. L. (1995). A Portrait of Transforming Teaching and Learning through Integrated Arts. Unpublished doctoral dissertation: University of New Orleans.
Finnan, C. (1996). "Making Change Our Friend." In C. Finnan, et al., *Accelerated Schools in Action: Lessons from the Field*, pp. 104–23. Thousand Oaks, CA: Corwin.
Finnan, C., E. P. St. John, J. McCarthy and S. Slovacek (Eds.) (1996). *Accelerated Schools in Action: Lessons from the Field*. Thousand Oaks, CA: Corwin.
Friere, P. (1985). *The Politics of Education*. New York: Bergin & Garvey.
——— (1989). *Pedagogy of the Oppressed*. New York: Continuum.
Gutierrez, G. (1984). *We Drink from Our Own Wells: The Spiritual Journey of People*. Maryknoll: Orbis.
——— (1988). *A Theology of Liberation*. Maryknoll: Orbis.
Hopfenberg, W. S., H. M. Levin, and Associates (1993). *Accelerated Schools Resource Guide*. San Francisco: Jossey-Bass.
Keller, B. M., and P. Soler (1996). "The Influence of Accelerated Schools Philosophy and Process on Classroom Practice." In *Accelerated Schools in Action: Lessons from the Field*, pp. 273–292. Thousand Oaks, CA: Corwin.

Levin, H. M. (1996). Accelerated Schools: The Background. In C. Finnan, E. P. St. John, J. McCarthy, and S. Slovacek (Eds.) *Acclerated Schools in Action: Lessons from the Field,* pp. 3–23. Thousand Oaks, CA: Corwin.

Miron, C. F., E. P. St. John, and B. M. Davidson (1998). "Implementing School Restructuring in the Inner City." *The Urban Review,* 30 (2): 137-166.

Oldenski, T. (1997). *Liberation Theology and Cultural Pedagogy in Today's Catholic Schools: Social Justice in Action.* New York: Garland.

St. John, E. P. (1995). "Parents and School Reform: Unwelcome Guests, Instruments of School Initiatives or Partners in Restructuring?" *Journal for a Just and Caring Education.* 1(1): 80–97.

St. John, E. P., G., Dell and Associates (1994). *Louisiana Accelerated Schools Project: Second-Year Evaluation Report.* University of New Orleans.

St. John, E. P., A. I. Griffith, and L. Allen-Haynes (1997). *Families in Schools: A Chorus of Voices in Restructuring.* Portsmouth, NH: Heinemenn.

St. John, E. P., B. Davidson, J. Meza, and L. Allen-Haynes (1996). In C. Finnan, E. P. St. John, J. McCarthy, and S. Solvacek (Eds.) *Accelerated Schools in Action: Lessons from the Field,* pp. 124–138. Thousand Oaks, CA: Corwin.

CHAPTER TEN

Spirituality of the Crows

Janine Pease Pretty on Top

Today, in Crow country, religious expression is commonplace and everywhere. Sundancers rise to greet the sun with prayers for the new day. The sweat lodge fires generate plumes of cottonwood smoke into the valley woods along the Big Horn and the Little Big Horn rivers, Pryor and Reno creeks. Four clan parents pray with anticipation and encouragement for a youngster celebrating his sixth birthday with a family feast in the school cafeteria. Hymnodies, or vision songs, of aboriginal patterns are hummed by grandmothers in their kitchens and sung as the Baptist and Pentecostal churches begin biweekly services. The Catholic priests recite prayers and read from the New Testament in the Crow language as mass proceeds. The boom box in the living room and the car stereo play Native American church songs, high pitched and fast paced, with words that plead for blessings on "the children." A young sun dancer in the sweat lodge pledges the intent to fast in the mountains. As evening falls, a young father lights a one-inch sphere of sage leaves with a match, and takes the incense from door to window to corner throughout his sleeping household of wife, five children, a son-in-law, and three grandchildren. A grandfather concludes his day, lighting a tobacco cigarette and praying to Akbaatatdia in earnest for the safe return of his son from Billings. A clan father and elder raises his palms skyward beneath an arch of stars in the Milky Way, crying, "the stars are bright . . . there is peace in Crow country tonight."

Crow Overview

The Crow Indian people reside in a beautiful place in Montana. The 10,500 members of this Plains Indian tribe live all across the 3,000 square mile landscape, especially in the river valleys. The Crows, Apsaalooke, are arranged in six geopolitical social districts, mostly reflecting the placement of historic groups when the current reservation was settled during the 1880s. Then numbering 1,800, the Crow have now regained their original-population strength. Of the buffalo tradition, the Crows are among those well-known Indian nations among the high plains states last settled in the emigration of the west. Although the Crow witnessed Lewis and Clark, their first encounter with white people happened in 1835 and included explorers and Jesuit priests.

The 1990s have been a decade of growth for the Crows. The tribal council's elected officers pursued noncrucial battles in court on the collection of a severance tax for a strip of coal inlaid along the reservation boundary line. These two decisions have resulted in an annual $10,000,000 income to the tribal government budget. The current tribal chairman, Clara Nomee, has instituted a comprehensive government service employing 700 tribal members. The policy on economic development improved and brought a flurry of business openings (casino and convenience store), and a new hospital with a dialysis center and nursing home.

About Religion

Among all Indian tribes, the Crow held the distinction of having a 61 percent high school completion rate. The tribal council chartered a tribal college in 1980 which, in 1990, became fully accredited at the two-year level. Since 1918, the majority of Crow children have attended public schools; the tribe gave land to the state of Montana for that privilege. The Crows are known, among other tribes, for their annual Crow fair, an encampment of 900 plus teepees, an all-Indian rodeo, races, parades, and powwows. The language fluency rate of the Crow people far exceeds that of any tribe except the Navajo. Of special note is the core of 150 Crow Indian teachers in the public and Catholic schools. The Crow breed horses, and the men's basketball teams are sources of genuine pride for tribal members. Some 7,900 of the 10,500 members reside on the reservation, while many of those who have moved off live in border towns, Billings and Hardin.

The Crow people would seldom characterize their lives as "religious"; however, at its very core, the Crow way of life is prayer- and song-filled. The very foundation of the most mundane activities is the pursuit of conversation and relationship with the creator, Akbaatatdia. The transcendent is actively involved in the Apsaalooke life as orchestrated through the natural world, through intercessors and directly through Crow human beings. Quite outside of dogmatic patterns, the Crows have a remarkable "matrix of varied views," which are curiously bound together and even, at times, contradictory. The "lodge" of the Crows, the Crow social order, has been called by themselves "driftwood lodges." The transformation of river-driven driftwood into a chaotic, but nonetheless tightly woven and cohesive "lodge" is the metaphorical name of the multiplicity of Crow life facets. Like river driftwood, the wood of the Crows is united in the swift current of life, one piece landing upon the other, tangential, connected, and tightly bound (Frey 1987). Rodney Frey, in *The World of the Crow Indian as Driftwood Lodges,* stated that the Apsaalooke participate in multiple, even occasionally contradictory, perspectives, not unified or even integrated, yet cohesive, bound.

The Sweat Lodge

The sweat lodge is the original way of worship the creator gave to the Crows (Frey 1987, 15). At dawn, the crack and pop of chopping of wood can be heard through the poplar and cottonwood groves. A middle-aged Crow man oversees the building of a huge, carefully constructed, woodpile. One by one, all kinds of rocks from double fist to soccer ball sized are placed in the wood and then the woods are lit. Almost two hours later, plumes of smoke announce the sweat up and down the valley. The sweat is convened once the rocks are placed just to the right of the door in a carefully carved two-foot-deep hole. The lodge was built by a sweat-way owner about two years ago in the spring when river willows were fresh and pliant. The lodge is well-framed, dome-shaped, and covered with many layers of canvases.

To the untrained eye, no sweat lodges reveal themselves from the road. For the Crows, a drive south from Hardin on Interstate 90 shows thirty-eight lodges in just a ten-mile span of the valley of the Little Big Horn River. For those families whose religious life includes the sweat lodge, it is a weekly (sometimes three to five times weekly) prayer service. The men sweat first for an hour or two, and then the women sweat. Related groups of blood, clan, and society sweat together. The sweat builder obtains the specific assistance of a sweat conductor who "has the right to sweat." The sweat builder has built the sweat and arranged the sweat conductor for a specific reason. The sweat builder would have the concern of a health issue with a family member, the success of an upcoming event, a "surgery" of a relative or a community member, or an unsolved problem.

The men's sweat is conducted in four rounds and has a prescribed ceremony, based on the pouring man's way of conducting a sweat ceremony. The focus of the ceremony is the purpose, which fits into the prayers structured into the pourer's service. The dippers of water are poured over the "cherry-red rocks" in rounds: first four dippers are poured, then seven, then ten, then an infinite number of dippers are poured in the final and fourth round. The women are generally less formal and more focused on the family and community, but follow the same format. Concluding each round, a prayer for the specific purpose is offered, as well as specific prayer directions. Altogether, the ceremony from the fire building and lighting to the last participant's departure from the sweat enclosure lasts for seven hours.

A Child Is Named

Parents and grandparents concern themselves with obtaining "a name" for each of their children. The family parents and grandparents convene a meeting to discuss the need for a name and which of the family's children must be named. The discussion includes possible "name givers" and the time and place of the "naming." The parents are looking for a name giver from among biological relatives and clan parents. With choosing such a person they will take into account that person's family division, religious commitments, community standing, and special achievements. Sometimes the choice of the name giver is under debate for an extended period, for the parent is choosing the person whose name will be a pronounced and consequential influence for the child's lifetime. The "name" is thought to provide a way to promote chosen characteristics in the child and, most of all, a full and prosperous life. Once a choice is made, a family representative is sent to the chosen name giver with a respectfully placed request for a name along with a "gift" of tobacco and a $5 bill or fabric. The designated name giver must accept this responsibility and blessing. Now, the name giver turns to a reflective posture and, after a time, designs two or three names that suggest a self-portrait/profile that may encapsulate a major life theme or attribute.

To give a name is a blessing, but the paramount and long-term importance of this "name" requires careful study, prayer, and even vision on behalf of the name giver. Many will turn to a dream. The name giver will design two or three "good" names. These will be offered to the family in the context of public feast and give away in the honor of those being named. The name giver will propose the names by telling the full background of each choice; sometimes each name will have an hour-long explanation.

The parents and grandparents review the choices: they confer in a brief discussion, and make a choice. The name giver confers the name after an extensive prayer, the child being named standing in front of them, both facing the people. The name giver reaches forward and, holding the child's shoulder, slowly turns him or her in a full circle clockwise, and announces the new name. Thereafter, in Apsaalooke gatherings, the person will be identified by this name. From now on the child has a new relationship and special tie that brings the name giver back to the home for birthdays and moments of achievement, advice, or correction of behavior.

On occasion, a name may not be well-suited to the child. This conclusion would be made after years of individual trouble, the happenstance of a serious illness, or a series of accidents. The blessing nature of a name is tenuous and follows the real fabric of life events. The Apsaalooke will notice the power has gone from a name, and seek another one.

An adult may request another name to replace his or her original one. This new name will be given in a gathering like the one described for an original naming. But once given away, the name giver must acquire a name to replace the one given. It has also happened that a person will merit an additional name through achievement or reputation. A name may be sent via spirit messenger that well suits an individual and his or her life. In this instance, a person may bear two names. More rare is the unsolicited gift of a name from a clan parent or blood relative based on dream instruction or a need that is considered critical. Also, then, this person will have a second name—not by asking, but by circumstance. Finally, a fasting vision seeker may be given a name in the vision context.

The "name" that is given to you has lifelong strength and relevance. As a child, your name is explained to you in words and concepts you understand and need. As you grow, the name giver's intent with the name expands and advances; parents provide more interpretation and relevant implications to life direction. Moreover, the name giver may be asked to serve as an advisor, even as mentor for more lessons and training.

Naming is a crucial pathfinder for a child. The child has a role model assigned through receiving a name. A child is connected and related to the name giver in a unique advising and mentoring relationship. Named children have assurance they are prayed for always by their name giver.

Crow Indian Hymnodies

The "sing-spiration" program notes "Crow Indian hymns." Most Wednesdays, all over town, church night is happening. The minister announces a Crow hymn and requests a leader. Standing in the pew where his family has sat since the 1930s, Dwain Bends clears his throat and then makes a few thoughtful comments about the struggle he and his wife have had this week with their granddaughters, due to absence from school. "Through prayer and the singing of my grandmother's song, my granddaughter has returned to health and school," he recounts.

With a pause and eyes toward the floor, Dwain begins the Crow hymns as a solo, "A he hele aa hee heele . . ." Two phrases into the song, Dwain's elderly mother, Agnes, joins in with the song along with the rest of the congregation. Halfway into the song, the congregation is singing in unison on the same note, the women, an octave higher, many with their right hands raised upward, palm open.

Singing it a second time, Dwain raises the tone one-half step higher. (Translated) "Hear me, hear me, oh hear me. You who live in the clouds." The song concluded, the congregation trails off, bringing the prayer song to a close. Dwain recites the name of this dreamer and the circumstance of the song received from Akbaatatdia. The congregation knows this event and the dreamer, and reverently acknowledge and relive the receiving of this dream song.

Almost ten years ago, a musicologist from Kansas, David Graber, moved to the Crow Indian reservation. He is a Mennonite by faith. He translated and transcribed hymns of the Indian people of the Cheyenne and Arapaho nations. His guest presentation at the Crow Agency Baptist Church over ten years ago started a series of recording sessions and translations/transcriptions and work sessions dealing with Crow Indian hymns, or hymnodies. Today, the Crow Indian Hymnbook Project Steering Committee represents over thirty-five churches, including the Catholic, Baptist, Lutheran, and Pentecostal churches in seven Crow Indian communities.

The Crow Indian hymnody is a unique hymn form to the Crow Indian people of Montana. The song has the form of Crow Indian traditional music and is original to the dreamer, or song receiver. Through extensive research, David Graber (1996) finds that only one other North American tribe has such a music form.

In the Apsaalooke worldview, the "spiritual creative forces act not only through the natural world, but through human beings as well" (Frey 1987, 178). The hymnody is seen as a special gift from Aakbaatatdia, as a blessing to the gifted song receivers and a message and gift to the Crow people. The Apsaalooke world provides social and spiritual distinction and attainment, both for men and women (Frey 1987, 35). The Apsaalooke have "always lived in close association with the land, its animals, its plants, and its season cycles. Through this kinship, they have been receptive to any lessons" (Frey 1987, 3). The Crow people have received songs, or hymnodies, through dreams and visions since the earliest Christian converts existed among the people at the turn of the century. The Crow worldview accommodates for individual spiritual interpretation and expression that supports the resilience and strength of the Crow community. Further, since every member of the tribe has a clan membership and is aligned, therefore, with a large number of fellow clansmen and clanswomen, in addition to the literal blood relations, the interpersonal difference and respect an individual receives generates a religious climate in which creative expression finds unique freedom and even encouragement. The interpersonal difference and respect, coupled with the immediate kinship of Aakbaatatdia and the relative association, promotes this song gift phenomenon. The words in the Crow hymnody are few, often specifically sacred and repetitious, conveying connection to the Creator and imploring for blessings. For the Apsaalooke, words have great power, and the knowledge of good words is medicine.

Recently, the Christian Apsaalooke have begun offering hymnodies as public praise songs. The clan father called to the public give away receives the fit and takes the microphone from the announcer, then sings the hymnody as a praise song. Relatives of the family giving away thank the singer nominally through bringing $1 and $5 bills to the singer, and placing these appreciative tokens in his hand while he sings. The praise song is an act of "public declaration, an acknowledgment that each individual is linked to others and can attain social distinction only through this connection" (Frey 1987, 52). Offering the hymnody as a praise song, indicated the Crow worldview adaptability, for the clan father's offer is a metaphorical connection to the honored Gift giver. The hymnody singer sings publicly, bringing blessings through the song.

Loud Speaker Preachers and Rocking Musicians

In our town, there are many home-based Pentecostal Christian groups. The first Pentecostal evangelist to arrive in Crow country was Nellie Stewart, who, in 1923, went with three other Crow people to study at the Angeles Temple with Anne McPherson. Here, after three weeks of study, they were designated "ministers" (McCreary 1993, 2).

Nearly any evening from April to October, it is possible to hear the enthusiastic high-volume and fast-paced preaching from the Carpenter Church, right in the center of the eight-block-square town of Lodge Grass. Loudspeakers attached to the four corners of the small wood-framed church building broadcast the fervent appeals of men and women evangelists and their testimonies. Rock-style bands accompany the preaching and testimony, complete with electric guitars, organs, and drums. In addition to the services in the church, outdoor birthday or anniversary celebrations often feature gospel singing on into the nighttime. Even after the partygoers have departed, the musicians sing on into the night. Popular gospel songs and some standard "hymns," including "One Day at a Time" or "Amazing Grace," can be heard from anywhere in town.

During the Crow Indian Fair, when rodeo and race meet in mid-August, the Pentecostal congregations come together and sponsor a "big top revival" across the road from the fairground entrance. Every evening, concurrent with the intertribal dances on the fairgrounds, a rousing revival attracts the Pentecostal Church followers. The tent meeting place is surrounded with thirty tent camps and many vehicles. At 2:00 in the morning, the rock band sings Christian songs and witnesses on into the nighttime. Sometimes only the musicians are left to carry on the loudspeaker ministry. The loudspeakers carry nearly a mile over the night air.

Black Whistle Singers in the Evening

Songs and social powwow singing accompany Crow Indian life. Five to fifteen male singers surround a bass drum, each with his own drumstick. Many important family events feature a tradition Crow Indian drum (group). Today on the Crow Indian reservation, there are eight well-known drums (groups). During the event, the drum will present songs of honor, country, praise, and celebration. Songs range into the romantic and social.

A fiftieth wedding anniversary was celebrated in the Catholic gym with over three hundred family members and guests attending a ceremony and feast. The drum was the Black Whistle Singers, a drum that started in the Lodge Grass High School Indian Club. Today, the members range in age from 16 to 22. Black Whistle sang a series of romantic songs called "round dances."

As the anniversary event convenes, the announcer introduces the honored couple and the drum sings the individual song made for the man's grandfather, probably around 1890. A recitation of marriage vows and a minister's soliloquy complete the ceremony. Now, the formal songs are complete, and the members of Black Whistle play hand-carried and hand-made drums. They proceed to the center of the gym, facing one another in a small circle. The lead singer takes up a song of love, and a "push dance" begins. Gradually, unmarried couples come out of the crowd and dance the "Crow Indian Two Step" or the "Push Dance" to the romantic heartbeat rhythm.

The ceremony started at 4:00 P.M., and by 10:00 P.M., the feast is served, the greetings of departure are said, and the drum sings until 2:00 A.M. Around 11:00 A.M., the lead singer strikes up the sun dance songs that accompany the three-day traditional fasting ceremony. Sun dance songs carry them on until 2:00 A.M. The whole town can hear these young male voices and know the songs are of the sun dance.

Song Making and Praise Singing

Crow Indian singers are in great demand for family gatherings and community events. The eight drums on the Crow Indian reservation are extended family groups who sing together most of their lives. Each group has six to twenty members and a lead singer. The lead singer usually owns the drum and is connoted "drum keeper." These drums have the names Night Hawks, Black Whistle, Mad Dogs, Black Lodge Wranglers, Wolf Mountains, Castle Rock, Crow Agency, Mighty Few, and Cedar Child.

The Night Hawks, Black Lodge Wranglers, and Mad Dogs are particularly well known for the knowledge of their lead singers. They perform individual songs, clan songs, district songs, warrior songs, ceremonial songs, social, and powwow songs for dancing. Their knowledge of individual songs entails a volume of works that dates back over a century, but among these works are songs made as recently as this year. Individual songs have specific melody and word passages that make them powerful in a medicine context. The song maker of these songs has a known blessing for "making songs." This gift, from Aakbaatatdia, is a special blessing recognized and evidenced in probably fewer than twenty Crow Indian men. At the Crow, people come to attention and stand for the singing of the individual songs and clan songs.

Praise singing occurs when a clan father chooses to bring out a time-blessed praise song on the occasion of recognizing a favored clan child of the praise singer. This song is one that has been given to the clan father by one of his male clan relatives. The most common occasion for a praise song is during a give away ceremony.

The give away Ceremony is one sponsored by an Apsaalooke family, to honor the achievement of a family member. Gifts of substantial value are given to the clan parent of the honored person. The clan parents are the members of the honored person's father's clan. The family calls on the clan parents, both men and women clan members, in recognition of their constant and unceasing prayers for their clan children, the children of the clan's male members. The family expresses gratefulness for the help and prayers of the clan parents, that have brought about this family achievement. The clan parents and the clan father come to the give away site from the audience and receive a pile of gifts from the family. The gift may be a Pendleton blanket, a packaged cotton blanket, a fringed shawl, a western shirt, cigarettes and, sometimes, western boots and hat. The clan parent pauses beside the announcer, and quietly conveys the prayer that they commit to take up in the ensuing time, the prayer about the honored family member. The announcer turns to the audience and conveys that prayer to the people. Still, the clan parent lingers near the honored family member. The announcer finishes the conveyance, and the clan parent and the clan father sing a praise song. Family and clan members bring $1 and $5 bills to the praise singer, in thanks for this unique and special song. Because the praise song itself is a gift from one clan member to another, usually between generations, their songmaking origins are not specifically known. What is known is that just a few people are honored with praise songs, and those are blessed ones.

The Sun Dance of the Crow

In late July, in the traditional campgrounds at the Pryor district, 170 Crow people are assembled in two long files. Side by side, they are poised and ready to encircle the huge sundance lodge twice. They anticipate entering the lodge. Right at sundown, the sundance leader sounds the call. It's time. Winter medicine bundle openings are complete and four rehearsal dances have been performed. Now, the dancers follow their leaders into the lodge, which will be their three- or four-day home. Each individual has made known to their families and the sundance leader their vow and commitment to fast for three days, going without food or water. Many of these dancers have already fasted for one or two days in the hills near their lodge prior to this moment. The dancers nod to their family members. Family members have made teepee and tent camps in a large circle surrounding the lodge.

The North American people are almost universally known for their fast and vision-questing characteristics. The Crow people have practiced this religion since time immemorial. The Crow religious questing through the sundance is expressed in five or six dances each summer. Nearly five hundred dancers take part in the ceremony each year, along with their families. There are five thousand adults among the Crow enrolled as members today.

The drums come at sunrise, to start the day's dance. The medicine man and sundance leader convene the sundance ceremonies, with specific prayers and vision songs brought to this generation from preceding sundance leaders.

The families witness the dancers' sacrifice and sit for hours in observation and prayer at the doorway of the lodge. Folding and lawn chairs are arranged neatly with a circumference of two hundred fifty feet around the lodge and only fifteen feet from the door. The drum is arranged to the left of the door opening. The announcer directs the dancers and drummers to observe a time schedule for the major ceremonies of the day. The dancers dance from sunrise until 10:00 p.m. The drums change off throughout the day, singing one song after another so the dancers may quest.

This year, the dancers were so numerous that twenty dancers were moved to the topmost hill to the west to fast and pray there, in full sight of the lodge. Thus, only Crow and Indian dancers were allowed in the dance. These potential participants of other origins were asked to stay within view of the camps on nearby hilltops. The sundance leaders explained the Crow peoples' commitment to the whole year of ceremonies, rehearsals, and feasts in preparation for this major time of sacrifice. The leader requested the non-Indian sojourner's understanding of the sacred Crow sundance and its prominence in the religious year of the Crow people.

The intermediary spirits of the buffalo, the eagle, and the otter are unique to this Crow sundance. The center pole and subsidiary pole display these representations of medicine spirit. The center pole is the focus of the dancer's path. Each time the dance must move about in the lodge, the center pole is touched by the dancer's hand. Crow people come from throughout the reservation of three thousand square miles to visit the lodge on the second day for doctoring at the center pole. The announcer brings forward two or three people at a time for the sundance leader and assistants to the doctor. Family members bring offerings of cattails, leaves, sage, and mint to relieve, in some small way, the destitution of their fasting family member. Cigarettes are brought to the door and given to the individuals, especially clan parents and children of the giver, requesting prayers of a unique nature. The announcer calls these dancers individually to come and receive these items. The path to the door, and from the door to the center pole, is trodden with the prayers and intentions and fasting sacrifice of the dancers, the drummers, and their family members.

On the final day, the water is brought by appointed women from among the families in the encampment. The bringing of the water is a celebration of life. All life is based on the water. The final closing sundance song is sung. The closing song is sung by the sundance leader and dancers. A woman of honor offers the prayer for the water. The water bearers, young men and women, serve water. The dancers are jubilant, cheering as the dippers plunge into the water buckets as they are brought around the lodge. One by one, the dancers partake of the blessed, life giving water. As the dancers pack their ceremonial belongings and prepare to depart from the lodge, clan parents are requested to enter the lodge and pray for the dancers. The dancers offer a gift to the clan parents. The ceremony is complete. The dancers file out, one by one, down through a two-sided tunnel of family members who are anxiously awaiting their return. Handshaking and greetings pour out the elation of a sundance completed in a good way.

Conclusion

The Crow people are deeply involved in religious expression. Whether the expression is traditional Crow Indian ways or Christian and Pentecostal, the communities and families are actively pursuing spiritual connections with Aakbaatatdia and the creator. The immediate kinship of Crow people with one another, family members, clan parents and members is evident, and the intermediary spirits of the land and animals penetrate their daily lives. The Crow people avidly practice their religious and spiritual expression in song, prayer, and ceremony, seldom noting any line, fuzzy or otherwise, between the sacred and the secular. The expressions reach all of us in the Crow Indian community, embracing and buffeting us around and through. At the present time, the way of the Crow people is an anomaly to the mainstream secular world that surrounds us. The Crow people frequently stay "within the exterior boundaries." Within the exterior boundaries of this Crow world exist a world quite apart and unique and richly expressive of religious and spiritual life.

References

Frey, Rodney (1987). *The World of the Crow Indians as Driftwood Lodges*. Norman: University of Oklahoma Press.
Graber, David (1996). "Hymnodies in Crow Christian Belief." Unpublished Manuscript. Little Big Horn College Archives.
McCleary, Timothy. (1993). "Akbaatatshee: The Oilers Pentecostalism among the Crow Indians." M.S. thesis. University of Montana.

Contributors

Jeanne Brady is the director of the Interdisciplinary Doctor of Education Program for Educational Leaders at St. Joseph's University, Philadelphia. She is the author of *Schooling Young Children: A Feminist Pedagogy for Liberatory Learning* (SUNY Press).

Dennis Carlson is a professor in the Department of Educational Leadership and director of the Center for Education and Cultural Studies at Miami University, Oxford, Ohio. He is the author and editor of several books on educational topics and has published widely in educational journals.

Bill Doll is Vira Franklin and J. R. Eagles Professor of Curriculum at Louisiana State University. He is the co-director of the Curriculum Theory Project and administers the Department of Curriculum and Instruction's Holmes Elementary Teacher Education program.

Glenn Hudak teaches in the Cultural Foundations of Education Program, University of North Carolina at Greensboro. He is co-editor of *Labeling: Politics and Pedagogy* (Routledge/Falmer) and *Sound Identities* (Peter Lang).

Kathleen Keeson is director of Teacher Education at Goddard College, a historic progressive college designed on the principles of John Dewey. She is the co-author, with Jim Henderson, of *Understanding Democratic Curriculum Leadership* (Teachers College Press).

Thomas Oldenski is an associate professor in the Department of Educational Leadership at the University of Dayton, Ohio. He has written *Critical Pedagogy and Liberation Theology in Today's Catholic Schools: Social Justice in Action* (Garland).

Janine Pease Pretty on Top is the president of Little Big Horn College, Crow Reservation, Montana. She became the first woman of Crow descent to earn a doctorate. Janine has been active in many areas related to the welfare and education of Native Americans.

Contributors

David Purpel is a professor in the Department of Educational Leadership and Cultural Studies at the University of North Carolina at Greensboro. He has written several books, with his latest book being *Moral Outrage in Education* (Peter Lang).

Elaine Riley is an assistant professor of Instructional Leadership at Northern Arizona University, Flagstaff. Previously she was an instructor in the Department of Curriculum and Instruction at Louisiana State University.

Edward St. John is professor of Educational Leadership and Policy Studies at Indiana University, where he also serves as director of the Indiana Education Policy Center. He has written and edited several books and articles on school reform.

Index

2001: A Space Odyssey, 22

Aakbaatatdia, 187
Absolute Other, 62
Accelerated School Project (ASP), 164, 169
  as a liberation process, 170
  critical reflection, 174–75
  description of, 171
  new model of, 176–77
  principles of, 172
Ackermann, Robert, 144
agape, 95, 156
  definition of, 96
Akbaatatdia, 180
Allen-Haynes, L., 164
American Educational Studies Association, 48
Anarchist Moment, The (Clark), 65
Anti-Oedipus (Deleuze and Gauttari), 59, 64
Apocalypse, 23
aporia, 11, 17, 19
Apple, Michael, 149, 151
Apsaalooke. *See* Crows
Arapaho, 184
Armageddon, 23
Aronowitz, Stanley, 141, 142
Astaunga Yoga, 51
axiology, 50

Bambara, Toni Cade, 145
Bateson, Gregory, 13, 14, 109, 111
Bateson, M. C., 14
Bauman, Z., 2
Bellah, Robert, 1, 54
Bends, Dwain, 184
Benhabib, S., 123
Bennett, Kathleen, 141, 151
Berne, E., 35
Bernstein, Richard, 15
Berry, Thomas, 5, 14, 16, 17, 44, 107, 111

Big Horn, 179
biophilia, 106
Black Whistle Singers, 186–87
Boff, Clodivis, 134, 140, 145, 148
Boff, Leonardo, 134, 140, 145
Bonino, Jose Miguez, 147
Book of Revelations, 23
Bookchin, Murray, 52
Border Crossings (Girouox), 133
bounded anarchy, 67
Bowers, C. A., 13, 14
Brahma, 68
Brannon, Lil, 80
Brothers Karamazov, The (Dostoyevski), 43
Brueggemann, Walter, 90, 98
Bryk, A. S., 163
Buber, Martin, 7
Buddhism, 8, 72
  and education, 108–11
  health and academia, 73, 74–80

Camus, Albert, 43
Capra, F., 109
Carlson, Dennis, 141
Carpenter Church, 185
Cartesian epistemology, 72
Casaldaliga, P., 8
Celestine novels (Redfield)
  discussion of, 26–45
  discussion of plots, 28–40
Celestine Prophesy (Redfield), 26
Center for a Postmodern World, 57
centered/de-centered self, 47
charis, 83
Cheyenne, 184
Chopp, Rebecca, 134, 139, 147
Civil Rights Movement, 6
Clark, John, 65
Clarke, Arthur C., 22

Cleary, Edward L., 164
Clinton, Bill, 120, 121, 122
Columbia University, 170
contemplative spirituality, 66
   and social transformation, 64–67
cosmogenesis, 33
cosmology, 11
Counts, George, 134, 150
Crazy for Democracy (Kaplan), 128
critical pedagogy, 133–60
   and Peter McLaren, 151
   as a form of border pedagogy, 150
   critical discourses, 157
   discourse of critique and possibility, 149–55
   integrative model for, 159–60
Crow Agency Baptist Church, 184
Crow Indian Hymnody Project Steering Committee, 184
Crows
   spirituality of, 179–90
   about religion, 180–81
   Black Whistle Singers, 186–87
   hymnodies, 183–84
   naming of children, 182–83
   overview of tribe, 179–80
   sun dance, 188–90
   sweat lodges, 181–82
Cultivating the Mind of Love (Nhat Hahn), 74, 75
Cupitt, Don, 60
curriculum, rise and fall of, 87–89

Daly, Mary, 96
Dante Alighieri, 11
Darder, A., 124
Darwin, Charles, 10
da Silva, Tomaz Tadeu, 136
Davies, Paul, 10, 12, 17
Declaration of Independence, 98
de la Place, Pierre Simon, 11
Deleuze, Gilles, 59, 64
Delpit, Lisa, 71, 72, 78, 117
deMello, Anthony, 4
Derrida, Jacques, 11, 14, 19, 79
Dewey, John, 134, 150, 151, 152
Divine Comedy (Dante), 11

Doll, William, 10, 106, 108
Dostoyevski, F., 43
dualism, 112

East St. Louis, 163
ecofeminism, 113
ecology, 109
Ecozoic era, 5
Eddington, Arthur, 10
education
   and Buddhism, 108–11
   and ecology, 109
   democratic form, 1
   funding for, 93–101
   holistic, 105–8, 108–11
   multicultural, 122
   progressive form, 1
   theology, religion, and, 7
Education for Critical Consciousness (Freire), 135
Education under Seige (Aronowitz and Giroux), 142
Einstein, Albert, 11
Eisler, Riane, 112
Enlightenment, 16, 88, 95
entropy, 10
epistemology, 50
esoteric religions, 46
Eurocentrism, 39, 124
evolution, 10

Fear and Trembling (Derrida), 16
feminist ethics
   and educational reform, 120–31
   nine general principles, 125–26
   of risk, 146
   on schooling, 126–30
Feuerbach, Ludwig, 60
Finnan, C., 164, 172
Flax, J., 123
Foucault, Michel, 10, 37, 78, 114
Fox, Matthew, 106, 112, 115
Frankfurt School of Critical Theory, 134, 150
Fraser, James, 120, 123, 126
Freire, Paulo, 134, 136, 149, 151, 156, 164
   Church and education, 140
   on conscientization, 164–68

Freire, Paulo *(continued)*
   pedagogy of denunciation and annunciation, 138
Freud, Sigmund, 34
Frey, Rodney, 181
Fromm, Erich, 104, 106, 112
fundamentalist spirituality, 6

Gablik, Susie, 116
Gadotti, Moacir, 134
Gaia hypothesis, 31, 39
Gayatri-Mantra, 61
Gift of Death, The (Derrida), 15
Giroux, Henry, 131, 133, 134, 139, 142, 151, 157
Grant, C., 124
Goals 2000: Educate America Act, 120
Gore, Jennifer, 78, 150
Gould, Stephen J., 23
Graber, David, 184
Gramsci, Antonio, 151
Grand Inquisitor, 43
Great Stochastic process, 17
Griffin, David, 57
Griffin, Susan, 105
Griffith, A. I., 164
Grumet, Madeline, 51
Guattari, Felix, 59, 64
Gutierrez, Gustavo, 146, 147, 164, 175
   individual in community, 168
   on critical practice, 168–69

Hale-Bopp comet, 46
Hall, S., 129
Heaven's Gate cult, 5, 24, 46
Heelas, Paul, 48
Hegel, G. W. F., 39, 42, 62
Heidegger, M., 2, 3, 12, 14, 29
   human values, 15
Hennelly, Alfred, 139
Heschel, Abraham Joshua, 7, 89
Hinduism, 8
History and Spirit (Kovel), 62
Holland, P. B., 163
hooks, bell, 117
Horkheimer, Max, 47
Huebner, Dwayne, 73, 76, 91
hymnodies, 179, 183–84

idealistic spirituality, 41
   See also metaphysical spirituality; subjective spirituality
"I-It" relationships, 7
Industrial Revolution, 15
Institute for the Study of American Religion, 46
introspective science, 56
"I-Thou" relationships, 7

Jaggar, A., 126
James, Charity, 98
James, William, 16, 34, 51
Johnson, George, 10
Journal of Curriculum Theory Conference, 48
Jung, Carl, 51, 59

Kane, Jeffrey, 91
Kanpol, B., 124
Kaplan, Temma, 128, 131
Kaufman, Stuart, 17
Keller, B. M., 172
Kesson, Kathleen, 91, 106, 107, 108
Kincheloe, Joe, 144
King, Ynestra, 111, 113
King Jr., Martin Luther, 6, 74
Kliebard, Herbert, 87, 122
Knoblauch, C. H., 80
Koran, 98
Kovel, Joel, 56
Kozol, Jonathan, 121, 130, 151
Krishnamurti, J., 60, 79
Kubrick, Stanley, 22
Kula-kundalini, 59
Kumar, Jayanta, 56
Kundun, 80

Lather, Patti, 150
Lazlo, E., 109
Learning to Labor (Willis), 150
LeCompte, Margaret, 141, 151
Lee, V. E., 163
Leonard, Peter, 143
Levin, Henry M., 169, 170, 171
Lewis and Clark, 180
liberation theology, 7, 133–60, 164
   critical discourse and method, 144–49, 157
   integrating into restructuring, 163–77

liberation theology *(continued)*
    integrative model for, 159–60
    six theses of, 147
Liberation Theology and Critical Pedagogy in Today's Catholic Schools: Social Justice in Action (Oldenski), 163
Life in Schools: An Introduction to Critical Pedagogy in the Foundations of Education (McLaren), 143, 151
"linguistic" health, 73, 80–85
Little Big Horn River, 179, 181
Living Buddha, Living Christ (Nhat Hahn), 80
Luke, Carmen, 150
Lydon, A., 113

Macdonald, James, 50, 67
Macedo, Donaldo, 142, 167
Macy, Joanna, 108, 109
Madhyarnika Buddhism, 60
Mair, Victor, 68
Malroux, Andre, 44
Man's Hope (Malroux), 44
Marcuse, Herbert, 62
Marshall, Paule, 145
Martin, Jane Roland, 91
Marty, Martin, 83
Marx, Karl, 4, 30, 42
Maslow, Abraham, 33, 43
matrilineal spirit, 111–12
Ma-Wang-Tui manuscripts, 68
maya, 52
McEwan, A., 121
McLaren, Peter, 6, 124, 134, 136, 143, 153
McKnight, Douglas, 15
McPherson, Anne, 185
Medellín Conference of Latin American Bishops, 139
Medcalf, John, 139
"media" Buddhism, 80
Melton, J. Gordon, 46
Menz, Johann, 147
Merleau-Ponty, Maurice, 59
metaphysical spirituality, 40
    See also idealistic spirituality; subjective spirituality
millennium significance of, 23
Miller, Ron, 91

Mind and Nature (Bateson), 110
modernism, crisis of purpose, 3
Moffett, James, 57, 67, 91
Moltmann, Jurgen, 147
Monod, Jacques, 12
Morrison, Toni, 145
Mouffe, C., 124
Movement of Education from the Bases, 141
Muktananda, Swami, 98
multiculturalism, 124
Munro, Petra, 114
mysterium tremendum, 14, 18
myth, definition of, 24

National Commission on Excellence in Education, 170
New Age texts, 25
New Constellation, The (Bernstein), 15
New York Times, 46, 54
Newton, Isaac, 11, 14
Nhat Hahn, Thich, 71, 73, 74, 80, 107
Nicholson, L., 123
Nieto, S., 124
Nietzsche, Frederick, 12
Nobel Peace Prize, 74
Noddings, Nel, 91
Nomee, Clara, 180
nonanthropocentric view of God, 13

Oldenski, Thomas, 147, 176
ontology, 50
Order of Things, The (Foucault), 10
Other People's Children (Delpit), 71
Outer Being (Nhat Hahn), 71

Palmer, Parker, 91
Paris Peace Talks, 74
Patanjali, 51
Patocka, Jan, 15
patri focal views, 112
patriarchy, 54, 113
Paulo Freire: A Critical Introduction (McLaren and Leonard), 143
"pedagogy of conscientization," 134
Pedagogy of Hope: Reliving Pedagogy of the Oppressed (Freire), 137
Pedagogy of the City (Freire), 137

Index

Pedagogy of the Oppressed (Freire), 134
philosophical idealism, 56
pharmakon, 80
Pinar, William, 51, 106, 141
Plato, 1, 34
Platonism, 41
poiesis, 15
Politics of Education, The (Freire), 167
Politics of Liberation: Paths from Freire (McLaren and Lankshear), 144
popular Catholicism, 149
Prajnaparamita Diamond Sutra, 60
Prigogine, Ilya, 10
process spirituality, 57
progressivism, 1
   and democratic forms of education, 24
   concept of the spiritual, 3
Prometheus, 43
Puritans, 15
Purpel, David, 3, 6, 141, 144

quantum mechanics, 109
Questioning the Millennium (Gould), 23
Quinby, L., 114
Quinn, Mary Elizabeth, 14

Rapture, 23
Reading, Writing, and Justice: School Reform as If Democracy Matters (Fraser), 120
Redfield, James, 22
Reed, S., 128
reflexivity, 37
religion and spirituality, 53–57
Reuther, R., 44
Robb, Carol, 125
Rugg, George, 134

sadhana, 58
Sanskrit, 58
Sarkar, P. R., 56, 63
Sautter, R. C., 128
Schooling and the Struggle for Public Life (Giroux), 133
St. John, E. P., 164, 172
St. John the Divine, 23
Second Coming, 23
Sedgwick, Eve, 79, 80

Segundo Juan Luis, 148
self, Eastern Understandings, 51–52
Seven Years in Tibet, 80
Shannon, P., 129
Shor, Ira, 136, 149
shunyata, 82
Sidel, R., 130
Slattery, Patrick, 134, 141
Sleeter, Christine, 124
Sloan, Douglas, 91
Smith, David G., 108, 117
Smith, Pamela, 134
social justice, 86–102
Socrates, 41
Soelle, D., 7
Soler, P., 172
Song of the Bird, The (deMello), 4
spiritual literacy, 71–80, 80–85
spirituality
   and education, 91–93
   and religion, 53–57
   definition of, 4
   educating educators, 49
   fundamentalist, 6
   progressivism, 6
   transcendence of human consciousness and culture, 5
   See also idealistic spirituality; metaphysical spirituality; subjective spirituality
Spretnak, Charlene, 112, 113
Spring, Joel, 141
Stanford University, 170
Starhawk, 103
Steiner, C., 35
Stengers, Isabel, 10
Stewart, Nellie, 185
Struggle for Pedagogies, The (Gore), 78
subjective spirituality, 41
   See also idealistic spirituality; metaphysical spirituality
sun dance, 188–90
sweat lodges, 181–82
Swimme, Brianne, 5, 44
systems theory, 109

Tadbhavananda, Ac., 56
Tantra, 55, 56

Tao te Ching, 65, 66
Taylor, Mildred, 145
Teachers as Intellectuals: Toward a Critical Pedagogy of Learning (Giroux), 142, 151
Tenth Insight, The (Redfield), 26
Texts Under Negotiation (Brueggemann), 92
Theology of Liberation, A (Gutierrez), 168
Theory and Resistance in Education: A Pedagogy for the Opposition (Giroux), 142
thymos, 1
Tillich, Paul, 16
Time, 80
Time-Warner, 26
Torres, Carlos, 141
Transactional Analysis, 35
Trend, D., 64, 142
Trungpa, Chogyam, 73, 82
Tyler, R., 106

Universal Declaration of Human Rights, 98
Universal Schoolhouse: Spiritual Awakening through Education, The (Moffett), 57

unqualified consciousness, 61

Vigil, J. M., 8
Vipassanya Buddhism, 64

Weaver, Juanita, 105
We Drink from Our Own Wells: The Spiritual Journey of a People (Gutierrez), 168
Welch, Sharon, 134, 145, 147, 149
Wertheim, Margaret, 13
West, Cornell
Whitehead, A. N., 14
Willis, Paul, 150
Wittgenstein, Ludwig, 76
Woodhead, Linda, 57
Woodroffe, Sir John, 53
World Council of Churches, 136
World of the Crow Indian as Driftwood Lodgers, The (Frey), 181

Zen Buddhist epistemology, 75
Zen progressivism, 34
Zukav, G., 109

COUNTERPOINTS

Studies in the Postmodern Theory of Education

General Editors
Joe L. Kincheloe & Shirley R. Steinberg

Counterpoints publishes the most compelling and imaginative books being written in education today. Grounded on the theoretical advances in criticalism, feminism, and postmodernism in the last two decades of the twentieth century, Counterpoints engages the meaning of these innovations in various forms of educational expression. Committed to the proposition that theoretical literature should be accessible to a variety of audiences, the series insists that its authors avoid esoteric and jargonistic languages that transform educational scholarship into an elite discourse for the initiated. Scholarly work matters only to the degree it affects consciousness and practice at multiple sites. Counterpoints' editorial policy is based on these principles and the ability of scholars to break new ground, to open new conversations, to go where educators have never gone before.

For additional information about this series or for the submission of manuscripts, please contact:
> Joe L. Kincheloe & Shirley R. Steinberg
> c/o Peter Lang Publishing, Inc.
> 275 Seventh Avenue, 28th floor
> New York, New York 10001

To order other books in this series, please contact our Customer Service Department:
> (800) 770-LANG (within the U.S.)
> (212) 647-7706 (outside the U.S.)
> (212) 647-7707 FAX

Or browse online by series:
> www.peterlangusa.com